The Heart of the Game

A Coach's Journey

Bobby McIver and Megan Macomber

Armsdale Publishing
COLUMBIA, TENNESSEE

Armsdale Publishing
2402 Hampshire Pike
Columbia, Tennessee 38401
www.theheartofthegame.net

Book Layout ©2013 BookDesignTemplates.com

Ordering Information:
Quantity sales. Special discounts are available on quantity purchases by corporations, associations, and others. For details, contact the "Special Sales Department" at the address above.

The Heart of the Game: A Coach's Journey McIver&Macomber. -- 1st ed.
ISBN 978-0-9894874-0-5

Contents

INTRODUCTION 1

THE PIED PIPER 19

"PLAYERS HIT THE FIRST SHOT" 35

WORKING SMARTER 59

LIFE LESSONS 91

NEXT! 111

HARMONIZED 133

OUT OF THE BUNKER WITH BOTH HANDS 149

THE ONLY CONSTANT IS CHANGE 177

'THAT GUY' FROM HARARE 199

KNOW YOUR ALL STARS 213

CHASING SEVENS 229

"ASK THE UNDERDOG" 247

DOUBLE EAGLE 265

WITHOUT A COURSE 279

ON THE BUBBLE 295

INTO THE SILENCE 313

GIVING IT TO THE MAGICIAN 345

THE DIRECTION YOU ARE GOING 361

THE 19th HOLE: GOING THE DISTANCE.........................381

AFTERWORD 391

INDEX...404

To Ruth

There are two ways to live: you can live as if nothing is a miracle; you can live as if everything is a miracle.

−Albert Einstein

Introduction

Before his career really started, Bobby McIver faced a challenge that would test the limits of the most experienced teachers. Newly hired as an assistant at Belle Meade Country Club just outside Nashville, Bobby not only lacked any prior coaching experience; he had never even had a golf lesson himself. When one of the kids he'd spotted hanging around the golf shop became the very first player Bobby coached, he had no reference point, no previous students to serve as comparisons. Despite this, the 23-year-old novice instructor saw talent when he saw it.

You read that right. Not all teachers can see talent. Even good ones can settle into merely praising a gifted student--or worse, undermining any student who threatens to out-perform them. Bobby had already achieved something special just by perceiving that twelve-year-old Matt King could be a champion . . . *"if I could learn how to get him there."*

Like Bobby, I had just turned 23 when I taught for the first time as a grad student. Some of my students, Navy veterans, were several years older. I stayed up all night before our classes, determined to give them something worth their time and effort.

Having managed to elude the teaching preparation program for graduate students at Cornell, I felt like a gigantic, newly blazered imposter. But at least I had *attended* some English classes before I walked to the front of one and wrote my name on the board.

The first classroom I entered as a real (assistant) professor was a stately wood-paneled room at Kenyon College. Thirty freshman faces greeted my nerves. I recalled my mother telling me "just remember, they're more scared of you than you are of them." But she was talking about the raccoons that lived in our attic, and besides, it wasn't true. Front and center sat a dark-haired, clean-cut young man, hands not just folded but locked under his prow of a jaw, eyes half-lidded. Definitely *not* scared of me. When I called roll he instructed me to call him by a nickname because he was "The Third." I wrote the nickname on my roster and scrupulously never called him anything else. The Third would dominate that classroom for the entire course.

At the end of that first week the class handed in their first writing assignment. It was just a page or two, to serve as a "diagnostic" and benchmark. Once home and blessedly barefoot, I dug these pages out my purse, grabbed a beer, and went out onto the porch to read the descriptive prose of thirty freshmen. The Third might have the loudest voice in the room, but out here on the edge of the little college town his paper put him on equal footing. Finally I could get to know my other students, one by one.

Late-summer evenings in central Ohio dematerialize into night like your last dream--the one where you sense something's askew, and then you're awake. The owls hadn't started their call-and-response and I wasn't aware of my eyes straining when I got to a paper that stopped me.

It wouldn't be fair to read another student's work after this one; I would start over the next morning. I read it a second time, really wrestling the darkness to extract every word. By the end it was all I could do to make out the writer's name: Laura Hillenbrand.

Squinting in the twilight, I did not see the author of *Unbroken*, a masterpiece of historical research and narrative prose that (as of this writing) has remained on the New York Times Best-Seller list well over two years. Maybe I glimpsed the shimmering potential of *Seabiscuit*, but that is most likely giving myself too much retrospective credit. What I did see: words struck against each other, shedding sparks, seized upon by a writer who was herself seized by her subject: whatever it was, Laura had to tell her story.

***

It is always a privilege to work with a gifted student. But for an inexperienced teacher this blessing comes wrapped in a shroud of anxious questions.

Am I wrong? Crazy? (Okay--but am I *wrong?*) Am I subconsciously competing with--or worse, undercutting--my student? How can I help create opportunities for her when I'm so bad at doing it for myself? (Just ask my mother.)

Some of the swing "gurus" mentioned in *The Heart of the Game: A Coach's Journey* relentlessly market their tales of success (with accomplished players) on social media. Bobby McIver has always taken on unproven beginners; together, coach and player embark on a voyage of discovery and mutual adaptation. "Success" is not an empirical concept, or a universal standard.

The quality of your *bad* shots matters most. One player's break-through might be another's bad day. We call these teaching moments.

But moments don't teach--teachers do. Bobby lets each student determine his teaching path. This is the "secret" of great teaching--except that it isn't a secret, it just requires talent and dedication to achieve. (The support of employers and/or supervisors doesn't hurt either.) Bobby McIver wanted to coach, but he questioned whether he would be an effective teacher. The only way to find out was on the job.

Matt King and his friends made up the "Belle Meade crew" that set the template for Bobby's coaching. Now, as an adult decades removed from that experience, Matt still attests to its long-term benefits.

Interviewing early readers of *The Heart of The Game: A Coach's Journey* introduced me to many of the key players in Bobby McIver's story. The more of his former students I talked to, the more each reinforced (with personal nuances) the others' messages. His players--and friends, family, and colleagues--brought up points that both illustrated and extended the book's themes. My first impulse was to weave these ideas into Bobby's narrative. But my weavings made Bobby seem to be praising himself, which he would never do. I decided to present these memories, observations, and insights directly.

As a coach Bobby McIver emphasizes goals--not just having them, but consciously and deliberately ingraining them. Goal setting is also a prime example of how a golf lesson can carry over into all aspects of life. Matt King related how Bobby taught him to ask, "What do I want to accomplish?" This mental practice routine, Matt said, fostered his "ability to focus mentally."

That focus always distinguished Matt's game, even when he was a teenager competing in Junior tournaments. But its benefits extended beyond golf. As an adult, Matt King has built a highly successful capital investment company with fellow Belle Meade player John Burch. When I asked what it was like working so closely with a lifelong friend, Matt said they had a rule: "friends first, partners second"; that way "we can be really, really competitive" without ever violating the bond of friendship. This was exactly the premise Bobby had established in bringing along a group of talented young golfers: they were competing together, not against each other.

"The things Bobby talked about carried over into so many things in life," Matt told me--not only the goal-setting skills and mental focus, but deeper lessons. Though they might not have used those terms, Bobby got them "talking about values" before some were even teenagers. Matt recalled conversations about "God, and something bigger than ourselves." This established that the group's spiritual foundation transcended trophies or prize money. That belief in *something bigger than ourselves* is the ultimate take-away for any student (or reader) of Bobby McIver.

***

Mark McMurrey was seeking golf instruction for the first time at age 15 when he arrived at River Oaks Country Club, where Bobby McIver had just been hired as an assistant by head pro Dick Harmon. As Bobby explains in these pages, he considers 12 (give or take a year) the ideal age for a child to start golf lessons; a significant delay can make it hard for a teenager interested in junior or collegiate competition to catch up. But when Bobby left River Oaks three years later, Mark McMurrey was on his way to join Matt King on the elite Wake Forest University team. His own talent and work ethic, and Bobby McIver's coaching, had made him a highly competitive collegiate player.

Bobby's players have won tournaments at all levels. Scott Verplank is a great professional golfer; many of Bobby's students have competed on the highest amateur levels; and some have made careers in golf as instructors and course managers. The first of Bobby's former students I talked to, Mark McMurrey told me that what he valued most about Bobby McIver's teaching was how it shaped his life beyond the golf course. As he recalled the achievements of Scott Verplank, whom he knew from River Oaks, and his former teammate Matt King, Mark underscored this point: these men have made a success of their lives in many realms--business, church, and family--and Bobby's instruction has played a key role in their development.

Mark McMurrey describes Bobby's overall contribution to the lives of the kids he's coached, including himself, as "building champions." He defines a champion as a person who has internalized the teachings that allow him to make a success of whatever he pursues--whether Matt King's prominent business career, Scott Verplank's decades of distinction on the PGA Tour, or achievements less susceptible to public acknowledgment, like raising a kind and generous child. In recent years Mark has arranged for his teenaged son Harry to work with Bobby--a testament to Mark's belief in Bobby McIver's coaching philosophy and methods.

***

Jack Larkin first appears in this book as the "weakest link" on the Battle Ground Academy golf team that Bobby McIver, then an assistant at Belle Meade Country Club, helped prepare for the Tennessee state high school championship. With his young players Bobby emphasized dressing, preparing, and carrying yourself like a champion. Jack said this paid off for him well beyond the golf course. The fundamental insight behind this practice--present yourself as the winner you aspire to be, and you will feel and become more successful--applies to men and women, all ages, golfers and non-players alike. All you need is an aspiration: a goal.

Jack Larkin's teenage years provide an inspiring example of the power of goals. Playing for Bobby on that BGA team, he said, "ingrained some grand principles." As an adult, Jack has concluded that Bobby McIver instilled these values more through his actions than what he told his young players. Conveyed on the golf course, these "invaluable" lessons, about setting goals and adhering to a strong work ethic, proved in retrospect to apply throughout life.

The same year Bobby McIver left Belle Meade Country Club for "graduate school" at River Oaks with Dick Harmon--and, unexpectedly, Claude Harmon--Jack Larkin's family moved to Atlanta. Leaving his school and golf friends behind, Jack found himself the new kid in a big, unfamiliar city. What did he fall back on? "I'm going to do what McIver set me to do," he resolved at the time.

When the boys on the BGA team first asked for his help, Bobby had challenged them: every team member had to show up for daily practices at 6 a.m. They called them "sunrise sessions." In Atlanta Jack continued Bobby's dawn practice sessions on his own.

Anyone who's ever tried to get a teenager out of bed in the morning will recognize how deeply Bobby had instilled the discipline and focus of the practice routine in Jack and his teammates. The bottom line, however, was that Jack Larkin had set himself a goal: "I was supposed to win that U.S. Junior." Even if his coach couldn't picture him achieving it, Jack believed that national title rightfully belonged to him. And he proved that when the test comes, you need only (but always) your own belief.

***

"I wish I'd had Bobby as a coach," George Creagh said. Surprised, I reminded him that the final chapter of *The Heart of The Game: A Coach's Journey* describes how Bobby helped George prepare to compete in the U.S. Senior Amateur at the age of 69. No, George told me, he wished he'd had a coach or mentor like Bobby McIver when he was a boy--someone to serve two critical roles: an inner game coach who could have trained him to silence his own inner critic, and a teacher to guide him on how to practice.

Bobby writes that his young Belle Meade students had an invaluable opportunity to observe great players. These included Bobby's fellow assistant, the local phenom Mike Whiteside, 1975 U.S. Open winner Lou Graham . . . and George Creagh, mentioned in the same sentence: Graham's equal. "But George," I said, "from what Bobby says, you've got such a great swing you don't need much coaching."

But that was exactly the problem. George Creagh always had that natural, repeating swing so many envied. But he had come to understand the difference between target golf and "the swing"--that concept so many players fixate on (and some teachers exploit), at the expense of giving attention to areas that might actually benefit their game. "A pretty swing is nice," George said, "but the point is putting it in the hole."

George Creagh is a thoughtful and intellectually voracious person with great insight. At the age of ten, he was inspired to play golf by the movie "Follow the Sun," about Ben Hogan overcoming the injuries suffered in a car accident. George's innate ability and "pretty swing" yielded dazzling collegiate success; a professional playing career was certainly a realistic possibility given his talent, and he tried to make the PGA Tour once.

But George had set himself an impossible internal goal: "I'm going to be good enough that I never lose a match." When the inevitable happened, the failure felt absolute. "I was very hard on myself," he said, underscoring the importance of the kind of psychological, or "inner game," coaching that Bobby McIver promotes and practices.

George Creagh believes that the ideas in this book can benefit golfers at all levels. Discussing Adam Scott's loss to Ernie Els in the 2012 British Open, he said that in the heat of a tournament, players "forget that they could win this if they don't make it earthshaking." His advice to young people: find a mentor, someone who can reinforce your belief in yourself through patient guidance and encouragement. Developing a positive and constructive outlook from the beginning is the ideal George shares with Bobby.

"I wanted to have a goal, something to shoot for," George said of attempting to qualify for the U.S. Senior Amateur in his late 60's. I asked if he planned to try again. As far as golf is concerned, he told me, "What I want to do now, the rest of my life, is really enjoy it." George Creagh still has his sights set on Belle Meade's club championship. But his primary intention now is to savor each moment, rather than come out with a winning score.

***

The Inner Game of Tennis, by Timothy Gallwey, played a formative role in the development of Bobby McIver's coaching philosophy. It has served him as a touchstone, springboard, and inspiration--and also as a "straw man" to argue against. Bobby locates its shortcomings in Gallwey's failure to acknowledge the years of practice or training one must invest before the body can be liberated from the conscious mind. This concept has recently been popularized by Malcolm Gladwell and David Brooks, among others, as the "Ten Thousand Hours to Mastery" theory.

Bobby was first introduced to *The Inner Game of Tennis* and spurred to read it by George Creagh. The book remains a powerful influence on George nearly four decades later. Like Bobby, he cites the timelessness of Timothy Gallwey's core messages about staying in the moment, focusing on the ball, and how a positive thought leads to a positive reaction. George believes that Gallwey's principles can help anybody, "even if they don't have the ten thousand hours, or even a thousand hours." Being a champion is a state of mind first, last, and always.

I first read *The Inner Game of Tennis* after being immersed for almost a year in the process of editing Bobby's book. Having played tennis as a kid, I could 'feel' the physical adjustments Gallwey described. My hands unconsciously tensed, clutching an invisible, weightless racket. I wished I could try out my serve with no one looking.

I started hitting a tennis ball around age ten, with a friend who had some old wooden rackets. We walked to the dilapidated public recreation center--tennis courts in the summer, the space was flooded to make an ice-skating rink in the winter. But we weren't court-ready. On the back of the square brick administrative building, at net height, someone had painted a yellow stripe about the width of my palm, all the way across the back wall. The ground behind it was paved with concrete--perfect, as far as a couple of ten-year-olds were concerned.

We wore flip-flops. Our hair hung in our eyes. Many of our swings missed the ball entirely. Sometimes this made us laugh until we cried and had to use our bare tanned arms as Kleenex. We brought sisters, hers older and mine younger. When my friend moved away my sister kept coming to hit balls with me.

I don't want to give the impression that I was a good, or even mediocre, tennis player. Bobby McIver truly possesses an inner Magician he taps into when he plays golf. I witnessed this myself when I saw him play the Yale University Golf Course.

Bobby had traveled up to Connecticut to compete in a U.S. Senior Open qualifier. That tournament marked the culmination of months of effort, self-discovery, and heartbreak, described in the "Back Nine" chapters of this book. The Yale course lies hidden amid a tangle of obscure streets in northwestern New Haven; when Bobby decided to spend a pre-tournament rest day playing this historic layout, I was proud of knowing how to get us there.

Bobby was playing for fun, and to acquaint himself with this hauntingly beautiful and challenging course, but I watched him come up with some quirky bunker shots that demanded an inspired imagination. And regardless of how they were falling, he swung his driver with a loose, graceful ease that made him look like a gray-haired teenager. I kept thinking I should really pay attention because I could learn something from carefully observing my friend in this context, and then reversing my internal course. *Bobby's enjoying each moment! Enjoy it with him!*

My point about my "tennis career" is that I didn't have one. I started at the right age, and for the reason Bobby emphasizes throughout this book: fun. I had fun playing with my friend, and for a time both my sisters. If only *The Inner Game of Tennis* had somehow found its way into my hands when I was thirteen . . . but it hadn't been published yet. By the time the book came out I had grown highly resistant to anything that might help me.

Like George Creagh, I wish I could have found a mentor like Bobby McIver. Or rather--realistically--I wish he or she had found me and then persisted like mad in affirming my essential self. I was privileged to have adults in my life who tried to give me positive reinforcement. But since I couldn't believe them, I didn't hear them.

Describing how his own father demanded "excellence" and withheld encouragement, George said "it took me some time to really mature." For me, maturing is a work in progress. Working on, inhabiting, and metabolizing *The Heart of The Game: A Coach's Journey* has helped me with that progress. Life is precious--I've always said and believed that--but this book helped anchor the elusive feeling that my own life is precious. I have even set goals.

Some might approach *The Heart of the Game: A Coach's Journey* as simply a golf book. Virtually every golfer who has read this book has reported playing better immediately, especially after finishing the "Working Smarter" chapter. Whatever his or her natural inclination, each has credited this to Bobby's instructions on staying in the moment--and trashing your swing keys.

A book this personal invariably has origins that reach back into all the chambers of conscious memory, as well as the landscape of the unconscious, the half-dreamed world a writer accesses in the flow of writing "in the spirit."

Bobby McIver conceived of this book before I knew him. In response to Miguel Coles' suggestion to "write how you coach," in 2001 Bobby started a project titled *Playing Great Golf: Less Is More.* Five years later he found himself mired in intractable writer's block. Realizing he had written "just another textbook," he abandoned the project. But an honest self-assessment can reveal opportunity, even within the most discouraging insight. Chapter 15 describes the moment of inspiration that carried Bobby from *Less Is More* into *The Heart of the Game.*

If you want to get Bobby's coaching from this book, the key lies in Miguel's specific words, way back in 2001. He did not suggest to Bobby that he "write *about* how you coach." What he said was: "write how you coach." The experience of reading this book is intended to replicate, as closely as possible, what his players have experienced while being coached by Bobby McIver--and to produce results.

Bobby coaches using stories. His most important lessons employ subtlety and repetition to overcome the reflexive impatience most of us carry around. You are not going to find bullet-pointed lists or diagrams in *The Heart of the Game: A Coach's Journey*--but you might find the soul of golf.

And if you "pay attention," as Bobby McIver recommends, you just might find even more than that. During every conversation about this book, even the most avid and successful players invariably move from talking about golf to describing how Bobby's teachings apply to life off the course. This I can validate from my own experience. This book has made me better at being me--or maybe just being.

Bobby McIver & Megan Macomber

When Farmington Country Club invited Bobby McIver to interview for the position of head golf professional, he made the trip to Charlottesville knowing that if he did not get the job he was essentially unemployed. An impulsive act of principle had cost him the head pro position he had held for eight years, and jeopardized the excellent reputation he had built. After an intense Q&A session, the Farmington selection committee asked Bobby to give two lessons so they could observe his teaching style.

So much was riding on this Charlottesville visit. The (by then) highly experienced Bobby McIver could have given a couple of simple golf lessons on autopilot. Anyone would have understood a lapse of concentration. But Bobby's account of these two lessons illustrates what he means when he writes that "the teacher must be fully present." From the moment he glimpsed his first "student," committee member Dick Funk, warming up, the great teacher took full charge.

True to both his philosophy and his own nature, Bobby attuned himself to each student, solving problems with spontaneous insight, creativity, and a dose of "Harmonized" humor. Witnessing teenaged Ellen Youel respond to Bobby's instructions--with a "better than decent" golf swing and a blooming enjoyment that initially seemed impossible--thrills me every time I read it. That's the beauty of teaching, viewed as a sporting event: no one has to lose.

***

"The question is not whether we are going to face trials, pain, and suffering, but what we are going to do with them when they show up. Life is a learning experience--we face ad-

versity and learn from it. Without pain there is no joy, or life."
These words come from a section of the book that did not survive the revision process (my account of how *The Heart of The Game: A Coach's Journey* evolved from Bobby McIver's manuscript to its current form can be found in the Afterword). But I could not consider this book complete without them.

Bobby McIver has faced unimaginable losses in the course of his journey. The death of a parent, while heartbreaking, is foreseeable by most of us who are beyond a certain age. Even the loss of a sibling, spouse, or a child to illness--because we fear these most, our minds conjure them. This is not to minimize these events in the slightest, but to differentiate them from those that come out of the blue, forcing you to come to grips with your loss while in a state of shock. Bobby went through this following the tragic deaths of two of the young men he had coached. For a teacher, finding out a student has died feels indescribably wrong. Life, God, the universe--it's just not supposed to be that way. Your students are supposed to carry on after you.

Dick Harmon's death from heart disease in his fifties had a different but just as profound effect on the man he had hired almost two decades earlier. The intervening years had sealed an irreplaceable friendship. After Dick's funeral in Houston, Mark McMurrey drove Bobby McIver back to where he was staying. As they got out of the car in the rain, Mark made a point of thanking Bobby for all he had given him, and they hugged. Bobby writes of that moment: "The Lord promises that He will provide. He says He will see us through. Mark let me feel something we tend to forget: what it is like to be in His hands."

Bobby McIver promotes the "Harmon way," not taking your-self too seriously and encouraging others to have fun. He describes his mother's essential "lightheartedness." This book contains many lighthearted moments, and Bobby's teaching is creative and fun.

Under all these grace notes runs a deeper current. Whether you are always conscious of it or not, you are reading a message of love. Every hour I have spent with *The Heart of The Game: A Coach's Journey*, I have felt what it is like to be in His hands.

Now I'll get out of the way, so you can make your own journey with Bobby.

Megan Macomber

"Daddy Will" Gordon and Bobby McIver, 1950.

The BGA Sunrise Service team: Back row, l. to r.: Jack Larkin, Matt King, Bobby, John Burch, Mike Keliher. Front row l. to r.: Jimmy Ward, Bruce Carillion, Robert Keene, Roy Matlock.

{ 1 }

The Pied Piper

*The greater danger for most of us lies not in setting
our aim too high and falling short; but in setting
our aim too low, and achieving our mark.*

–Michelangelo Buonorrati

*Logic will take you from A to B.
Imagination will take you everywhere.*

–Albert Einstein

My father introduced me to golf. He never played well
enough for me to emulate his game--he broke eighty a few
times--but his passion for just playing probably exceeded mine.
I always saw him with the same group, three men who were a
good many years older. Playing for the exercise, they used pull
carts and played incredibly fast. My father, an accountant,
wanted everything organized and just right. He would sweep the
ball with his irons instead of swinging down and taking a divot,
because he wanted his irons to stay like new.

I only played with him a handful of times but I can remember
him telling me, "You should be a golf professional." Though I

was no more than ten or eleven, I can still hear those words and even picture the spot at Graymere Country Club where we were playing when he said them. Graymere, the little nine-hole club in Columbia, Tennessee, had no golf professional; with no idea where to go, I didn't even think about getting lessons. At a junior clinic when I was about eight or nine, all we did was hit a five iron. Lacking any role model, I knew nothing about the life of a club pro and wouldn't consider it as a career path until I stumbled onto it more than ten years later. I came in the back door, so to speak.

I pretty much taught myself to play golf. Although I often glimpsed him observing from a distance, my father stayed out of my way; he allowed me to develop naturally, without the pressure of his presence. He took me to the club, let me learn on my own, and picked me up.

I used to caddie for Tillman Knox, known for many years as one of the best players in the region. Admired for his gracious manner as much as his great game, Knox taught me more than how to play: he epitomized the true gentleman. Like all young people, I learned by watching and imitating him. I'd enrolled myself in a golf-professional preparatory course--without any thought of making golf my career. But a game that started out as fun would soon serve as my refuge.

One summer afternoon before my eighth grade year my mother called me aside. "Daddy Will has cancer," she told me. "He's not going to make it."

Will Gordon was already in his eighties when I was a child, growing up on the 175-acre farm my ancestors settled in 1807. Generations of Gordons, an African-American family who moved onto our farm in 1912, lived as our neighbors until 2011.

Daddy Will taught me to fish, whittle, play checkers--if it had anything to do with fun, we did it. Daddy Will spoiled me like grandfathers do, and I was his shadow.

Two-a-day football practices were about to start. Our junior high school team counted on my speed at the tailback position and for kick returns, but after several days of practice I went into the locker room, showered, put my clothes on, and never returned. I went to sit at Daddy Will's bedside every day instead. Will Gordon died on October 13, 1961, at 10 o'clock in the morning. It was the first time I'd lost anyone close to me.

Shortly after that my school had tryouts for the basketball team. As one of the top two or three players, I got assigned to the best group as the tryouts proceeded. On the final day the coach called us together to tell us that two players had been cut. "One was very hard," he said. "The other one was easy because he's a quitter." We went into the locker room where the coach had posted the final team roster. My name wasn't on it: I had been labeled a quitter.

In a small-town junior high school this was hard to shake. Nobody knew why I'd left the football team. In those days of "Colored Only" drinking fountains, they wouldn't understand even if I told them.

Four diverse elementary schools fed this junior high school, pooling 1,000 students, and discipline was stern. A bullying assistant principal delivered licks with big paddles that sent me home black and blue. After a session with that assistant principal--for something I didn't do, this time--my 8th-grade homeroom teacher met me coming down the hall. Having heard the licks echoing down the hall, she asked what was going on. I told her.

I could handle that paddle, but when Mrs. Leah Hays grabbed me in her arms and said "I believe you," I fell apart. Recently Mrs. Hayes told me she almost resigned from teaching over what was going on that year. She is one of only a handful of my teachers I remember now, and hands down the best teacher I ever had.

To a boy who lived for sports those years were hell, but the pain and adversity of that time contributed to my passion and affinity for coaching young players. I've never coached a young person who didn't want to be a winner, and I wouldn't use a paddle for any reason.

Finally my parents pulled me out of the public schools and sent me to Columbia Military Academy, where I regained my confidence and experienced great coaching for the first time. CMA's basketball team competed in a prep school league; half of our schedule had us competing against college teams. Coach Bill Wade would start practices by telling us, "Men, we will be smaller. They'll think they are better. We'll win more than our share, but we'll have to do it differently."

Coach Wade got us in tremendous shape and drilled us until we could run the plays blindfolded. After we lost a close one, he would come into the locker room and say something positive. "We sure made those big ol' college boys work for it tonight!" "Men, we didn't lose this one, we just ran out of time." "You showed 'em some heart. We out-hustled them--I'm proud of our effort." He never called us anything but men. "Okay, men, it's time! Time to take the floor and show 'em what we've got. Let 'em see it!"

I had continued to develop my skills, shooting alone with imaginary defenders. I always defended our opponents' best outside shooter. Many times he would be 6'6" or so, five inches taller than I was, but when Coach Wade told me "Bobby, they can't score without the ball," that's all it took. I did anything I could to deny their guy the ball.

During those years in public school, I had focused mainly on golf. Playing golf to win involves an inner battle, and success requires a tractor-trailer load of competitive passion. My father enjoyed watching competitive sports, but it wasn't in his nature to compete; he couldn't give me something he didn't have. My mother didn't have a clue about anything related to athletics, so I had my space. Seeking to avoid dealing with the coaches who'd labeled me a quitter, I discovered in the safe and protected world of Graymere that I had a natural gift for this game: the more I gave golf, the more it gave back.

Our golf teams at CMA were the best in the school's history. Coach Lewis Moore carried himself with such presence that he inspired our confidence without saying a word. Like most coaches on the high-school level, Coach Moore also taught an academic subject--history, in his case. The day Sir Winston Churchill died, he lectured extemporaneously with tears in his eyes, telling us how Churchill saved the western world by the power of his voice. It stuck with me. Coach Moore always followed my career with interest, and I became a big Churchill fan, something I had the pleasure of sharing with Mr. Moore before he died.

Encouraged by a group of CMA friends from the Mississippi Delta, I applied to the University of Mississippi. The following spring I was riding a tractor on a Saturday when my father brought the acceptance notice for me to see.

College revealed that I had another gift: getting along with people. A club professional interacts with club members, their children, grandchildren, in-laws, guests, and others you can't even imagine, to say nothing of club staff. Like diplomats, we juggle, reflect, and soothe myriad personalities. In order to succeed, as one of my mentors said, we have to be "public relations geniuses." With its reputation for football, parties, and supplying a disproportionate number of Miss Americas, Ole Miss gave me a world-class education in this fine art.

I showed up in Oxford, MS, in the fall of 1966, totally naive about college and equally lacking in career ideas. I chose the business school, figuring I might go into "business" one day, and joined SAE, a CMA friend's fraternity. I continued to play golf at Ole Miss and competed during the summers, but playing for the Ole Miss team never entered my mind. The team members knew I had game, and I would play any of them for a dollar or two, but college golf hadn't become the big deal it is now--plus I was too busy, what with fraternity parties and trying to keep my grades mediocre. I had to go to summer school to maintain my 2.0 average and stay one step ahead of the draft board. I knew guys who got drafted as soon as they fell behind in their hours, and others who joined the national guard to keep from going to Viet Nam.

In January, 1971, I managed to graduate with exactly a 2.000000 average. Leaving Oxford caused my heart to sink. Forced to start thinking about what to do with my general business degree, I didn't have the slightest idea.

I was playing golf at the club back home one day when someone asked why didn't I get an assistant's job and try the golf business. This man said to contact Ewing Pomeroy, who had served as the pro at Graymere many years earlier and was now head pro at the Lakewood Golf Club at the Grand Hotel in Point Clear, AL. Mr. Pomeroy offered me a job without an interview. I spent six months at Lakewood serving as a "ranger"--the guy who rides a cart monitoring pace of play--all day, seven days a week.

That summer my mother called; according to her cousin, Mrs. Mary Kimbrough, Belle Meade Country Club, outside of Nashville, had hired a new head professional from New Jersey and the whole golf staff was leaving, so there would be some openings. Mike Whiteside, a good friend from the CMA team, was just graduating from Middle Tennessee State University. I let him know about the openings and took a weekend off at the end of July. Willie Gibbons, Belle Meade's new head pro, interviewed us both at the same time. Mike was shy and didn't know how to sell himself, so I ended up making the pitch for both of us.

Before going to work for Mr. Pomeroy at Lakewood, I had submitted resumes to all the golf manufacturing companies. Back in Alabama, I got two calls on the same day: the sales manager for MacGregor Golf Company offered me a job, and Willie Gibbons asked me to return his call. As he gave me the message, Mr. Pomeroy advised me to take the MacGregor job. The life of a club professional wasn't nearly as glamorous as people thought, he explained. I had seen how much time he had to work. When MacGregor made a financial offer, I asked for time to think. Then I returned Willie's call. He offered me a position, too--for less than half of MacGregor's deal. But I liked the idea of coaching.

My heart told me to forget about my wallet: I was off to Nashville.

I hadn't even seen Mrs. Kimbrough, my mother's cousin, in ten years, yet she had thought of me when the position at Belle Meade Country Club became available. Walking in the door at Belle Meade with Willie Gibbons on August 15, 1971, I knew I'd gotten a break.

Mike Whiteside had also been hired. We found an apartment and settled in to learn our new jobs, leaning on Willie to teach us what was expected at a swank club like Belle Meade. The three of us came from similar backgrounds. Just 30 years old, Willie Gibbons was originally from Texarkana, AR--he may have worked in New Jersey, but he wasn't a Yankee after all. Willie's father had been a barber in Texarkana. Mike's dad worked in maintenance at the Monsanto plant back home. My dad was an accountant on the small-town scale, but I identified more with working on our farm for Horace Gordon, Daddy Will's son.

Belle Meade wanted us to bring new life to the golf program. I decided to focus on the basics: greet every man, woman, and child by name and with a smile, four or five times, whenever they came into the shop. It works--people love to hear you say their own names. I spent hours behind the counter registering players: writing each name in a journal, collecting a dime per player for the caddie fund, and using an intercom to call the names back to our bag room manager, Jeff Sales. Getting to the first tee at Graymere Country Club never took so many steps, but this was the Belle Meade program. Columbia and Graymere might be only 45 miles away, but this was another world.

At first, Willie Gibbons seemed anxious about his position at Belle Meade. I believe he may have had an oral agreement, not a written contract, with the club. At Echo Lake Country Club in New Jersey he had worked as an assistant for the great pro Bob Moser. Moser had worked for Jack Lumpkin, then the pro at Oak Hill in Rochester, New York, a famous club that has hosted U.S. Opens, Ryder Cups, and U.S. Amateurs. And Lumpkin, Willie told me proudly, had worked for Claude Harmon at Winged Foot. Not only was Claude Harmon the last club professional to win the Masters, he had also appeared on the cover of Sports Illustrated--unheard-of for a teacher. "We come down from the Claude Harmon line," Willie said, like he was talking about the pedigree of a Triple Crown racehorse.

Willie hadn't been at Belle Meade for a month when Echo Lake called wanting him back; Moser had announced he was leaving. Willie said, "I have no idea what income this job will generate. I know what I can make at Echo Lake." A club pro's salary was small in those days. The better the job you did the more you would make from bag room storage fees, the driving range, the golf shop, and lesson income. Willie's wife and daughter hadn't even relocated to Nashville yet. "Bobby, how'd you like to move to New Jersey?" he asked, halfway serious.

As a worldly-wise twenty-three-year old who had been an assistant pro for maybe two weeks, I took a moment to collect my thoughts. "I'm not thinking about going to New Jersey," I said. "This is *Belle Meade*. And you don't need to be thinking about it either."

Willie already knew this, he just needed to hear it for reassurance. "This is the best club in the state, and maybe the south," I continued. "There are some heavy hitters and big league players out here--if you pay attention, you can make more playing the stock market than you can from this job." Willie Gibbons would remain Belle Meade's head pro for a remarkable thirty-five years. I think he did all right in the stock market, too.

Belle Meade had an old Donald Ross course that had been renovated by Robert Trent Jones, a really great test of golf, but I was lucky to get nine holes in before the sun went down. Once Willie hired shop lady Sandra Martin, pressure on our staff eased; early on, however, Willie, Mike, and I were stretched thin, and my game suffered from the constant, competing demands on my time.

With his strong short game Willie could bring in a good score regardless of how he was hitting it. Mike Whiteside, a great player before coming to Belle Meade, routinely finished with a 64 or 65 when he got it going. One day several club members approached Mike, offering to stake him for three years on the PGA Tour. Jimmy Holt even volunteered his private jet. But Mike declined. "I don't want to be having to do all that traveling," he told them. To this day, people in Columbia speculate whether Mike Whiteside could have made it.

During my first month at Belle Meade I kept an eye out for kids who might want some coaching, and I'd noticed a few "regulars" hanging around the golf shop. Late one afternoon I spotted a young man seated quietly on a chair behind a clothing display, flipping through a magazine. "What's happening, big man?" I asked. He was waiting for his mom, he said. His name was Matt King and he was twelve.

He also told me he wanted to be a player--but not in words. It has been said that communication is 75%, 80%, 90% non-verbal.

For me it's about 95%. I could see something in his eyes as we talked. I can't tell you what exactly, but there is a spark or twinkle that tells me a kid has something. If you know how to look you can spot it, even during a brief encounter like this. I told Matt I'd be looking for him; he needed to round up some friends, so we could see how good we could get. I was saying "we" because I didn't know how good a coach I would be. My heart was saying *Hey, let's go!* but I didn't know if I had what it took to make it happen.

When Matt's mom came into the shop to retrieve him, flashing a radiant smile and bringing her joy with her, I said to myself, "Lord have mercy, you brought me one! This boy has something special. Just look at his mother."

Matt King was lean and tall for his age, with long, slender fingers that fit well on the club. He just walked up confidently and made these silky-smooth swings. Too many players, young and old alike, lash out with a sense of urgency, as if the ball were a rattlesnake. Matt's swing, sound grip, and unconscious rhythm and timing added up to effortless power. Recognizing his natural swing, I had enough sense to leave it alone. I had taken on the mission of coaxing out as much of Matt's potential as I could without messing him up. Sensing a future champion in my very first student, I was teaching by instinct--a combination of intuition and memories of my own early experiences, from the encouragement of Coach Bill Wade to the nonverbal inspiration of Lewis Moore.

I did not remain exclusively Matt's coach long. He soon introduced me to some of his friends. Jimmy Ward, a little blond kid, had such a pure swing that Willie Gibbons started calling him "the Cub," a reference to Jack Nicklaus, "the Bear." I still have some old graph check sequence photographs that show Jimmy's flawless move. John Burch was taller, like Matt; the quiet and studious type, John might not say much, but he knew everything that was going on around him. Bob Jackson, a year or two younger, mainly tagged along at first, but he would catch up in time.

King, Ward, Burch, and Jackson: this group would generate my career. In its soon-to-be expanded form it would produce my first national champion. But I could never have predicted when, where, or especially by whom this would be accomplished.

After I took responsibility for Belle Meade's junior program, kids started flocking to the clinics. Hugh Entrekin was among the older juniors who were good players; but in their last years of high school, they wouldn't be around long enough for me to do anything with them. I wound up focusing on the younger ones. Watching my pupils march with me to the range, club members smiled and called me the Pied Piper.

I was never partial to males over females. A young lady named Lissa Bradford came through a year or so before I left Belle Meade. Although I really had little to do with Lissa's development, I did tell her there were two types of golf-- competitive golf and social golf--and she got to choose. Since she related this years after the fact, it obviously made an impression.

Lissa definitely wanted to play real golf. Maybe I set the hook and some others brought her along; she played well in college and won two Tennessee Women's Amateur tournaments.

***

I didn't see Matt King or the other boys much after school started. The golf staff at Belle Meade filled out foursomes when club members dropped out of a game. One Sunday at the end of January, 1972, Matt's father, Jim, and two other members asked me to play. The weather was damp and cloudy, but the temperature stayed pleasant for mid-winter. These guys were true gentlemen, and it was a great day. What I remember most is that Mr. King was one of these guys who played around with a pipe. You know: fooling with it took more time than smoking it.

The next morning, headed home to the farm in Columbia for a meal and to get my laundry done, I was cruising along in my canary-yellow Oldsmobile Cutlass when the radio announcer cut in. "Mr. Jim King, President of Martha White Foods, died suddenly of a heart attack last night in his home."

I pulled off the road, stunned. Matt King, the young man with such natural ability, had lost his dad. I'd known Mr. King only briefly, but long enough to perceive that he was a class act.

***

I knew Matt King could be a champion if I could learn how to get him there. Matt and Jimmy Ward were both naturals with great swings. With such limited time early on, my aim was simply to make it fun, so they would make golf their game.

I kept it very basic, emphasizing a good grip and set-up. The grip aligns with the clubface. A good set-up means an athletic stance with the legs bent to provide spring. It's like guarding someone in basketball: the spine naturally tilts forward so the hands and arms can just hang, giving enough room to swing. The other element in set-up is alignment: the club faces the target while the player stands to the side to let the club swing towards it.

Golf is a target game. Pick a target, focus on it, and hit it. Don't make it complicated. This minimalist approach may have been born out of my early fear of messing up these talented young players, but it eventually evolved into the core of my teaching philosophy: *Less Is More.*

I'm talking about working with a complete beginner around the age of eleven or twelve. Because the motor skills to really handle a club well don't typically develop until age twelve--plus or minus a year--I advise against starting lessons before this. If the clubs are too heavy or light, too long or too short, the swing must compensate; our brains and nervous systems latch onto our swings, good or bad, and the move will be grooved.

I withhold the ball until the player experiences a natural, balanced swing. Then I place the ball on a tee, making sure they have plenty of loft with something like a seven iron. It's important not to put the ball in front of them until they can make solid contact: nothing discourages a young player more than whiffing their first shots. A coach should evaluate each player, start where they can succeed, and keep the attention on the motion, not the ball--this goes for everyone, not just beginners.

When I asked Matt King how he first got the idea golf was his game, he said his dad had taken him to see Lanny Wadkins and Steve Melnyk compete in the Southern Amateur at Belle Meade when he was ten or eleven. This is a typical story. Hey parents, what's the best way to get your child interested in golf? Start by taking them to a tournament--let them witness excellence and they won't need any commentary.

Matt King and the crew inspired my philosophy for coaching this age group: "Say Little, Be There More, and Make It FUN!" Once the school year ended, the boys' parents dropped them off at the club every morning when we opened. Then, after playing or practicing all day, they waited for me to get off work and we would play nine holes or until it got dark.

***

My family never took a vacation together because we didn't have the money. But my father used to pull me out of elementary school to go to Vanderbilt University, where we watched the entire Tennessee state high school basketball tournament; that was as close to bonding as we got. During golf's off-season I took my young players to Vanderbilt basketball games.

After Mike Whiteside got married I moved into a member's guesthouse across from the club. Glancing behind my new place one day, I saw Jimmy Ward shooting baskets and immediately went out do a little basketball coaching pro bono. I was happy to extend this role. Matt King's family had a very nice barn complete with backboard and basket; it was a little tight, but we could play regardless of the weather.

Matt King and Bob Wolcott both played high school basketball. The schedule doesn't overlap golf season, and I'm convinced playing basketball made me a better golfer. Basketball requires good hands, fitness, and being part of a team; like golf, it is a game of rhythm, balance, and finesse. Young golfers benefit from getting involved in a second sport. These year-round junior golf tours are a formula for peaking too soon and burning out, while participating in school athletic programs lets young players take a break and *have fun!*

I loved hanging out with these kids. I was coaching when they didn't know it, and they were teaching me what they needed. Yes, I do believe the player is the teacher--as long as the teacher pays attention.

Mark McMurrey playing at River Oaks in 1979.

"Players Hit the First Shot"

You can't divide the swing into parts and still have the swing.
A cat is a cat. If you dissect it, you'll have blood and guts
and bones, but no cat.

–Ernest Jones

Somewhere I'd gotten the idea that club pros were supposed to play great all the time, just a notch below the touring pros, and at Belle Meade I started to feel self-conscious about my game. During my college years I had competed in summer events on the fried chicken circuit in Mississippi: two-day, 36-hole events that always served potato salad, sweet tea, and--yes--fried chicken. With little preparation and no expectations, I beat some good players.

By the spring of 1973, breaking 80 had become an accomplishment. I practiced whenever I could, often staying on the course well past sundown as I searched for my old magic, the game that had always come so naturally. I experienced spurts of my old self, but mostly it felt like I'd slid into a slump that just clung to me. I started wondering if I had the game to make it as a club professional.

I was discovering "the revolving door": the worse it gets the harder you try, and the harder you try the worse it gets. The key word is "try." In this game or any other, you need to *let it happen.*

A year and a half at Belle Meade hadn't convinced me that the golf business was for me. I missed my college friends, wasn't used to working sixty hours a week (plus weekends), and couldn't get my game together. The mounting frustration drove me to search for help, and when *Golf Digest* started promoting a new teaching concept I latched right on.

The magazine first presented a thorough history that linked the evolution of the golf swing to advances in equipment. The next step in this evolution was supposed to be *The Square to Square Golf Swing,* by Dick Aultman, who derived his approach from a clinic given by Jim Flick. Start with the club-face square, set the angle early to remain square, then turn to the top and swing; weaken the grip by turning the left hand under the handle with the back facing the target and the thumb stretching down the middle in "a long thumb" position.

Golf Digest touted this new "system" as a paradigm shift in how the game would be played, and it made a big splash in the early 1970's. To follow the instructions, however, requires an early cocking of the wrists. The flat left wrist is desirable at impact, but not at the starting or address position. Now, with the benefit of thirty-plus years of experience, I know this is anything but natural. But I was young, it was *Golf Digest,* and I bought into the concept . . . with little or no success.

I had also begun to study Ben Hogan's *Five Lessons: The Modern Fundamentals of Golf.* These two conceptual methodologies did not square up (pun intended). The Hogan book provided a solid understanding of grip, posture, alignment, and balance, and it had great illustrations by Anthony Ravielli. I'm very much a visual learner, and these images of grip, set-up, and other parts of the swing were helpful--except for one.

Swinging on-plane is essential to consistent ball striking. If the club isn't on-plane when it starts down, it's too late to compensate--everything is happening too fast. Ravielli's images depict Hogan, a large pane of glass resting on his shoulders with a small hole for his head to go through. The bottom of the glass rests on the plane line, the bottom of the swing where the ball sits. One particular image shows Hogan at the top of the back swing, left arm and club on-plane and *the left shoulder under the glass*. Guided by that drawing, I started trying to keep my left shoulder under an imaginary pane of glass while getting everything else in proper alignment. No matter how hard I tried, I just couldn't get it.

I finally figured out on my own that it is anatomically impossible for that left shoulder to turn "under the glass" while everything else works properly. Trying to achieve it caused my back swing to be too steep, requiring me to try to drop the club on-plane coming down. That was a seriously flawed drawing. The editors hadn't caught it, nor had Hogan himself.

Or perhaps, Claude Harmon explained to me years later, I'd failed to take into account "the fallacy." As Ben Hogan's best friend, Claude Harmon knew his swing; but Claude Harmon knew the swings of almost every other top player in the game then, too. "Never trust what a good player says they are doing," he told me. "They cannot see their swings and what they feel is never real. Let me see the swing and I'll determine for myself what they are doing."

Claude Harmon had an infectious sense of humor. Every time they saw each other, he would ask Mr. Hogan how his book sales were going. When Hogan, as usual, indicated sales continued to be good, Mr. Harmon would laugh and say that was great, because club professionals could keep making money from all these confused and overwhelmed players whose games needed straightening out. The simple truth is that more knowledge and better play aren't companions. In fact, it works the opposite way: *less is more*. It took me years to drop the notion that studying others' methods was the answer for me.

***

I had spent the second half of 1971 and most of 1972 trying to find my old natural swing. With my mind focused inward rather than on the target, I got nowhere.

For a time I just worked on my short game. Then I got creative: swinging left-handed, one-handed, cross-handed, with my feet together, even practicing in the dark. Improvising in this era before heavy clubs, I would bundle three clubs and swing with my eyes closed. These techniques all helped me make incremental progress.

But none of the effort I put in directly on my game helped as much as working with the kids. When I demonstrated shots for them, my thoughts were no longer focused on myself. Slowly my old swing showed up. I realized something so simple nobody thinks about it: any method that advocates something new is very likely unnatural. If it doesn't *feel* natural, then it's unnatural—forced--and you don't want anything to do with it.

Tom Watson, a year younger than I am, was a good college and amateur player, but dozens of college players could beat him. In just a few years on the PGA Tour, however, he went from "lucky to earn his card" to elite status. Everyone-- including Byron Nelson, who became his mentor--took notice. Confident and aggressive, Watson worked as hard as anyone who ever hit the Tour. His red hair and quick smile inspired reporters to nickname him Huckleberry Finn--my own boyhood nickname.

A guy named Randy Hudson used to play in some money games at Belle Meade. Randy knew golf. One Sunday morning word got back to me of Randy saying, "'Bobby's worked so hard, he's Nashville's Tom Watson.'" I had gone through the very hard process of unlearning something grooved. Because my progress had been slow and steady--which is best--I couldn't see how far I had come. Randy Hudson's compliment gave my confidence a huge boost. Once Randy, a credible and keen observer, validated my achievements, I stopped focusing on how my body was moving and started hunting targets and flags.

When I was younger, quicker, and stronger I would attack a course; if I could see the pin, I was going for it. If I got four or five over par in a round I declared war.

I drove the ball really *long*. A mature hackberry tree about fifty feet tall stood at the end of Belle Meade's range, about 280 yards away from the practice tee. If the boys were around and I spotted a foursome I knew playing the eighth hole, I'd launch a couple of those extra-hard, low-performance range balls over that tree into the middle of the number eight fairway; off persimmon-wood-headed drivers, they carried well over 300 yards.

The members were stunned at my power, when in truth I was fast: distance comes from club-head speed, not strength.

***

Every spring the Tennessee PGA held an education seminar. In 1973 Davis Love, Jr. was scheduled to speak during the two-day event. When he fell ill, he contacted Dick Horton, the executive director of the section, to say that Harvey Penick, from Austin, Texas, had agreed to substitute for him. Dick didn't know who he was. Harvey Penick was in his seventies, Davis Love said, and someone would need to assist him while he was in Nashville. The seminar was only days away when Dick asked if I would help Mr. Penick during his visit.

My contemporaries might not know him, but I was well aware of Harvey Penick. He had coached Tom Kite and Ben Crenshaw at Austin Country Club since they were strong enough to swing a club; both had been named NCAA First-Team All Americans in 1972. I saw Crenshaw play in his first Masters in 1972, finishing as Low Amateur. With Matt King and Jimmy Ward already showing promise, I needed to learn a lot more about coaching--helping younger players in particular--and judging from the players he had coached, I figured Harvey Penick was likely the best in the game. I quickly agreed to assist him.

At the airport I recognized Mr. Penick immediately from pictures in *Sports Illustrated.* Extremely thin and frail, his skin wrinkled from years in the sun, he had a presence about him that communicated dignity and humility. He looked me in the eye when speaking, listened and thought before offering a reply, and selected his words with care. There wasn't the slightest hint of pride. A gentle man in every way, Harvey Penick treated me with respect and courtesy. It didn't take me long to appreciate his wisdom, or to share his conviction that the game should be played (and taught) with common sense and simplicity. This marked a refreshing departure from the nonsense of *Square to Square* and the highly technical *Five Modern Fundamentals*.

Mr. Penick believed that simplicity is essential for consistency. But anyone can say those abstract phrases--what made him a genius?

With a few carefully chosen words, he *kept* things natural and uncomplicated.

Harvey Penick possessed exceptional intellectual power and creativity. Using his experience and genius to hone his coaching to a critical core, he instructed each player as an individual, not by some one-size-fits-all system. With all the complexities of the game, mastering golf requires assimilating an enormous body of knowledge; some instructors, unable to filter it, overload players with what they consider "fundamentals." Harvey Penick winnowed the countless aspects of playing great golf down to a minimum of essentials. This gives any player the best chance to play to his or her potential. Finally, he had the crucial--and rare--ability to read a player's body language.

A player learns more visually and by feel than from what you say. With a desired result in mind, a great teacher like Penick can process a world of information and come up with a very simple adjustment. Claude Harmon displayed a similar ability. Very different in personality, they shared the same brilliance in diagnosing a player's core problem and then prescribing a simple, fundamental fix that would resolve it.

Each day during his visit Mr. Penick spent an hour delivering his TPGA conference messages. Aside from that, he would sit and talk with me for hours. Taking notes in his presence seemed a little over-the-top, so whenever we parted company I wrote everything I could recall in a green spiral notebook. Harvey

Penick's *The Little Red Book*, published in 1992, became the top-selling golf book in history. I appreciated the profound wisdom it contained, applying not just to golf but to life; but my little green spiral notebook already contained at least 80% of the book. Ditching the *Square to Square Golf Swing* and Hogan's *The Five Modern Fundamentals*, and ignoring any other system or new concept that came along, I went over Mr. Penick's ideas so many times that eventually they became a part of my subconscious. Every player I've ever coached (indirectly) receives the teachings of Harvey Penick.

A generation before Penick, in the late 1930's, the great teacher Ernest Jones used to complain that his students had "paralysis by analysis." Harvey Penick and Claude Harmon both rejected systems, and coached the individual. I bet all three would be appalled at what is going on today: 24/7 Golf Channel broadcasts, internet instruction, magazines, books, schools, inexperienced teachers, sports psychology, and network telecasts of the PGA Tour . . . no wonder players get overwhelmed.

What does knowing more about golf get us? A 2005 study by the National Golf Foundation revealed that in spite of tremendous technological advances in equipment, better courses, and supposedly better coaching, golf handicaps had not shrunk. For all the money he spends, the average golfer isn't getting any better.

Harvey Penick focused primarily on scoring, and playing golf to the best of one's ability. He never uttered one word, to me or in his two lectures, remotely related to technique. He offered nothing resembling a swing key. The focus was always outward: "commit to a specific target on every shot." The body will try to give you what the mind is picturing. The steps in playing a shot should always be the same: visualize the shot you see in detail. Picture it and feel it simultaneously, set up holding your picture, and let it go.

Holding the picture of your shot and target in your mind's eye makes it impossible to think about a swing key, because the mind cannot focus on two things at a time. "Take dead aim" was Mr. Penick's mantra; he called it the best advice he could ever give anyone. *The Little Red Book* lodged those three words in the minds of nearly every serious golfer on the planet.

In response to my questions about Ben Crenshaw and Tom Kite, Mr. Penick said their personalities were so different that Penick wouldn't let either one observe the other taking a lesson. Crenshaw was more of an artist; Kite a thinker and technician. Crenshaw wanted to play 36 holes a day, while Kite would practice hours at a time. A healthy balance was best, Penick said, but he couldn't change their basic personalities, so he just went with it. He expected Crenshaw to succeed earlier, whereas Kite would likely be a late bloomer. He reasoned "Players learn to hit the first shot. Practicers learn to hit the third one." I didn't want my players practicing too much; their concentration had limits, and could give way to carelessness.

Harvey Penick told me he had wanted to play tournament golf . . . until, he said, "I practiced next to Sam Snead at Pinehurst--I knew then I needed to specialize." I decided that if I was going to make golf my profession, my specialty was coaching younger players. "The young ones can make you famous," Harvey Penick said of Crenshaw and Kite, "but the older ones pay your salary." Developing some talented young players could be my ticket: there was a lot of competition for the best jobs, then as now, but all clubs want a good teacher.

Harvey Penick liked to say that a good professional "guides the learning" of a young player, as opposed to "teaching" him or her. He shared some common sense: don't proceed with your coaching until the player has learned grip and stance--if you have a bad grip, he reasoned, you don't want a good swing. He was right; the stance takes care of the essentials of balance and alignment. Ball position fell right behind the grip and stance in importance.

Small changes, he emphasized over and over, could make dramatic differences: "If I prescribe an aspirin, please don't take the whole bottle." A professional does any player a grave disservice by trying to make radical swing changes, the kind of "fix" or makeover that has recently gained popularity.

Harvey Penick didn't like using the clichés, such as keep your left arm straight and your head still. He wanted his players to make a free swing that came naturally to them, stand in the finish position, and watch the shot. You will make instinctive and natural changes based upon what your eyes are seeing. Since the desired outcome was strong concentration without thinking too much--the player totally committed to a target, his mind made up on each and every shot--he said that staying mentally present was universal wisdom. I had been looking for help in making this game easier. Mr. Penick was the right man at the right time.

Four days with Harvey Penick yielded fifty pages of notes. The hands and fingers simply swing the club head, he believed, while the shoulders, stomach, hips, legs, and feet react. You shouldn't have to *think* about turning the shoulders and hips if you just swing the club-head with the hands and let everything else trail along the way the body moves naturally. The wrists cock naturally. The left hand needs to lead the club-head through the shot on every swing. Mr. Penick emphasized the flat left wrist--nothing new--and believed a heavy training club was a must for everyone; swinging it at half-speed would allow the brain and nervous system to latch on to a good move quickly.

It was all so logical. The brilliance came in the simplicity, as in his stated belief that the three most important clubs are the putter, wedge, and driver, in that order. A good short game can give a player "par for a partner," he said, so "good players ask for putting lessons."

Don't forget this wisdom that Harvey Penick, Ernest Jones, and Claude Harmon passed on to guys like me. If you truly desire to play to your full potential, you need to think about and embrace this philosophy: "Perfection is achieved, not when there is nothing more to add, but when there is *nothing left to take away*." Originally these words were Antoine de Saint-Exupery's. I got them from Ernest Jones, and the message is Penick and Harmon to the core. Find a coach who is good enough to work himself out of a job.

Great teachers do not embrace systems. Harvey Penick taught uniquely different human beings how to play and enjoy the game. This demands intuition and creativity: the teacher must stay present, too. Make it simple, stick with just the essentials, and teach everyone according to how they can best learn.

I picked up on a nonverbal quality, as well: great teachers know that silence is also an effective form of communicating. Mr. Penick had a gentle and humble manner I can only call noble. I was impressed with how intently he listened, and how thoughtfully he responded. Just as choosing the right words mattered to him, he clearly felt that there was a right way of doing things, with integrity foremost. I knew Mr. Penick had endeared himself to the Austin Country Club, where he served for a half-century as head professional, and because of him I was realizing that I wanted to make a similar mark. I wanted to excel in coaching golf.

The ripples from those four days with Harvey Penick in 1973 touched my life in every direction. What he shared with me convinced me to make a commitment to the golf business. I now knew where I was headed and what I hoped to become. I internalized these ideas so completely that today, reviewing my notes on the now-yellowing paper in the "green spiral notebook," I cannot see where Harvey Penick ends and Bobby McIver begins. I have rarely looked elsewhere for knowledge.

Mr. Penick liked to coach using stories, too. Players not only enjoy them, they stand a much better chance of remembering what's essential. Give them what they need and forget the rest. That's how Harvey Penick and the other great ones did it. I wanted to master their wisdom . . . and pass it on.

**

My grandfather was a Presbyterian minister and the family moved every seven or eight years. After spending his early childhood in east Tennessee, where he recalled sitting in his father's lap at the Scopes trial, in the early 1930's my dad lived and attended high school in Jeffersonville, Indiana, across the Ohio River from Louisville, Kentucky. Although these were the years of the Great Depression, he recalled that time with great fondness, and the main reason was basketball.

In Kentucky they never took to football because "the ball didn't bounce right." It didn't bounce right in Indiana, either; there was some kind of organized basketball twelve months a year. My father told me even the church had a basketball court. He played in a summer league representing Jeffersonville. Among his opponents was a reedy but motivated high school kid named John Wooden, playing for his hometown of Martinsville.

Mike McGraw, the golf coach at Oklahoma State University, recently sent me an Oklahoma State Camp notebook. Looking it over one morning, I said to my wife, Ruth, "this seems familiar."

She glanced at it. "I guess it should, Bobby, because you wrote it!"

I was looking at my version of Coach John Wooden's Pyramid of Success. I'd tweaked Wooden's original, with its team-sport focus, to make it apply to golf; even if a player is competing for a college team, the golfer has to go out there and get it done by himself.

After my experience with Harvey Penick, I'd made a decision to study the coaching philosophy of John Wooden, gleaning as much as I could over a period of several years. I never met Coach Wooden, but countless television appearances, books written about him, and his own *They Call Me Coach* showed what he and Harvey Penick shared: common sense, a focus on the essentials, and the understanding that every player is unique.

UCLA might recruit the best athletes, but it took great coaching to keep winning championships one after another. Before Wooden's retirement in 1975 UCLA won ten NCAA titles; after being defeated in the 1964 semi-finals they went years without losing another tournament game--and almost three complete seasons without losing *any* game. This win streak reached eighty-eight games before Notre Dame finally beat them in January 1974 on national television. I've never forgotten the calm, poise, and class Coach Wooden displayed as he told reporters afterwards that the streak couldn't last forever, and his players had given all they had every time they went on the floor. After commending Notre Dame, he said it was time for UCLA to put this win streak and game behind them, and focus on the next opponent.

Coach Wooden had taught high school English. He considered himself a teacher first and coach second. He spoke with eloquence, sincerity, and substance, always focusing on process, details, and emotional state: the things a coach and a player can control. You can't control outcome, so invest your thought and energy where it will benefit, such as paying careful attention to the details. Explaining that "a basketball player with blisters isn't much good to the team," he started practice each season by demonstrating how to put on your socks and shoes correctly. Every practice was organized to the minute, including thirty minutes spent with his assistants, reviewing the previous practice in order to make that day's a masterpiece.

His players knew Coach Wooden would not tolerate compromising core values. Showboating--dribbling behind your back, making blind passes--put the player before the team. Walt Hazzard was, in the Coach's own words, the best ball handler he ever had. But when Wooden put him on the bench for being overly flamboyant, Hazzard realized that Coach Wooden was willing to lose if the game wasn't played right.

Bill Walton showed up for his senior year with long hair and a beard. When he came to Coach Wooden's office to proclaim his right to wear his hair any length he wanted, Wooden affirmed that his All-American center did indeed possess this right. "We're going to miss you," he added--"we" being the basketball team. The following spring UCLA defeated a strong

Memphis State team for the NCAA championship, with Walton hitting 21 of 22 field goal attempts for a 95-plus percentage that has never been matched. Photos showed his red hair cropped short. Steadfastly devoted to his coach, Walton was there when Wooden died in 2010, at age 99.

John Wooden said, famously, that for every peak there is a valley. He wanted his players to stay on an even keel. Champions control their emotions and stay in the moment. Victories and defeats alike are quickly dismissed from everyone's mind, the focus directed to the next practice and the game ahead. Coach Wooden believed in correction, as opposed to criticism: correction presents a teaching opportunity, whereas criticism hurts the player's self-esteem and ultimately damages the team. He never corrected a player without having his hand on his shoulder and first offering a compliment--not yelling at him or embarrassing him in front of his teammates. I believe the greatest gift a coach can give his players is to simply let them know he cares. Once they feel your compassion, they will follow you to hell and back.

John Wooden possessed the rare combination of genuine humility coupled with a very high level of confidence. When the Sporting News ranked the Top 50 Coaches in sports history in 2009, John Wooden was number one. But Coach Wooden declared that Maryland high school basketball coach Morgan Wootten was truly the best of them all. Wooden said he himself had wound up in the spotlight simply because he was placed in a position that resulted in great recognition.

I set about emulating Coach Wooden by organizing his ideas on note cards. The personal computer may have turned them into antiques, but one of those old metal file-card boxes still has a place on my desk, because of its contents: hundreds of coaching ideas from Mr. Penick and Mr. Wooden. You can see stains on the cards where I handled and reviewed them for years: the mind needs repetitions just like the body.

What I accomplished--starting with Matt King at Belle Meade and proceeding through four decades, countless trophies, hearts broken and full--isn't for me to say. I gave my players all the heart and soul I had in me--in essence, that was how Coach Wooden defined success. Harvey Penick didn't offer a definition that I'm aware of, but it would likely have been very similar. The great ones think alike. Always follow the best, even if you have to study them from a distance.

***

When I was four or five my parents had left me with Daddy Will and his wife, Mama Grace, instead of taking me on a vacation. When they returned, my mother said I came up to greet them and then headed back to Daddy Will and Mama Grace's house, ready to stay with them. I'm not sure it's totally true, but my mother loved to tell that story. Mama Grace and I shared a birthday, June 24. I didn't like cake, so I used to gather us a bucket of blackberries (and chiggers) and she would make us a birthday cobbler.

In the summer of 1973 word reached me at Belle Meade: Mama Grace was asking for me. Less than an hour away by car, she wanted to see me before she died. As a thirteen-year-old I had summoned the strength to sit at Daddy Will's bedside every day for over two months, until the morning he died. Now, at twenty-five, I couldn't go see Mama Grace. I gave her son Horace some money to help with the expenses, but I couldn't even bring myself to go to her funeral.

My next day off I drove down to Columbia. Walking up the driveway to the Gordons' house, I sat in Daddy Will's old rocking chair and cried. Horace's wife Lillian told her young grandchildren I was sad, and to just let me be alone. After a half-hour or so she came over and hugged me, wiping my face with her apron like she had done many times before.

It took me almost ten years, plus counseling, to finally forgive myself. Before writing this book I never told anyone about this, except my wife Ruth.

I see things differently now. Death is part of the journey, not the end. It might break your heart, but the only way to avoid that pain is to never give your heart away: never love.

***

Belle Meade had a fleet of E-Z-GO golf carts, manufactured in Augusta, Georgia. E-Z-GO held workshops once a month. Mike Whiteside and I had little or nothing to do with maintaining our golf cart fleet, but one day it occurred to me that maybe we should make the trip and learn as much as we could. With Willie's approval, Mike and I enrolled for February, 1974.

Oh . . . Augusta National Golf Club, home of The Masters, *just coincidentally* happened to be located where we were going.

Getting a Masters ticket is tough, playing the course now virtually impossible. But five Belle Meade members belonged to Augusta National as well; Sam Fleming, chairman of the board of Third National Bank, would make it happen if it was possible at all. Excited at the idea of Mike and me getting to play, Mr. Fleming called one of the co-professionals at Augusta.

Mike and I could play after lunch Thursday, Mr. Fleming said when he got back to me. The club security guard would tell us where to park and what door to enter.

We tried to listen to the E-Z-GO man conducting the seminar, but just about all we could focus on was the weather. It rained every day. After the seminar ended Wednesday the clouds hung low and dismal and the rain showed no sign of relenting. Mike and I tried not to think about the worst-case scenario. When we walked outside Thursday morning, however, there wasn't a cloud in the sky. It was still cold, but the sun was shining on us that day.

We headed to the Augusta National Golf Club at noon, as instructed. After we had passed through security the guard called inside. One of the assistant pros came out to greet us and give us a quick tour of the locker room, clubhouse, and golf shop. We would be playing at 1 o'clock, with a professional from the Atlanta Athletic Club making up the foursome.

Under a clear, cool sky the ground was still soggy from three days of rain. Augusta National couldn't play any longer. Their beautiful greens were rye grass back then, which provided great putting surfaces. As Masters scores kept getting lower they've made changes, including a switch to bent grass years later, and the pace of Augusta's greens is so quick now, it's unreal.

One of our opponents asked, "What would you guys like to play for?" Thrilled just to play, we hadn't given the game much thought. "We'll play for whatever makes you comfortable," I told him. He came back with a figure about five times what we played for around Belle Meade. His partner was acting so cocky that it almost rose to arrogance. With Mike listening from a distance, I shot back, "We'll play for whatever suits you. You name it--we're easy."

The bet and game were set: a Four Ball match, or a $25 Nassau. We were playing $25 skins, too--they thought they had some easy money in their pockets. I turned and walked the ten or fifteen yards to where Mike was standing with our caddies. Winking at him, I said, "Big Man, these boys don't know what they're getting themselves into."

Staring down the first fairway while putting his glove on, Mike Whiteside had that look. I leaned in so our opponents couldn't hear me but our caddies could. "Come on, Mike. Let's rub something on these boys so strong that Ajax won't take it off. Tell me you're ready!" Our caddies had huge grins. Mike's dad, a Marine, had fought at Okinawa. That stuff gets passed down. My ancestors were Scots and we couldn't spell quit. Don't take me wrong--it was a cordial match. They just threw out a number they thought would be hard for us to swallow, and we were ready.

Nobody at Belle Meade could handle Mike Whiteside, not even 1975 U.S. Open champion Lou Graham. Mike's game was rock solid and he couldn't be intimidated by anyone. He never got loaded down with conceptual baggage since he never had a lesson, and unlike me he never went looking for something new in a book or magazine. When we played together as partners Mike always teed off first. He was like a machine with his driver, and he hit his irons so solid that you just never saw him out of play; he rarely missed a green. Coming behind Mike let me turn it loose. If I could see the flag I was chasing it, and I could really roll it with the putter. I just needed to give myself as many good looks at birdie as I could.

I left a putt two inches short for a birdie on seven. When it happened again on eight, my caddie came over. "Don't be leaving these putts short," he whispered in my ear. "We got some good money on y'all." I liked that--you want your caddies in the game with you. Walking down nine, I told Mike that because of these caddies we needed to reach for another gear.

I finished with six birdies, close to a miracle for a first time out at Augusta. Mike and I were in the flow together. Mike made four birdies and one bogie to shoot a 69. I offset those six birdies with two triple bogies, maybe the best even-par 72 in the history of Augusta National. I tripled the par-three number 16, trying to make a hole-in-one--Mike was already fifteen feet away, so what good was another three? I gunned it at the flag, landed in the water, then did it again. This was team golf; my score didn't matter with Mike that close.

We shot ten under on our better ball, won every bet and press they made, and took every skin, winning around $300 apiece--a pile of money back then. With less than $50 in my pocket, I had never played in a game like that.

Our caddies were waiting to be paid. Mike and I both handed them our entire winnings--happy just to play this great course, we weren't there to gamble. Those caddies showed some heart by getting behind us like they did, and we wanted them to have the money. We all gave each other big bear hugs. I think I saw tears in my caddie's eyes.

I have never played Augusta National again. I have been to the tournament many times, especially during the 70's. After the touring pros started bringing their professional caddies, the club put their regular caddies on the course in white coveralls doing different jobs. My caddie always spotted me first; he'd come over with that big smile and we would stand there and visit. I'm getting old and I can't remember his name, but I can remember his face and his smile. According to him our match was unique--he said he never caddied in anything like this again. I always ended our encounters by asking him, "Do you think those boys remember us?"

He would bust out laughing. "They'll never forget you, and that whoppin' we put on them! There's no way they'll forget it."

Notice the "we" directly after the "whoppin'"? He put himself in the game, the way caddies do when they talk about something special like this. And that's right where our caddies belonged. There's no way those boys could handle the four of us.

***

I was always a streak player. For the 1974 Tennessee State Open, held at Stones River in Murfreesboro, my personal goal was to succeed in a stroke-play tournament. In match play I could compete with anyone, whereas in stroke play, I was forever getting in my own way.

On the first hole, a short dogleg left, I hit my ball five yards out of the fairway, next to a newly planted tree. The tree was no problem but the strong steel wires supporting it only let me hit it about ten yards. Rattled, I three-putted from twenty feet and ended up making a double bogey. On the next hole, a medium-length par-three with an accessible pin, I failed to factor in my adrenaline and hit one or maybe two clubs too much. Since you run into trouble long on most holes, the maxim is 'avoid being long.' My ball sailed over the green and came to rest in a washed-out, cherty spot without a blade of grass around: a terrible lie and an extremely difficult shot. Another double bogey.

The third hole was a good straightaway par four, with Stones River down the entire left side. I looked at the hole, glanced at the river, told myself to blast it *away* from the river . . . and watched it roll into the river.

I didn't know how the mind worked then. It's a "don't think about a pink polka-dotted elephant" deal. Once I looked at that river and told myself "don't hit it towards the river," my sub-conscious mind grabbed the concept—except for the abstract part it couldn't understand: *don't*. I took my drop, hit it on the green, and two-putted for an easy bogey. That put me five over after three holes in the biggest tournament we play, with statewide media coverage.

Jimmy Ward was caddying for me; I wanted the boys to see the action and feel the adrenaline pumping. I looked at Jimmy. "What are we going to do?" I asked him. "Are we going to lay down like a dog and quit? Hell no, let's go! Let's start playing!"

The fourth hole was a par-five. I reached it in two and made eagle. I then proceeded to birdie five, six, seven, eight, and nine. Seven under for these six holes, I turned two under. Jimmy was beside himself.

But on the back nine I started playing safe. Protecting what I had, I lost the magic and ended up two over for the round. This was my mojo all the time: four or five birdies, two double bogies, and a triple. I hit the driver long, but with the wrong zip code about twice a round. I really was a great putter; with my Arnold Palmer Wilson 8802, I thought I could make them all. Calm on the outside, inside I'm aggressive and even combative, especially when it comes to sports. In better-ball, match-play money games, if I knew I had a solid player as a partner, I would get totally free and turn it loose.

Years ago I found a profile, based upon the Myers-Briggs personality test, that applied your basic personality to golf to determine which style of play fits you best.

I learned that I'm a "Magician." Magicians feel most comfortable taking chances. Conservative strategies--going for the center of the fairways, and taking the safe angle to the pin--cause us more stress than letting it rip and trusting our intuition to create whatever shots we need. I've seen it in myself: missing the easy shots, then coming up with something brilliant when forced to rely on my intuition and creativity. I usually play difficult courses really well, whereas I could go to sleep and shoot an 80 on an easy one. Some touring professionals in the Magician category include Severiano Ballesteros, Ben Crenshaw, and yes, Tom Watson.

Harvey Penick told me that two great champions he coached, Ben Crenshaw and Tom Kite, learned and trained very differently. Which one found the right way to play?

There is no *one* right way. The right way is what is natural for you.

Bobby McIver & Megan Macomber

Augusta National GC in February, 1974, with Mike Whiteside

{ 3 }

WORKING SMARTER

*Target oriented players figure out how to get it in the
hole, even when they're not swinging well. Swing oriented
players can't get it in the hole when they hit it perfect,
and ball oriented players have no chance.*

–Claude Harmon

In 1974 Jack Perry, a Belle Meade member, offered me a spot
in one of his self-empowerment courses. A dozen people--most
of them influential Nashville businessmen--met once a week for
six months. Between sessions, our homework included listening
to audiotapes by Earl Nightingale, a pioneer of human development. Mr. Perry instructed us to play these tapes twice a day, six
days a week.

After years studying the lives of successful people, Nightingale discovered they shared certain uncommon traits; put simply, we become what we think about. The course focused on
developing human potential, but it couldn't be reduced to just
"positive thinking." We explored the workings of the human
mind, mapping out ways to use it to achieve our desires.

That often-used image, the tip of the iceberg, represents the conscious mind. The 90% we cannot see is the vast and powerful subconscious, storehouse of every memory, emotion, and sensory perception we have ever experienced. The subconscious encounters the world in pictures, sounds, colors, smells, emotions, and anything else we perceive, but it is passive and only acts upon what is fed into it. It does not differentiate between a real event and something vividly imagined, which is why visualization can be such a powerful practice.

But whatever we desire must survive the process that Earl Nightingale called our "screen of logic," in which the conscious mind determines what is possible for us. The good news is we get to choose--the bad that most people sell themselves short. Experts have theorized that we use only 5-10% of our mental capacity. Nightingale believed that we allow the conscious mind's screen of logic to deny our true potential. In other words, when we consciously desire something we deny the possibility of success, and thus stop the very process we might have used to achieve it: channeling those desires into the subconscious mind.

Earl Nightingale called *attitude* the magic word because it predicts your outcome in life. Attitude is the single most important quality of a champion. Two aspects of attitude especially foster playing golf in a peak state: gratitude and positive self-expectations, or genuine confidence. They will pay big dividends, but you first have to decide to embrace these qualities as yours.

How do you form a good attitude? *Act as though you have a positive attitude* towards life, and you will see change. I coach *acting like a champion* before you become one, asking my players to act confident before they feel that way. The feeling of confidence always follows, and they begin playing great. It never works in reverse.

Success or failure has more to do with attitude than even mental or physical capacities. Champions are different from the general population because of their attitudes. The major difference is how they perceive situations: confronted with challenges, they see opportunities for success. Consciously, golf champions picture hitting the perfect shot, which feeds the subconscious. Where others feel anxious and distressed, champions experience an increased level of arousal, which prompts them to play better. They reinforce good shots with positive emotions and detach from poor ones immediately.

Most successful players also develop the habit of enjoying those they are paired with; instead of pulling against a fellow competitor, they see their opponents as teammates. This attitude reduces tension, of course, but there's more to it--the better an opponent plays, the more it pushes you to excel. In fact, "compete" means to "seek together."

Our homework for Jack Perry's course also included a workbook with weekly assignments. Among these assignments was an exercise on setting goals. First Mr. Perry asked us to list ten goals; then we were to take these and, if possible, expand them beyond our screen of logic. By the end of the process I had settled on these six goals:

1. Help my players receive major college scholarships.

2. Develop a national champion.

3. Take two players from beginners to first team NCAA All Americans in the same year.

4. Become a head professional at a metropolitan club by my early thirties.

5. Be known and respected by my peers in the PGA as a good coach or instructor.

6. Write and publish a book of substance that would be well received.

That was as big as I could dream back then. I looked at the list four or five times a day for three months but kept it hidden, afraid that anyone who saw my goals would think they were impossible and I was a fool to come up with such a list.

Some don't just fulfill their own potential—they expand possibilities for everyone. Before Roger Bannister ran a mile in 3:59.4 in May of 1954, people thought that a human being could not break the four-minute barrier. Once Bannister did it, others--including American high-school athlete Jim Ryun--accomplished the feat. What was holding them back? I can only conclude that they also believed running a mile under four minutes was beyond human capabilities.

Scott Verplank was just finishing his junior year at Oklahoma State University when he became the first amateur to win a PGA Tour event in 29 years. He took the lead in the opening round of the 1985 Western Open at Butler National in Chicago and never looked back. Since then several others, including Phil Mickelson, have accomplished this, but there always has to be a pioneer willing to dream bigger.

The most important decision you will ever make is what you want from life. Don't be overly concerned with when you are going to achieve your goals; once they get anchored in the subconscious, they will show up on their own time schedule. As Albert Einstein said, "Imagination is more important than knowledge." If you are capable of imagining it, you are most likely capable of accomplishing it.

The Heart of the Game

***

At the first meeting of Jack Perry's course I had been glad to see my friend George Creagh, a Belle Meade member who routinely shot 64's and 65's. Shortly after we finished the course he told me, "Bobby, you have to buy this new book--it's about the mental game and it's receiving great reviews." I wasn't looking for excellence in a book now, but George was very smart, in addition to being the best player at Belle Meade. When he told me the title was *The Inner Game of Tennis*, I asked him what in the world a tennis book had to do with golf. "It's about the mental game," he said. "The tennis part doesn't matter. Trust me and buy a copy."

After losing the U.S. Junior Tennis Championship, Timothy Gallwey spent four years on scholarship at Harvard trying to figure out why match point is harder than any other. Majoring in psychology and becoming captain of the tennis team, he still couldn't satisfy himself with an answer. After graduating he went to India and studied the problem from the eastern perspective. *The Inner Game of Tennis*--an enduring classic--resulted. Exactly as George Creagh had promised, I found Gallwey's insights about letting go with the conscious mind, relaxed concentration, and focus invaluable. But his discussion of the natural learning process had the impact of a revelation. Gallwey's analysis made me not only revisit but really think deeply about the ways I'd learned to play and coach--my role models, discoveries, and what I realized was my personal philosophy taking shape and focus.

At Columbia Military Academy, basketball coach Bill Wade had us drill to the point that every move was reactionary. Our shooting guard, Ernie Hampton, was a smooth left-hander from

Kentucky. Thirty feet from the basket, diagonally behind the left side of the free throw line--an NBA three-pointer today--Coach Wade outlined a two-foot box with adhesive tape and declared it "Ernie's spot." Every practice for three months Ernie made twenty-five from that two-foot box. When opponents tried to play a zone he would force them out of it by racking up points from "Ernie's spot," routinely making the shot under pressure.

Which came first? Ernie had the shot to begin with. He made dozens every practice. The more he practiced, the more shots he saw go in. The more he saw go in, the more confident he became. When we had one shot to win and only seconds left, it was unconscious in the huddle, too: just put it in Ernie's hands in his spot. Repetition, repetition, repetition, and *more* repetitions free a player's ability. Whatever the game, *getting ready makes the difference.* Good coaching means working on the right stuff. Get your players ready, and then trust them to get it done.

Trust is the second most powerful motivator a coach can use. The first is a combination of kindness and compassion. It may sound soft, but it's awful strong.

Bill Wade died in a car wreck before I got to tell how much his coaching helped me. I can hear him now: "Men, it's not how tall you are, it's how tall you play. They don't have any idea how big we are."

Bill Wade coached the mental game without ever labeling it as such. He made sure we got to an out-of-town opponent's gymnasium two hours early and did a walk-through of their facility in silence. Looking at the scoreboard, we visualized ourselves winning. Coach Wade had trained us to let our minds become still on our own, a process Timothy Gallwey describes as "quieting down" to reach a state of relaxed concentration. In the locker room 90 minutes before tip-off, our final, solitary routines included stretching while breathing deeply, then relaxing with our eyes closed. There was little or no outer chatter, and not much inner chatter either. These techniques are almost identical to those Gallwey describes, but our CMA team was practicing them nine years before his book came out.

But even now few young players in any sport get anything like what Coach Wade gave us. I see no sense in the current golf-world fad of having a swing coach *and* a mental guru. The last time I checked, my brain was in my skull and part of my physical being. And the game of golf (even more than tennis) allows plenty of time for mental interference anyway.

Many ideas from Earl Nightingale appear in *The Inner Game of Tennis*: attitude is probably the single most important essential; if your conscious mind indulges fearful thoughts the body will respond with shallow breathing, tightness, and other physical reactions. In the lesson "The Miracle of Your Mind," Nightingale explains that we respond better to images than words because the subconscious can't understand words--words occupy the conscious mind, or ego. In order to play without inner chatter, the ego has to shut up and let it happen without advice, reminders, corrections, or other conscious-mind sabotage.

Gallwey calls this interference Self 1 as a label, but it's the ego. I read somewhere that the ego is the source of every man's misery, which holds whether you play golf or not. Every great coach understands that detaching the ego and replacing it with an attitude of nonjudgmental awareness is essential to playing at one's peak. That is the only way to access the subconscious--

Gallwey's Self 2--where intuition, creativity, super-intelligence, and the spirit reside.

Begin with a still mind, allowing time to relax and settle down so your attention can be focused. Your mind needs an object of its attention. Awareness of sight (the target, the ball in flight), awareness of sound (the club-face striking the ball and taking a divot), awareness of feel (the grip in your hands, the snapping of club and ball through impact), and even awareness of your mind: these skills are available to anyone who seeks. The mind will give them to you, but you have to know what to ask from it.

Peak state or flow may be the single most essential element of playing great, whether your game is golf, tennis, or electric guitar. Emphasizing its elusiveness, Timothy Gallwey rightly says you cannot try or strain for peak state. I knew almost nothing about peak performance when I first read *The Inner Game of Tennis* in 1974; since then I have contemplated and studied it thoroughly. Later in this book I will present a process that gives players their best chance to reach a peak every time out.

But I really want to teach you how to *stay* in the flow for eighteen holes, which is exponentially more challenging than getting there.

***

Whether by oversight or omission, *The Inner Game of Tennis* has a blind spot. Timothy Gallwey never says that it takes thousands of hours training the body before these inner game concepts can really help.

I heard a story of a family finding an old violin in an ancestor's home. They took it to an authority and found out it was a valuable instrument greatly in need of attention. After the violin was carefully and expertly repaired, the owners went to retrieve it. A violinist from the local symphony happened to be present. When the music store's owner asked her to play, beautiful melodic tones emanated from the violin. Excited, the couple brought it home, and one of them attempted to play a few notes, just letting the bow pass over the strings. The result was what you might expect. What was the difference?

It's true these artists are really gifted, but it takes thousands of hours of dedication and hands-on practice to approach mastery in whatever your passion may be. The key word here is *passion*. No matter what mindset I bring to playing a piano, it makes absolutely no difference: I can't play the piano. Some of the inner-game ideas concerning internal chatter and attitude *might* help a thirty-handicapper, but I doubt it. If the body can't give it to you, the inner game is not the answer. You have to be able to trust your body and your training completely to play at peak levels in flow. The Ten Thousand Hours to Mastery theory (based on research by University of Florida psychologist Anders Eriksson and popularized by Malcolm Gladwell in *Outliers*) contends that to really *master* golf it will require twenty hours a week, fifty weeks a year . . . for ten years. Excellence requires work, and no book of any kind can provide a shortcut.

Golf may truly be the ultimate inner-game challenge. With so much time between shots, the conscious mind can seriously undermine a golfer who lacks training in how to make the mind work for him. *The Inner Game of Tennis* gave me some great coaching ideas. I recommended Gallwey's book to my players, knowing each one would have different parts that registered with him.

I never attempted to coach *The Inner Game of Tennis*, however, or any other mental game concept. As soon as you begin conceptualizing, the unconscious flow of coaching is lost. The concepts become more important than the players.

***

Most players who are naturally gifted know it. But I don't think a coach should assume that players can truly envision their full potential.

Matt King, around fourteen, tagged along with me one evening while I taught on an indoor golf course at the YMCA. As we drove home, I told Matt that his potential was unlimited and all his ambitious long-term goals were attainable. Anything was possible with him. It would take thousands of hours of work-- his attitude and desire would make the difference. The journey would be hard at times: there are no shortcuts to greatness. I said I would help him get there and give him all I had in me. After pausing to let him take all this in, I asked, "Do you want it?"

Matt was taken aback by what I'd said, but I could see it working on him. Finally he said, "I want it. I want it badly." Some time later Matt told me he didn't sleep a wink that night.

Later I came to call this anchoring. I hadn't planned in advance to do this. My intuition just told me it was a good time for Matt King to hear it. Older players have told me they never had a teacher pull them to the side like this. That's a shame, since it can make the difference between being good and going beyond to competitive greatness.

***

I started taking the boys to local tournaments for the experience. One of the first was at Shelby Park, the old municipal course in north Nashville. I got them there in time to warm up and then got out of their way. In golf the coaching is over when the event begins: giving advice is against the rules.

I was sitting around the clubhouse thinking about nothing in general when I spotted an unfamiliar young man. His posture, relaxed focus, and sense of awareness--even his white Hogan cap--impressed me. The way he walked did too; these racehorses have a way with their feet. When the round ended I made my way to the scoreboard, just in time to see his pretty mom put her arm on his shoulder. The scorer posted the totals: Mike Keliher. I didn't know the name.

On the ride home, I interrupted my guys' laughing and joking to ask if anyone knew him. Sure enough, they told me Mike Keliher had moved to Nashville from Lexington. He belonged to Hillwood, a neighbor club little more than a mile away from Belle Meade.

Matt King was already making some headlines with his play and our names had become associated in the local papers, the Nashville Tennessean and the Nashville Banner. Nowadays, with their coverage reduced to a few wire service paragraphs alongside the scores of PGA Tour events, larger newspapers no longer cover local golf. Back then it was an art form. The Banner, an afternoon daily that has dropped by the wayside, boasted superb writing by Waxo Green and legendary Sports Editor Fred Russell. Mike Keliher read about me in these articles, and one day he called to ask if I would help him. I had been hoping for this. "Do you want to be a champion?" I asked.

It was a rhetorical question. Before long our group's silent leader emerged. Those are the best kind, because nobody even knows they are leading. With the addition of Mike Keliher, my group now comprised the Battle Ground Academy golf team.

Everyone knew them: it wasn't *if* they were going to win, but how badly they were going to kick everyone else's butts.

Then Dr. Bob Wolcott of nearby Dickson asked if I'd take a look at his fourteen-year-old son (also named Bob). When I told the guys that Bob Wolcott was coming over, Bob Jackson burst out, "You won't believe this guy--he can play golf, and I mean *really play!*"

Bob Wolcott still recalls showing up at Belle Meade to discover the entire BGA golf team waiting to greet him, as a show of respect. Bob hit four seven irons that first day. "That's enough," I told him. "Put your clubs on the cart." He looked down, thinking he'd done something wrong. "Bob," I said once we got on the cart, "your swing is so pure I don't want to mess with it. We're going on the golf course and I'm going to show you how to play. Anybody can swing a club--it takes someone special who can have the heart to play and be a winner."

That was our introduction. It was nothing but playing lessons for Bob Wolcott, from that point on . . . through eight years on the PGA Tour.

Matt King, Jimmy Ward, John Burch, and Bob Jackson were all children of Belle Meade members. Mike Keliher joined the group in 1974, Bob Wolcott in 1975. In 1976 Jack Larkin became the seventh member of this team.

Paradoxically this group grew tighter as it expanded: a powerful synergy developed. We used to say, "somebody's going to win this tournament--it doesn't matter who, but it's going to be one of us." They played with greater courage, boldness, and confidence because of their closeness. You can't coach this or make it happen. It just happens or it doesn't.

***

Matt King, Jimmy Ward, and Bob Jackson played in the 1974 Southern Junior Invitational in Perdido Bay, AL. The Invitational included a father-son event; Bob and Jimmy's fathers were participating, so I asked to play with Matt without competing, but my request was turned down. We forgot about this disappointment pretty fast, however. Jackie Nicklaus was playing, and *his* father showed up unannounced to put on the most impressive clinic I have ever witnessed. He said that Byron Nelson had inspired him--Jack Nicklaus witnessed golf at the highest level as a young person, and it left a profound imprint.

Matt was in contention late in the final round when he encountered a hole cut on a steep slope. He had a ten-footer for birdie--with that slope, he'd either make it or have a twenty-footer coming back. After three-putting for a bogey, he let out a string of expletives. Beyond the roped-off greens a couple stood watching. I pulled Matt aside, informed him a lady was present, and told him to apologize, which he did immediately.

The husband wouldn't let it go. Trying to prevent him from becoming a distraction, I told him, "These young men are new to this. This is how they learn." The guy wasn't merely refusing to accept the apology--he wanted Matt disqualified. I managed to keep him at a distance from the players. When the event concluded and Matt went into the scorer's tent to check and sign his card, I finally raised my voice. "I'm your problem now, and I've had enough--either back off or come get some of me."

The fight died in his eyes. His wife looked mortified. Matt finished second in a good event, making this experience a confidence booster.

***

These boys came to me healthy and strong. Every one had a good mind. Along with physical skills, I nurtured the decision-making ability that gave them their best chance to win. And as I saw it, my role also included supporting each one spiritually.

Some might think of "spirit" or "spiritual" only within a religious context, but every human being has a spirit. We are all spiritual beings. This spiritual dimension can be called heart: the courage, compassion, and conviction to be a winner.

Golf has been split into two games, mental and physical, while the most important isn't even discussed: every person is the interconnection of Body/Mind/Spirit, *one system that cannot be split*. It takes heart and soul to win at anything. My background and what I learned from Coach Wade, Harvey Penick, and John Wooden have only strengthened my belief that spiritual qualities absolutely and unequivocally make the difference.

These young men already had strong spiritual lives. Maybe more than any other coaching duties, I considered it crucial to keep them in touch with that core. In fact, the spiritual focus they came to share was what made them champions, because winning always boils down to who can haul the most heart to the course.

When Mike Keliher's sister, Diana, praised me for how I developed my players, I replied, "They had what it took when I got them." They all had champions for parents and family. I never raised my voice with one of these young men, much less disciplined them; but had I needed to, I would have had parental support. This is not always the case today—ask a coach.

***

As a coach, I always invoke the Hippocratic Oath: "First, do no harm." No coaching whatsoever is better than too much (especially verbal) coaching. Claude Harmon used to say that he couldn't do anything about talent other than mess it up. I over-coached Matt King early on, putting too much on him too fast. Willie Gibbons cared enough and had the good sense to be aware of what was happening. Explaining the phenomenon of "paralysis from over-analysis," Willie said I was giving Matt too much information. It was a very helpful piece of advice.

I was the primary coach of this group, but also a member of a very strong team. The kids learned more than they probably realized from just watching Mike Whiteside play. Three great shop ladies enthusiastically supported my work with the juniors. Everyone was friendly and encouraging. Willie and Mike always had them laughing. Too many young players today walk around with solemn and serious faces; keeping these boys loose was critical in getting them ready to play.

Most days, Mike Whiteside and I stayed in the shop past dark. We would take turns, one of us closing up so the other could leave a couple hours early. One summer evening Mike closed so I could play golf with our bag-room attendant Jeff Sales and a hometown friend. As we played along we started to hear sirens. Thinking it was a routine medical call or some such thing, we kept playing. By the time we came up number 18 it was almost dark.

In front of us were six police cars, blue lights flashing. We found all the officers inside the shop, gathered around Mike. They were asking him what kind of shotgun it was, as in the gauge. "I have no idea," Mike answered with a straight face. "It looked like an anti-aircraft gun."

On a sultry summer evening, the robber had come in the side door and through the bag-room. "When I saw him in a trench coat," Mike said, "I knew something wasn't right."

We busted out laughing. I nudged Jeff. "It's a good thing you were on the course--the guy probably knew he couldn't leave you as a witness."

The shop money was kept locked in a safe. The lock had loose tumblers and even being very careful it might take us four times to open it in the mornings. I asked Mike how many times it took with a gun pointed at him. "I got it the first time," he said. "The big man up there only knows how." Willie, who had arrived back at the club from home, asked Mike, "Why did you let him have the cash?"

"If he wanted a check, I would have written him one," Mike replied.

Finally the assistant manager brought Mike a big glass of what looked like iced tea with lemon . . . and was later revealed to be straight Scotch.

We passed a little of this on to the young players. In tournament golf you need a sense of humor--even if you find it, like Mike did, at the wrong end of a sawed-off shotgun.

***

I gave each of my players a blue three-ring notebook. These contained some basic instructional and inspirational material, their tournament and practice schedules, and a place to journal. Right up front I had them declare their goals: what they hoped to accomplish that season, followed by their intermediate (five-year) goals, and finally their long-term aspirations, where I asked them to DREAM BIGGER. This exercise was based on that assignment from Jack Perry's course; like me, they committed to look at their goals over and over. As adults, many have told me that the written goals made all the difference not just when they were players then, but later in their professional lives, too.

Human beings perform better with structure. This is the only "system" I advocate. Our practice habits had structure. We never hit a practice shot without going through the on-course process. Whenever we played, we holed out and had a score. Always practice with a purpose, playing shots, not beating balls. No goofing around on the course and picking up. Over-long training sessions can hurt rather than help; even touring pros can benefit from taking a five-minute break after twenty minutes and then refocusing.

To facilitate practicing with a focus, it helps to *simulate tournament conditions* as closely as possible. I got each of my players a nice shoe bag containing twenty-five brand new balls. Because the typical range ball responds nothing like a good Titleist, I urge players in training to work on their short game only with the balls they play. Bob Wolcott says this made a huge difference in the development of his game.

***

The PGA Tour Pros that they show on TV rarely seem to miss short putts. In truth, their average from six feet is only 50 percent. This means that the average golfer might be squandering a lot of resources (time *and* money) in the quest for length and power. As Harvey Penick said, good players--players who want to *win* rather than show off--ask for putting lessons.

For training with the putter I gave each of the guys a six-foot 2-by-4 that I had painted white. I started them out making twenty-five in a row from three feet, using the plank to measure distance and line them up. Soon all of them could do it at six feet. Not only were they making more, but once they *believed* they could make everything within six feet they became very confident with their entire short game.

As an adult Jack Larkin once stopped to visit with me at the Greenville Country Club in South Carolina. He and his sister had established a successful wine distribution business, so when he said "come with me out to my car" before leaving, I thought he might be giving me some wine. But what he pulled out of the trunk was that six-foot 2-by-4 I had given him twenty years earlier. "This is like my American Express Card," he said, "I never leave home without it." We both laughed. I've switched to using chalk lines because they're less cumbersome than the old board, but whatever the method, the point is to get your alignment right every time. Your head must swivel and your eyes track the line consistently, too.

I trained my players to focus on all the sensory aspects of a well-struck putt, including the sound, and the feel in the right index finger and thumb. They learned to stroke the putts and then hold the finish; this eliminates "hand slapping," a fear response to not knowing how hard to strike the putt. My guys visualized holing every putt. It seems like this would be a given, but you might be surprised how many players squander their potential by playing defense on the greens without knowing it.

Two-thirds of our overall practice time was dedicated to the short game, divided between putting and the other short shots. The routine was the same: see the entry point, set the chin, and let it go, unconsciously and with a quiet mind. We worked on making six-footers by engaging as many senses as possible, feeling the stroke with the thumb and index finger of the right hand and paying close attention to the sound (every putter sounds a little different). We aimed for a higher level of awareness with everything, but we really wanted to be dialed in while practicing our putting because the short game is particularly vulnerable to ego interference and trying too hard.

Once my players were putting great from six feet we addressed pace, or hitting it the right distance. Unless you get the distance right, line makes no difference.

I wasn't joking earlier when I mentioned practicing in the dark. Shut down one sense and the others step up: when your vision is limited, your balance and timing improve. Putting at night can also curb worries about spike marks or other visible issues with the surface. Removing the anxiety factor helps to mute the chatter of the conscious mind. I will have much more to say about this later.

Harvey Penick believed the putter was the most important club, and that good players, realizing this, "ask for putting lessons." Ben Hogan, on the other hand, said the most important club was the driver. Raymond Floyd, who holed out from off the green more than any player I know, said it was the sand wedge. Anyone aspiring to be a champion needs to master all three.

I want my players to have a driver they can hit long without sacrificing accuracy; more loft, along with the right shaft, provides that combination. A strong three wood suits those situations when the driver doesn't fit a player's eye. Ben Hogan's three wood was driver length, with 13 degrees loft when 15 degrees was standard, and he could hit it out there when other players were hitting driver. Weak driver and strong three wood--that's my advice.

Learning to handle the sand wedge puts a player on track to mastering this game faster than any other club. Playing shots requires intuition and creativity, and learning to play every conceivable shot with the sand wedge will teach you how to handle any club. To play great recovery shots you have to control club-face angle and loft. Handling the shaft and grip, along with the club-head, lets you create shots. Once you get it with the sand wedge, you have it for everything: you can make birdies from off the green more often and have "par for a partner" practically.

Players learn best visually. At Belle Meade my players got to watch the great swings of George Creagh and Lou Graham over and over and then imitate what they had witnessed. Lou Graham allowed me to film him with a Super 8 millimeter and I made copies for all my players: nothing but Graham's image, but he won the 1975 U.S. Open with that swing, so my boys were feeding their subconscious minds a very sound motion. Constantly looking at video of your own swing, however, causes more problems than it solves. The golf swing is a target-oriented motion. Only the target ultimately matters. And in competition, players have to figure things out in the heat of battle through feel, making adjustments without a video camera to provide an image. Video has a place, but it's now over-used.

If a player's full swing is out of synch, I want them to hit thirty- to forty-yard pitch shots. The pitch shot is the bottom of the full swing, and every shot in golf has the same fundamental timing. The duration of a swing with good rhythm should be the same, regardless of the length of arc--you will be working on the full swing without knowing it. Swinging a heavy club at half speed is another great way to keep the swing grooved.

The Heart of the Game

When we think "grip" we think of our hands, but if you can train your hands to swing while your feet grip the ground, the middle (and the rest of the motion) follows naturally. Just let the chin move where it wants to go--the body goes where the chin goes. It doesn't sound like much, but once you get it you'll understand how profound it truly is. Your body will follow, giving you good balance for free.

Rhythm and timing will come naturally, too. Count 1-2-3-4 as you make your most natural walking stride, then match it up with your swing. Your body will tell you how fast it wants to go. Good rhythm and balance will give you power, while straining for it will take it away. Winning is not about having a pretty swing. In competition everyone has a good one, and if you're looking for it with your swing, it's like looking for love in all the wrong places. My seven players had seven different swings, but each knew how to use his own. The guy who wins will trust what he's got and have something extra in his chest.

I started having my players record performance data for every round, keeping track of the major areas that influence *scoring* the most: fairways hit, greens hit, putting inside six feet, and one-putts outside this range; up-and-downs or holing out with all short shots (chips, pitches, and bunker shots); eagles, birdies, pars, bogies, and "other" (double and triple bogies). I didn't want my players to get tied up analyzing too many individual-round statistics. The goal was for them to gather the information and then use ten-round averages to determine their strengths and weaknesses on their own. This data helped them decide what they needed to practice and allowed each one to know his game better than I did.

As a group we focused on the areas that lead to winning tournaments. I got them driving with confidence--missing three or four fairways didn't bother me--and we practiced a lot of shots with the seven iron. "Mastering the sand wedge and putter gives a player par for a partner" and "Getting up and down is our strength" got lodged in their psyches. So did "we can make them all--six feet and in is automatic."

I coached them to walk, talk, act, and carry themselves as the champions they hoped to become: "Heads high and shoulders back." This included dressing really well, several notches above their opponents, and having shoes shined, clothes ironed, bags and equipment cleaned and looking good. I made sure they had extra gloves, an extra towel, a bag full of tees, and plenty of balls already marked. Taking care of as many details as possible ahead of time let us keep our cool and our focus: "Never let 'em see us sweat." We had another motto: "If it isn't going to kill us, we can handle it." In the country we call it being tough.

Matt King's swing and demeanor on the course made him a role model for the others. Projecting confidence, he had his game face on without being cocky. His family took me with them to the Masters every year. We sat in the bleachers for hours, Matt observing intently as I pointed out players with similar body types--tall and slim--noting the important fundamentals I was seeing as these players practiced their short games.

College coaches have told me they could identify my players by their posture and starting position, where grip, alignment, and posture come together all at once. Get that right at the start and your swing will require fewer compensations. This is just common sense.

Players I've coached also display a flat left wrist at the top and the club in an ideal position. I've never had to coach this-- their set-up, coupled with an athletic swing, *put* them in the right positions. Having the club in a good position at the top makes it much easier to get it down. This sounds obvious, but it's too important to leave unstated: the downswing happens so fast that once the club is out of position, or off-plane, it's impossible to swing on-plane (without loops or wobbles) coming down. There's no time to make a correction.

Think of the swinging club as a spinning bicycle wheel. Ideally it's tilted the proper amount and the swing path is circular in shape. A good *set-up* puts the club in a good position at the top. A swing that starts with the club out of position at the top will be like a wheel with a bent rim, ineffective and inefficient, wobbling worst at impact. Clubface angle, path, and angle of descent determine the shot, assuming center-face contact. The laws of physics that govern how the ball responds to the clubface at impact are *laws*: they work every time. Starting the downswing off plane--with your wheel wobbling--makes the game extremely challenging.

Golf ultimately requires doing only a few movements really well. Is there some wiggle room for personal preferences? Sure, but not much. For every action there is an equal and opposite reaction. Personal variations require compensations--the more quirks, the higher the maintenance. With any wobbles, loops, or variations from the proven basics, the timing has to be exact. I saw a golf book photo array showing numerous great players; although they differed in other respects, they were all in the same position at impact. Swinging the club-head properly through impact always results from soundness of form in the swing *before* contact.

We play best with *sensory perceptions* rather than logical concepts. A conception is an abstract idea. For whatever reason, our western minds tend to become absorbed in pursuing abstract knowledge, thinking this is how one plays great. The true power is underneath the surface, deep in the silence. Take your choice.

I want my players to totally *detach ego*--anything having to with me, mine, I, or self. The ego is like a professor who thinks too much, believes he knows more than he does, and--worse-- talks too much, making all the noise in your head. Get him out of your way and give it to your soul and unconscious mind. If I'm repeating myself, good! I will cover it again.

Preparing to compete in a recent US Senior Open qualifier, I found that immersing myself in music helped me get in the flow. Attuned with my unconscious, I didn't have to think. My training and mind let me react instinctively, picture the shot, and play it. In Zen, this is rightly said to be spiritual. Great music is not only inspirational but unquestionably spiritual, too.

Golf and music are both creative art forms. A player who becomes absorbed in the technique of either one may become a technician, but never an artist. Until this unconscious and spiritual place is attained, the technician knows nothing about playing. An artist will whip a technician and his concepts almost every time.

Every great player I know talks about the sensation of being carried along, "like riding a wave." That's *flow*, the peak state when a player, regardless of the game, gets a glimpse of their true potential. The potential already exists in everyone, but fulfilling it involves years spent learning how to eliminate or minimize any obstacles and interferences. Obstacles are anything external that gets in your way, while interferences occur when you get in your own way. When you realize your primary opponent is yourself, you're facing the greatest challenge of all: the inner game, which is primarily the ongoing battle with your ego.

Excellence in coaching is when there is nothing left to take away--including the coach. Get rid of the swing concept baggage any way you can. Find yourself a coach who says little, is present more, and knows how to have fun. He might coach himself out of a job; if he's any good, that's *exactly* what he'll do. Learn how to put low numbers on your card. Manage your own game and you will soon learn how to score. Let the swing-key aficionados parse their diagrams, sit around the 19th Hole, and talk about it. Players play.

Picture the shot, hold the mental image, then just swing with an empty mind and let the ball go.

You can draw your own conclusions regarding my coaching style. I've always trusted my intuition. Starting with this group in Nashville, I developed seven essential practices.

1. Goal-setting is the heart of my coaching: a player with a purpose will find a way.

2. Find the moment to tell promising players they can accomplish whatever they want and you can ignite a young imagination ("Anchoring").

3. Focus on what players are doing right--those areas that clearly lead to outstanding results--and let them figure out what needs attention. Effectiveness comes from doing the right things.

4. Prepare to win, gearing your training to peak at the time of the next event.

5. Have players put down their clubs two days before the event, convinced they are ready to compete, for a confidence boost as well as a rest.

6. Nurture a strong group synergy--young players will work towards team goals.

7. Have fun--more fun than you ever expected!

I look for a neutral grip, a good stance and posture, a smooth takeaway and start down, and a flat left wrist at the top. Propelled by the hands, the club-head snaps as both arms straighten past impact. As the feet grip on the backswing and push off, everything else follows: control the extremities and you control the middle. The swing should coast into a balanced finish. This is as technical as it gets with me.

Most players will naturally get all of this through *visualization*. Holding a picture of the shot makes golf exponentially less complicated.

***

I once gave great South African player David Frost a ride from Charlottesville, VA, to the Greensboro Open. He couldn't believe how quickly we were bringing players along in the United States. "In South Africa," Frost told me, "we want to hit our peak at twenty-five to thirty-five. Here, with all the competition, your young players are out of steam when they get out of college."

It was a good point 25 years ago and an even better one now. Young players today compete in so many events that they burn out prematurely. And throwing kids in over their heads by sending them to the biggest tournaments only teaches them to lose. Limiting kids to twelve good events, including the state amateur, lets them play well, take a short break, and get ready for the next one. Starting with local events allows them to win, build, and grow into bigger events . . . when they *will* have a chance.

To prepare my group of juniors for specific tournaments, we focused on winning and playing the course. We talked about working harder, but mainly *smarter*, than everyone else. Championships are won playing golf on the course, not looking pretty on the practice tee, so I prescribed two-thirds of their time spent playing and one-third practicing. This translated into a four-hour round and two hours on the practice tee--thirty minutes warming up prior to the round and ninety minutes practicing after the round. When they were swinging really well I wanted them hitting lots of balls. Hitting poorly? Practice the shorter shots. I wanted my players to manage their time, striking a healthy balance that included taking time *off*, the most overlooked fundamental of all.

Not playing practice rounds the day before let my players rest and bolstered their confidence. If they didn't know a tournament course, we found a time other than the day before to play it. I always told them they were ready and everything looked good, whether I believed it or not. I never tinkered, even if I saw something a little off. They would probably fix it themselves and my noting flaws would provoke them to worry, which would only hurt their chances. On practice-round day I always gave them the same words of encouragement: "They may not be able to see y'all, but they know you're coming."

In early spring we scheduled the tournaments we wanted to play, usually ten to twelve events. The 1975 U.S. Junior Amateur Championship was going to be played in July at Richland Club, right in Nashville. The qualifier at Belle Meade had two spots for thirty or forty players. Mike Keliher qualified. Matt King, the first alternate, got a call two days before the national championship: the player couldn't make it, which meant show time for Matt, too. Mike qualified for match play but losing an early match took him out of the running.

Matt had my caddie, Jerry Elam. Jerry could keep me calm outside while a fire burned hot inside. Worth several shots a round to me, he proved invaluable to Matt as well; they took off, leaving a vapor trail. I watched from a distance as Matt, playing with grace and poise, took on opponents one at a time. In the round of thirty-two he sent a kid named Harry Zaruba home to Ohio. In the round of sixteen he was playing Maxie Cupit, Jr. from Yazoo City, MS. I'd played there as an amateur. Maxie's dad was the pro. Maxie put up a good fight--he and Matt went extra holes--but Matt had that look in his eye. Local papers and television stations were featuring his achievements daily.

In the quarterfinals Matt faced a player from Chicago named Gary Pinns. After good weather all week, by the time of their afternoon match dark clouds were coming in. It was soon raining hard, and casual water started pooling on the greens. In my opinion the course was unplayable, but the USGA kept playing. Gary Pinns struck me right away as polished and experienced. As conditions deteriorated, Pinns impressed me with how he handled his umbrella and towels, kept his glove dry, and dealt overall with a situation Matt had never faced.

Finally Matt asked for relief from casual water, and officials moved it to the side about fifteen feet. He had a twenty-footer and left it ten feet short. After observing all this, Gary Pinns elected to chip over the casual water with an eight iron rather than putt. He gave it to his intuition, dreamed up an incredible shot, and had a tap-in for the win. All Matt could do was shake his hand and go home to get ready for next year.

Mike Keliher won the 1976 Tennessee State Junior, played at the Country Club of Jackson. Bob Wolcott won the 12-to-14-year-old age group. Later, playing well in the Southern Junior, Bob had the misfortune of losing a ball with officials standing right there. They searched in vain. It cost him the win. Bob would be named as a junior to the Tennessee Men's Amateur Cup team.

Mike Keliher didn't have a mean bone in his body. He loved to laugh. Just hearing him made me laugh, hard, even when I didn't know what it was about--so hard sometimes I would bend over and almost cry. Mike was crazy about everybody. Super-smart, he knew the game inside and out, but that never made him a show-off. A natural encourager, he loved to tell the other players how their swings were so PURE.

In early spring of 1976 Mike Keliher and Matt King came to talk to me. Along with John Burch, Jimmy Ward, and Jack Larkin, they made up Battle Ground Academy's golf team. The school was named for its location, the site of a ferocious battle in the War Between the States. The team had cranked it up all year, but the looming state championship had them anxious. Mike explained their quandary: because daylight was increasing only a minute or two a day, they were limited to playing nine holes during afternoon practices.

I didn't know what they expected from me; I had nothing to do with when the sun came up or went down. Then an idea popped up. They would find me waiting for them at Belle Meade at 6 in the morning, I said, but everybody had to show up. No picking and choosing just for those who want to. I wanted some men who would dig in at 6 o'clock and do it as a team. "6 o'clock works for me," I told them. "Nobody's going to beat me here." They looked at each other, uncertain. But when Mike Keliher came back the next day he had wrapped it up: everyone wanted to come for our "Sunrise Service."

I got to the club ahead of them by at least a half hour--when they turned the corner I was going to be ready. "Okay, how good are we and how much better do we want to be? We've got work to do. Let's go. Are y'all ready? Come on, we're wasting time!" I kept firing at them, loud enough so they could all hear me invoking Battle Ground Academy's rival, Montgomery Bell Academy. "Hey, those ol' boys at MBA, what are they doing? They're still lying in bed. Oh, we got something for them! You know what it is? All we have to do is let 'em see our heart. Have mercy, we got work to do!"

The line-up fell into place: Mike, Matt, John, Jimmy, and Jack Larkin, the youngest. Getting Jack ready became our priority. The other four understood: we needed to work from the bottom up. If I could get Jack thinking he had par for a partner, the short game would pull him through. Jack did anything I asked: "Big Jack, pull out that sand wedge and putter--I want you to sleep with 'em in bed and take 'em with you to school, too." Jack was just getting started, but he had that look. "Bear down on your short game," I told him, "it doesn't make any difference how many greens you hit or miss." Jack was the key but I didn't want him feeling the pressure, so we acted like it was no big deal. Big Jack was "the man," I said--he could handle it.

The Friday before the state championship I told them they were ready, to forget about it, just take it easy. We were coming to win a tournament. Everybody had a job to do. We needed to shoot a number and it would require five scores, but for now our work was done. Whatever happened, they were still the best.

The state championship was held on Monday at the Henry Horton State Park course, not far from where I grew up. My men played well both rounds, Big Jack showed us his stuff, and together they earned a good team score.

Just when I thought we owned the state championship, another team out of east Tennessee shot their all-time best and won it outright.

We did everything we could do. The other four would be back next year, but Mike Keliher was graduating. Holding up the rear, Mike was the last to finish playing.

We couldn't win and we knew it by then. I was stretched out on a hillside thirty or forty yards above the green, where nobody would see what I was feeling, staring off into space. Toni Keliher, Mike's mom, came over and sat close to me. We didn't say a word. As Mike was approaching the green, she reached over and patted me on my back. Unable to watch, I just buried my face in a towel. Toni cried. I did, too.

Ruth Johnson during her Vanderbilt days

{ 4 }

LIFE LESSONS

There is a law in psychology that if you form a picture
in your mind of what you would like to be, and you
keep and hold that picture there long enough, you will
soon become exactly as you have been thinking.

–William James

After the state high school championship we moved on. For the first time, my guys were going in different directions: having graduated from high school, Mike Keliher was now too old for Junior competition. Mike had received a scholarship to the University of Arizona, my first player to accomplish this.

In those days the U.S. Junior Amateur Championship in Evergreen, Colorado, was the U.S. Open of Junior golf. We wanted that trophy. Matt King had made it to the quarterfinals in 1975. Bob Wolcott was playing better and better. I believed either one of them could win.

I'd never told Matt or Bob my goal of developing a national champion because they didn't need the added pressure. Instead I anchored their own long-term, intermediate, and short-term goals in their subconscious minds by repetition and the emotions that attached to them. I kept their ambitions in the foreground, intending to push their potential to the limit. "When it's 102 degrees in the shade and 115 in the sun," I told them, "the player with goals will have a purpose for doing the work." Following the example of Chicagoan Gary Pinns, we were now prepared to handle rain better than anyone else; I knew the wet weather procedures but never coached them until Pinns put on that clinic in the 1975 U.S. Junior Amateur. We would train harder than everyone else, with the tournaments as the reward, when we had fun.

In the 1976 U.S. Junior qualifier at Belle Meade, thirty-five players were competing for two spots. After Matt King finished, Bob Wolcott was still on the course and very much in contention. Parked by the number 17 green, I saw that a kid from another club, in the group in front of Bob, was at even par with number 18 to play. A delay on the tee allowed Bob to walk over. He was one over after 17, he informed me. Telling him what was happening ahead, I urged him to get to the tee and let the guy see him. I always preached no gamesmanship, but anything that didn't violate a rule or wasn't disrespectful to a fellow competitor was OK.

To his credit, Bob elected to stay back. He was not going to let his presence intimidate this kid. When both made pars on #18, Bob was left first alternate with no chance of a spot. Matt King finished first and ended up medalist with a 70.

The national championship would be held in Colorado in July. Matt's grandparents were accompanying him to the event, and they invited me to come along, too.

Matt's confidence and game had improved since the quarterfinals in 1975. I didn't change his routine too much. He was playing more, practicing less, and when he did practice focusing carefully on the right things. Intensifying his prep work would just add pressure. I kept picturing him getting that trophy. By now, however, I had enough experience to stay calm, collected, and consistent around him--we didn't talk about it.

Belle Meade's shop lady, Miriam Moore, had been talking for months about this nice girl she wanted to match me up with for a blind date. I kept putting her off; I didn't like blind dates, and I was kind of involved with someone. Miriam had gone to the University of Mississippi too, after my time. When she invited me to a party at her apartment complex, about a week after Matt qualified for the U.S. Junior Championship, I figured there would be plenty of Ole Miss friends to catch up with. I arrived to find the party underway, complete with a DJ, music, and dancing.

I saw her from behind. She was on the dance floor, her long dark hair flowing as she moved to the music. Wow, this girl could dance. I couldn't tell if she was making the music or dancing to it--she was *more* than graceful. I kept staring, fixated on her. Then she spun around so I could see her face: she was simply beautiful, her smile radiant and something truly special in her eyes. I had never seen her before.

She was dancing with Lock Ross, who had played basketball for Ole Miss. In the same class, Lock and I knew each other well. Lock was 6'10" and as we say in the country, as graceful as a cow on ice. This beautiful girl could really dance. Lock was married and headed in a different direction when the dance was over, so when he went outside, I approached. "Hey, Lock, tell me . . . who was that lady?"

"Oh, her name is Ruth Johnson," he said. "She lives out here." I recognized the name: this was the girl Miriam wanted me to meet. I kept my distance that night and just watched her dance, but at work the next morning I lit on Miriam like a duck on a June bug. "What's taking you so long?" I asked her. "You need to get in gear--come on, let's go!" A puzzled look on her face, Miriam asked me what I was carrying on about. "Ruth Johnson!" I practically shouted. "I saw her on the dance floor last night--she's beautiful! I'm ready. Set it up."

On Saturday, July 4, 1976, Ruth met me at the door of her apartment and flashed that lovely smile again. We had dinner at Willie's home and watched the nation's bi-centennial celebration on television.

I didn't say much, which was out of character for me. They asked about it at the shop the next day. I had no answer then, but now I know that you can only focus on one thing at a time; my attention was on my heart, not my mind. I taught my players to trust their hearts over their heads. If they could see the shot and believe in it, let her rip.

I saw something extra special on my first glance. I can take you to the place and stand on the spot. At Ole Miss I'd dated several beautiful girls that I cared a lot about; I was the one who held back and prevented the relationships from getting too close. But Ruth knocked me flat off my feet. It was love at first glance for me and, surprisingly, the same for her. We clicked. We didn't want to be apart. We had a date every night--two weeks without missing a night--right up until it was time for me to leave for Colorado with Matt.

I'm seeing stars, my heart is fluttering--Ruth would be on my mind every day. When I imagined Matt winning, I pictured him handing *her* that trophy.

But we had a job to do. Friday, the night before we left, I took Ruth out to dinner. She knew how much I wanted to see Matt compete. This was her first experience with Bobby the coach before a tournament that really mattered. Bear Bryant said every coach has a partner behind the scenes. Ruth understood the passion behind all of this, and she was leaning into it, big time. As Matt and I headed to Colorado I felt her support for the very first time.

***

The U.S. Junior Amateur Championship starts with a field of 154 players. After 36 holes of qualifying on Tuesday and Wednesday, the low 64 move on to match play, weeding each other out until the last two meet in the finals Saturday. We planned on being there. Traveling the Saturday before, we would have Sunday for a practice round and a good look at the course, saving Monday to rest, relax, and get ready.

The Hiwan Golf Club course was well suited for a U.S. Junior, neither overly difficult nor too easy--a fair test. No trick holes or blind shots: the golf course was right in front of you. The pace of the greens was quick. The grass had a silver tint and rolled faster down-grain, whereas into the grain, where the grass was a darker green, putts would be slower. Matt knew how to handle this. At that elevation the air is much thinner, so the ball carries further with every club. Matt quickly came up with a system for factoring the altitude, settling on a 10% adjustment factor: a club he normally hit 150 yards would go 165.

Getting there early for the practice round, we had the course almost to ourselves. I coach my players to make as many decisions as they can *ahead of time*. With each club and target already determined, Matt wouldn't have to worry about these things during the tournament. After a good look at the course his experience would take it from there--he wasn't attempting anything new. The USGA erects hole signs so we knew within ten yards where the tees would be. The first step was determining "the club to the center," then what to do with different hole locations. After nine holes, Matt mentally reviewed each one. We came up with a plan for birdying each par 5 and determined the right club for each par 3. Every course has three or four harder holes; we now determined where to be aggressive and where to use common sense. As Matt made notes in his yardage book I sauntered alongside, trying to project total confidence and ease.

When the round concluded Matt re-played the entire course mentally. If there is any work to do, the time is after the round. Then he spent some time putting, just to get the pace--a great putter, he wasn't searching for a stroke. After playing some shots with his sand wedge he hit some six irons, the three wood off a tee, and his driver, every shot hit with a purpose, the routine the same. The course suited Matt's game well. Always focused, he rarely made a mental error.

Our prep work done, we went to get Matt's Tuesday tee time. As a quarter-finalist the previous year, he was paired with Doug Clarke from La Jolla, California. The top collegiate recruit in the country, Clarke was a genuine prodigy, winner of the California State Golf Association Amateur and the Trans-Mississippi Amateur. Gene Littler, who played with him regularly at the La Jolla Country Club, said publicly that Doug Clarke could win on the PGA Tour while still in high school. Another name caught my attention, Bob Clampett from northern California. This cat could play. There were other good players in the field, but these two from California were in another league.

While we rested and took it easy on Monday, I took the time to write a message on a note card. Writing notes from a tournament site was not typical behavior for me, and Matt asked what I was doing. "I'm writing this girl I just met," I told him. "Known her two weeks, and I'm going to marry her." Matt King was the first person I told that I'd met the lady of my dreams. Matt would soon meet Ruth and understand my instant attraction to her.

This rest day gave me the opportunity to show Matt something new. I introduced him to a technique I got from *The Inner Game of Tennis*: simply sit erect in a chair and *focus on your breath*. This calms your mind, heightens awareness, and helps you to control your emotional state and concentrate. Matt got it quickly. Always very systematic, Matt already had a pre-round routine. To give himself twenty minutes to meditate plus twenty minutes margin, I suggested finishing the warm-up about forty-five minutes before the tee time. He could scout out the clubhouse ahead of time and find an isolated and quiet spot.

***

Doug Clarke had the total package: the game, composure, and shots that were well beyond his age. Growing up in California and playing with Gene Littler--a very successful PGA Tour pro with years of experience and one of the smoothest tempos in golf--at La Jolla Country Club, Clarke got some natural-

learning training few have access to. La Jolla's head professional, Paul Runyan, was the greatest short game coach alive. This
attracted pros like Phil Rodgers and John Schroeder to hang
out, and made it a true players' club.

Matt and Doug Clarke cruised through a good first round.
With scores right at par, they put themselves near the top of the
scoreboard. Clarke knew that Matt could play and they seemed
to pull each other along, like drafting in NASCAR racing. Matt
played Tuesday afternoon in the same group. Again, he and
Doug Clarke were playing great and knew it. They were both in
the flow--you could tell by the grace and ease they demonstrated while playing. No straining or trying, just comfortable in
their own skin, trusting their eyes, and letting it happen. While
taking care to stay out of Matt's line of sight, I could see a mutual respect developing.

Match play is like the NCAA basketball championship: everyone waits to see how the brackets get put together. The field
is separated into four brackets, within which qualifying scores
determine the seeding; players with lower scores face those who
shot higher. I didn't say anything, but we didn't want to be in
the same bracket with Clarke or Clampett. Finally the brackets,
seeds, and first-round matches were posted. As Matt and I approached the scoreboard I noticed Doug Clarke scanning it too.
One glance confirmed that the two of them were in the same
bracket. If both made it, they would meet in the quarterfinals.

We couldn't think about that yet, however. Matt knew better
than to get ahead of himself or take any win for granted. Everyone still playing had two matches on Wednesday. Matt won his
first easily and the second without much straining; in events like
this, with the adrenaline pumping, young players don't get

tired. With the field down to sixteen players there were two matches on Thursday. Still playing well Thursday morning, Matt won his third-round match.

For the second year in a row he had made the quarterfinals. In the quarterfinals of the 1975 U.S. Junior, Matt had lost to the very good Gary Pinns in the rain. Once again three wins away from the national championship, this time he would indeed face Doug Clarke.

Between the morning and afternoon matches, about thirty minutes before the match, I noticed Matt sitting on the ground by himself. Something told me to go sit with him.

There wasn't much talking. Whatever round they met up, Matt would have to beat Clarke to win, I'd told him the night before. He knew his dream hinged on beating this extremely gifted player. Now I said I was proud of him. Nothing could happen to change that in one match, and everyone who cherished him would feel the same way.

"Hey," I said, "we've seen Clarke. We know what he can do. I hope he brings all of his game, every bit of it. Then it's my prayer that you can bring all the game you have . . . if that happens, this could be a match people will never forget."

Somehow Matt knew that one of my goals was to develop a national champion. I didn't want him to know it, but he did. This was his dream, too, and I could see he was carrying too much on his shoulders. Fifty yards up from the starter's tent I gave him a one-arm hug, holding on long enough to say, "You've got the game. Get out there, turn it loose, and let 'em see your heart. Remember, you're *Matt King* . . . And you're bringing all you've got, too." Those words seemed to loosen him up.

Matt and Doug approached the starter's tent, both carrying themselves with confidence. A crowd was already gathering; it didn't take these knowledgeable spectators long to know who the real players were. Hoping to seize the lead, Matt hit a beautiful, pure drive. Clarke came right behind him with a great shot and then proceeded to birdie two of the first three, to go two up. Matt hadn't missed a shot, but par wasn't going to win any holes in this match.

The gallery was building. After birdying to win the 9th, Matt was two under and two down at the turn. As he addressed his ball, a young guy with a camera drew near the tee. Backing away, Matt asked him politely not to use the camera. At the top of his back swing: CLICK. Matt's ball sailed way right into some tough rough. The guy spared Doug Clarke the click. Making bogie, Matt lost the hole and went three down. Finding the photographer--a rookie sportswriter with the local paper, using a 35mm camera without a zoom lens--I asked him not to take King's picture anymore, or Clarke's either.

On the eleven hole, a par three, both players were on the green with nice birdie putts. Just as Matt was getting ready to set up, this guy dropped into a picture-taking position. I stepped over to block his view and turned. "I'm going to ask you politely one more time to get lost with that camera. If it happens a third time, I will stuff it down your throat. Are we communicating?" He said he got it. A hole or so later an older gentleman approached. Informing me he was the publisher of the paper, he complained that I was keeping his employee from doing his job.

I stared at him. "Your guy doesn't have the proper lens to be taking pictures," I said. "And by the way, I came from Tennes-

see to do *my* job. I told him what comes next. Write it down."
Finally the pictures stopped.

Matt was three under when Doug Clarke closed him out, 4
and 3. Clarke was seven under: Matt just ran out of holes.
Clarke's experience made the difference. He knew how to keep
making birdies, rather than protecting and playing safe. I think
his respect for Matt factored in his game strategy; having seen
him for two days, Clarke knew no lead was safe. Between them
they made eleven birdies. It may have been the best match I
have ever witnessed--at any level.

We walked back to the clubhouse together. Matt was not
pleased with losing; no champion ever is. He had hoped to get
further and win, but Clarke was just that good. I told him they
put on a show, and there would not be a better match.

Two days later Doug Clarke lost in the finals to a player I'd
never heard of, Madden Hatcher III, from Georgia. Bob
Clampett had been beaten too, somewhere along the way. In a
72-hole stroke-play event there might be eight or ten with the
game to win, but match play opens things up. The winner will
be worthy, but the best player can lose his first match--it happens. Any player making it to the round of 32 has a chance.

Doug Clarke may have been the best junior player I ever got
to see. He went on to play some great golf at Stanford. He made
the Walker Cup Team and played in the 1980 Masters, and then
he disappeared. Sometimes playing that great so early--and
having a guy like Gene Littler throwing that level of praise in
public--can hurt a young man.

Bobby Clampett went to Brigham Young, became the college
player of the year, and started on the PGA Tour with great
promise. In the final round of the 1982 British Open Clampett

had a meltdown that cost him his seven-stroke lead and then the tournament. After that loss, to Tom Watson, he seemed to lose his passion for playing. Bobby Clampett trained for years with Ben Doyle, the teaching professional at Monterey Country Club and the first proponent of Homer Kelley's *Golfing Machine* system. Having devoted a lot of time to Kelley's ideas myself, as I will discuss later, I've wondered if those concepts might have gotten in Bobby Clampett's way. That book was written for physics professors, not players in the real world.

That Colorado trip capped a unique experience: in five years the skinny twelve-year-old I met in Belle Meade's golf shop in 1971 had reached the upper echelon with his game. The neophyte assistant pro who couldn't break eighty and didn't know how to coach had made some progress, too. We were both winners. The more I gave Matt King, the more he gave me.

I would never be able to give a player that kind of time and attention again. This was our time. It didn't end in Colorado, by any means. But like the Rocky Mountains we left behind to come back home, this was where it peaked.

***

Every October Lou Graham lined up a field of touring pros to play in the Music City Classic in Nashville, a full-blown Pro-Celebrity tournament. Twenty-five or thirty pros were paired with celebrities, mostly from the music business. Minnie Pearl participated in the banquet. With tournament sponsors, amateurs paying a hefty fee to play, and good crowds in the ticket-paying galleries, the pros got appearance money in addition to playing for a purse. It was a relaxed, fun event with a concert, cocktail party, and feast; back then the touring pros still did things like this and truly enjoyed it. Martha White Foods, always a sponsor, employed Tennessee Ernie Ford as the company's advertising spokesman. I had gotten to know him during my trips to the Masters with Matt King's family. In town for the tournament, he and Cohen Williams, Matt's grandfather and president of Martha White, kept everyone laughing.

For the second year, Matt was playing in his grandfather's place. This event was a very heady deal for a teenager. His partner was Tom Shaw, a steady touring pro at the time. Any time young players get up close and play with someone at this level, the natural learning process kicks in. Being around Matt's family showed me how a close family functioned and had fun in the process--a natural learning experience for me, too.

After putting my heart and soul into my coaching, I usually felt exhausted and worn out in the fall. This year was different: when I watched Matt play, Ruth was with me, and together we attended several of the parties that only crop up during a pro-celebrity. That Saturday night I asked her to marry me.

I didn't see this coming, either.

Most proposals and engagements include *some* prior discussion, often followed by a well-thought-out, clever proposal event. None of this had taken place. In golf, if you are committed and keep showing up, good things will happen. You can never tell when or how, but it works this way. On this particular Saturday night my heart took over. The words just flowed out, and Ruth accepted. Three months after we met we were engaged to be married.

I was happy, humbled, and a bit frightened. How could I support a wife on an assistant's salary? Am I good enough for her? Oh my, she was a keeper . . . but I questioned whether I was a worthy match.

Soon afterward I was working in the golf shop when Kim Kimbrough came in. We were distantly related; it was his mother who had passed along the news about the opening at Belle Meade. Glancing around the shop, Kim asked what I was earning at Belle Meade. When I told him, he promptly offered to double my income. After the original developer of a planned community called Nashboro Village went bankrupt, the lender had hired Kim to manage the property until a buyer could be found. Kim wanted me to become his head professional. Already concerned about making enough money to get married, I accepted without much thought.

On the other side of town from Belle Meade, Nashboro Village had an entirely different clientele and no practice range. Kim and I had a job to do. Almost anything I suggested would receive his blessing--in spirit, if not in funds. Responsible for the entire golf operation, I had gone from coach to business manager of a course on the ropes. Every day brought a stronger realization that I truly knew my *calling*: I was meant to be a coach.

***

Ruth's parents came to Nashville for Thanksgiving. Ruth and I went to where they were staying. The Johnsons were gracious, but my palms were sweating as we sat on the bed. "Mr. Johnson," I said, "Ruth and I have made a decision we hope meets your approval. We would like to get married and I would like to ask for your daughter's hand." His exact words blur in my memory, but he gave us his blessing.

Ruth's parents met mine at Thanksgiving dinner on the farm. I had asked my mother to see if Horace Gordon's wife Lillian could serve that night. Even in her serving uniform Lillian was more like the second hostess, charming the Johnsons with tales of her "baby" (me). We settled on April 23, 1977, as a wedding date so my accountant dad could get the April 15 tax deadline behind him beforehand. Then I made plans to go to Louisiana for Christmas to meet Ruth's entire family.

I was having second thoughts about Nashboro Village. *Now* I realized how important coaching was to me. I didn't know what to do--resign my job and call off the wedding?

In early December the PGA held a seminar for daily-fee course professionals; I had signed up when I started at Nashboro Village in late October, hoping it would pump some enthusiasm into my new position. Worried about missing my flight, I scrambled to pack and wound up in Oklahoma City without a winter coat. A freezing cold wind was blowing hard when Ruth's oldest sister, Marty, and her husband, Robert Margo, retrieved me from my hotel for dinner. They immediately noticed my lack of a coat--we all laughed--and Robert just happened to have one for me.

It was a big seminar, about two hundred participants. If you observe assemblages like this you will see the big group splitting into smaller clusters--it's human nature to seek out people with whom you have something in common. I met a sharp guy from Ohio who had served as an assistant at Scioto Country Club in Columbus, where Jack Nicklaus grew up and developed his game. This guy told me he had been named head professional at an established private club in that area. During his transition a long-time bag-room employee proved uncooperative, even insubordinate. He gave the man chance after chance before finally letting him go. When his board insisted that he reinstate the employee--this can happen when boards get involved in operations--my new friend told me he had resigned instead, as a matter of principle and ethics.

He was now working at a nine-hole daily-fee course, a huge step down. Over the four-day course of the seminar I told him some of my own dilemma, but mostly I marveled at how calm and at peace he seemed with his world coming apart--he even had a wife and family. Finally, over lunch, I asked him where he found his strength.

He said there was a bigger plan that he was incapable of understanding. Things had always worked out in the past, and the Bible had helped him. He told me to look in the drawer of the nightstand in my hotel room. That evening I read only the one Book he suggested--The Gospel According to John--but it was so powerful and hopeful that the world seemed to come off my shoulders. My feelings of unworthiness were resolved. I realized more clearly that life is a process. Everything is a learning experience and happens for a reason, even when we can't see it. Life isn't about being perfect, but rather being forgiven and moving on. We try to make the best decision we can at a particular moment but if it doesn't work out, just follow your heart and keep playing. I have never seen this man again. I've forgotten his name. He was a total stranger, but he showed up at the right time for me.

Going to that seminar changed my life. I learned several things. First, don't show up in Oklahoma City in December with no coat. Second, I had a cool future sister- and brother-in-law who made me feel welcome in their home. The main lesson, however, was to give strangers your attention and respect: you never know what will happen. I had a Bible at home and I lean on it all the time now. It's strong--steel sharpens steel. Life isn't about me. Tough times don't last, but those who can stay in the game and trust in something bigger than themselves do.

***

Three of my grandparents were dead when I was born. My father's father lived in Macon, GA, so far away (for those times) that I was fortunate to see him once every two years--and then he was so deaf I couldn't talk to him. My grandfather was a distinguished and handsome man with hair so grey that it was white; when my father's hair turned white in his forties, it just made him look older. My grandfather had graduated from Davidson College and Union Theological Seminary. A Presbyterian minister beloved by his congregation, he could really preach. My aunt Margaret saved all his sermon notes in boxes, holding onto them until I was old enough to appreciate the gift. She had three sons of her own, but she wanted me to be the steward of these invaluable documents and memories.

My father attended Hanover College, not far from Jeffersonville, Indiana, where he'd played John Wooden in high school basketball. He loved Hanover, but in 1937 his mother died and shortly thereafter his father was called to the Garden Street Presbyterian Church in Columbia, Tennessee. My father dropped out of college and moved to Columbia. I never knew him to stay in touch with any friends from those Indiana years; he was a reserved and private man, very different from my mother and the complete opposite of Marty and Rense Johnson, Ruth's parents.

My family had festive holiday gatherings, but nothing like the assembly I confronted when I met the Johnson clan in Lafayette for Christmas. Ruth's parents were both only children, but all of Ruth's grandparents and most of her great-aunts and -

uncles were still alive. Which one was Grandpa Johnson? Grandpa Downing? It was fun but stressful trying to keep track. I had never been on display like that, or met so many family members at once. I didn't know when to talk or remain silent. So unless I was spoken to directly, I kept quiet. It was a good policy.

Or would have been, if I had adhered to it more strictly. I had previously told Ruth that I loved giblet gravy and dressing more than the turkey. After I went through the Christmas buffet and returned to my seat, Ruth looked at my plate. "I thought you loved dressing and gravy," she said.

I hesitated. "I didn't see any dressing," I confessed. Thus I came to learn about "Yankee dressing," made from bits of white bread--unlike "southern dressing," made with cornbread. I stand by my initial assessment: I didn't see any dressing. But I wasn't just marrying Ruth, I was marrying her entire family, and they did things differently from us. They never hid their affection for one another. Warmth was their trademark and I was proud to be one of them.

Back in Nashville, I knew what steps I needed to take. My heart wasn't in Nashboro Village. What's a coach going to do at a course without a practice area? I was not meant to be an administrator, regardless of compensation. Ruth and I discussed it and she supported me. Meeting with Kim Kimbrough, I told him we had made a mistake. I appreciated what he had offered, but it just wasn't me. He understood. We agreed that resigning was the best thing.

I was now engaged with no job or income. My position at Belle Meade hadn't been filled. When I spoke with Willie Gibbons he told me nothing was decided. I knew I'd done an excellent job for Willie, but he clearly thought I hadn't given Nash-boro Village long enough; a month went by before he finally called and asked me to rejoin the staff.

Returning to my comfort zone, I breathed a big sigh of relief. My players were happy. But I learned a lot from that experience: never take a job because of the income. Be certain you are fully committed to the next opportunity. I believe Willie left me hanging to help me mature and learn some life lessons. At some point I would leave Belle Meade permanently for something else. Now I was ready to do it right.

Bob Wolcott at Belle Meade

NEXT!

Someday, after we have mastered
the winds, the waves, and the tide
and gravity, we shall harness for God
the energies of love.
Then, for the second time in the history
of the world, man will have discovered fire.

–Pierre Teilhard de Chardin

My flight to Lafayette for the wedding was supposed to include a change of planes in New Orleans. When a huge gulf storm dumped fourteen inches of rain on Lafayette, closing that city's airport, the airline put us on a Greyhound bus for the last leg of the trip. The New Orleans Open was being played that weekend. As he transferred my golf bag--with the PGA crest and my name--to the bus, the baggage handler looked at me. "You miss the cut?" he asked.

I smiled and winked at him. "No," I said, "I've got something more important to play in."

He grinned back. "Play well, tighten up, and let 'em see what you've got."

People talk about being nervous before their weddings, but I felt calm as I walked out with my father that Saturday afternoon. We took our places, turned, and faced the crowd that filled the First Presbyterian Church. Outside, there wasn't a cloud in the sky. The church had huge stained-glass windows and sunlight was streaming into the sanctuary. I knew the Lord was shining down on us. Here came the processional of friends, mothers, and grandmothers escorted to their seats, followed by Ruth's bridesmaids and my groomsmen. The organist began playing the music Ruth had chosen. Then, from the back of the church, she made her entrance.

The word beautiful doesn't begin to describe how she looked to me that day. Her dad walked beside her and both beamed as they made their way down the aisle. I tried to take it in, all of it. Then I looked at my groomsmen and nodded.

Time seemed to speed up. We were taking our vows and exchanging rings. We were taking sacred oaths. This was for keeps as far as we were concerned, a lifetime deal with no 36-hole cut. We have to keep playing, no matter what trouble or hardship comes our way, the same as a golfer who wants to be a champion. Quit? No way. Then I was kissing my WIFE.

Nellie Wooden preceded John Wooden in death by twenty-five years. After she died, Coach Wooden wrote her a love letter every month until his eyesight failed, just months before his death. In my book, this may top all those NCAA championships.

Claude Harmon's wife Alice died of cancer at age fifty-one, after thirty years of marriage. His sons told me their father was never the same after losing her. Mr. Harmon had impeccable manners. Speaking to my juniors about etiquette and doing things the right way, he would say, "It doesn't cost a dime to be nice and treat people with respect." A lady never entered the room without Claude standing to honor her presence. He understood the art of being a gentleman, something his sons attribute to their mom, Alice. They never heard their parents exchange a cross word. Claude treasured and revered Alice, whom he survived by close to twenty years. I don't know what I would do without Ruth, so I have instructed her to outlive me.

In our marriage service, the pastor talked about two being joined together as one. After all these years, I take this literally. Marriage isn't a 50/50 partnership, as some say. By throwing all we have into the game, we become and function as a 100% whole. Wooden, Bryant, Penick, Harmon, and other great coaches have acknowledged the roles of their wives in their careers. Trust me: their contributions cannot be fully comprehended. Ruth has always been there for my players and me. Many of them traveled great distances just to spend a few days, gather the courage to keep competing, and feel better about themselves. Some would confide in her things they wouldn't bring up with me. Ruth sent them away feeling much better about *everything*. If you played for me, you were family in her eyes, always treated with love and respect. She called them "Bobby's boys," but everyone knew they were hers, too.

***

The engagement ring, a wedding present for your bride, the honeymoon . . . It takes cash to get married. Six months earlier I'd bought some stock in a new company. Jack Massey, married to my third cousin, took three companies to the New York Stock Exchange, first Kentucky Fried Chicken and last the Hospital Corporation of America.

I found out about the second company without any illegal inside information provided; the news was floating around the club. When I got wind of it I'd decided to take action, buying 2,000 shares of Wendy's stock for $1.00 a share. As soon as Wendy's went public, the stock shot up to $6.00. David Patterson, a sophisticated stockbroker with plenty of gray hair, advised that I sell, because the fast food chains were risky. "You can't go broke making a profit," he added. So I put in a sell order and cashed in my chips to cover wedding expenses.

Fast-forward to 1999 and the lesson tee at The Golf Club of Tennessee. I was giving a lesson to Bob Frist, Senator Bill Frist's younger brother. Their father, Dr. Tom Frist, had founded Hospital Corporation with Jack Massey, and Bob Frist owned and managed every Wendy's in North and South Carolina. After our lesson I told him this story, then asked if he had any idea what those 2,000 shares would have been worth that day.

Bob put his hand on my shoulder. "Bobby," he said, "we just met and I like you. I can't do it to you." Finally he told me there had been five two-for-one splits, and the stock was now around $30 a share.

Five two-for-one-splits meant 36,000 shares, times $30 equaled . . . $1,080,000. I had to laugh when I told Ruth about it: "You see what this wedding cost us?"

***

Half the Belle Meade membership vacationed at Sea Island in Georgia. The Cloister resort there gave newlyweds a good honeymoon rate, betting they'd return for the rest of their lives-- many did. Making a living at golf took it off my list of recreational activities, but the Sea Island Golf Club had three eighteen-hole courses and we played a couple of times. Shortly after we began dating Ruth had asked me to pick her up at the airport; when she came back with a bag and set of clubs I'd thought 'something is clicking here.' She was a novice, but Sea Island had some really forward teeing areas that made it much easier on the ladies.

For a wedding present Ruth had given me an 8-millimeter movie camera. Early in our nine-hole round, playing a par four, Ruth hit a good drive and only had a seven iron to the hole. She played a beautiful shot--better than she knew how--that came to rest three feet from the hole. Hey, I thought, I can take my camera and capture her making a birdie. She tightened up, so I told her to breathe and relax. She took dead aim . . . and while I was filming, her three-footer turned into a nine-footer. Later, watching the film, we both laughed at her reaction.

The Cloister offered horseback riding along the beach, on very tame animals. Ruth wanted to ride. I wasn't excited about it, but she was my new bride, so I agreed to go. Climbing on the broken-down mare, I smelled the leather of the saddle first. Then, as my mount warmed up, a smell that anyone who rides will remember vividly replaced it: the smell of a horse. In an instant my mind went back to my childhood.

I rode a pony every day from the time I was five until I outgrew it around age nine. On the last day of first grade I was riding bareback like an Indian--I used to switch between this mode and cowboy-with-a-saddle--while the farm hands were taking up hay late in the day. Trying to get everything in the barn before sundown, the young guys had overloaded the wagon, which was pulled by our mules. When the wagon made a turn the load of hay tipped over, and the mules bolted like a runaway stage-coach in those western movies.

This happened behind me and I hadn't seen any of it. Perched bareback, I got jerked violently out of make-believe when my pony reacted by exploding forward.

I did okay for three or four hundred yards, but the pony was flying. Pulling back on the bridle had no effect. We came to a downgrade on a chert farm road near Horace and Lillian Gordon's home. I saw Lillian putting out laundry to dry. Once my pony started downhill, I slid forward every time her front legs hit the ground. I dug my knees into her sides as hard as I could, but I couldn't hold on. Finally I toppled off, hit my head, and got knocked cold.

Lillian saw this. She also saw those out-of-control mules, headed in my direction going wide open. The young guys couldn't make them respond even by hauling back on the reins. As I lay there, limp, Lillian instinctively took off in my direction as fast as she could. She was a large lady in her late forties then. There was no time to pull me out of the way. She managed to step between me and the oncoming mules, grab her white apron, and fling it up just in time to make them turn and run up into a grove of locust trees.

As I came to I heard Lillian giving those teenage boys a piece of her mind. Way up at the top part of the farm, my pony was still running--we could have won the Kentucky Derby that day. I suffered a mild concussion and the chert tore the skin off my face.

Years later I stood where Lillian had been at the laundry line. I remembered where I fell. I could also see how far the mules had to have stampeded before she could see them. Checking it all out and walking the distance, I just shook my head--it seemed impossible. But I was her "baby." Lillian could have gotten trampled, but she took that risk to protect me.

At nine I'd graduated from the pony to Black Beauty, a registered Tennessee Walking Horse with great conformation. We used her as a brood mare and bred her to champion studs.

Most of the time you have to chase a horse to bridle them. All I had to do was walk into the pasture and hold up the bridle, and Black Beauty would come running. She was so big, however, that I had to have someone help me onto her. One day I couldn't find anyone. There was a large metal drainage culvert next to the farm road. After managing to get her bridled and saddled myself, I walked her over to the culvert. There I thought I could mount her easily.

Black Beauty had a lot of spirit. She would perk up and you knew she was ready to go. As I got in the saddle she swung around sharply to her right for some reason. We made it about fifty yards before I realized she was limping badly. Jumping down, I saw blood squirting from her ankle--she must have hit the sharp metal edge of the culvert. I walked her the short distance to Horace and Lillian's house, yelling as loud as I could. "Help me! Help! Black Beauty's hurt--somebody help me!"

People gathered quickly. The blood was squirting two feet. Hearing Horace say she might need to be put down, I held on to her and cried, "God, please save her!" When the vet finally got there, she wouldn't keep her foot still. I grabbed her by the neck and put my face next to hers, pleading, "Be still, girl. Let 'em help you." Twelve years old and a skilled rider, I couldn't understand how I had let this happen. I kept crying, blaming myself.

Finally my mother and Daddy Will walked me away from her, to our patio.

Daddy Will broke in. "Bobby, *hush!*" I had never heard him raise his voice that loud. "We can get another horse. We can't find another Bobby."

It took them well into the night to sew up Black Beauty's ankle. She limped for the rest of her life. I hadn't ridden since that day, not until Ruth got me on that horse at Sea Island, but Daddy Will's words have resonated in my soul ever since he uttered them.

During our honeymoon week we got lessons in shooting skeet--or trap, I can't tell the difference. As a boy I just slung a shotgun up to my shoulder and fired at dove, quail, or rabbit. I was pretty decent; it's just hand-eye coordination. I'd never even heard of someone giving shooting lessons. The pro at Sea Island made some good points, and I could hit a few clay pigeons as long as I didn't think about what he told me. But with all that instruction rattling around in my head I quickly succumbed to paralysis from over-analysis. I did better just picking up my target and letting my body do what came naturally. Ruth, on the other hand, had learned to shoot as a girl. Her dad, a duck hunter, had showed her the basics and she could really shoot.

I met Sea Island Golf Club's professional Jimmy Hodges, and we formed a lasting friendship. Ruth and I returned to Sea Island repeatedly for a winter pro-am, and Jimmy and I always picked up where we left off. When I started a golf school at the Country Club of Jackson, where I had become head pro, I brought in a half dozen of the best teachers I knew--including Jimmy Hodges. Jimmy once called to ask if I was interested in being co-professional with him at the Atlanta Athletic Club.

Although nothing came of it, I was pleased he thought enough of me to consider it.

In 1988 a private charter airplane flying in poor visibility went down in a marsh near the Jacksonville Airport, killing Jimmy Hodges, Davis Love, Jr., John Poppa, and the pilot. It was a reminder to savor each day: you never know if this one is your last. Jimmy Hodges was a great teacher, and a better friend.

***

The honeymoon passed so quickly. Ruth and I departed Sea Island to begin our married life, heading back to Nashville on top of the world that we had been dreaming.

Ruth was working shifts (mornings, evenings, midnights) on an antiquated surgical floor of Vanderbilt University Hospital that resembled the set of the TV show "St. Elsewhere." I used to buy dinner and bring it up so we could eat together in the nurses' lounge. The floor had a motley crew of patients, from prisoners hand-cuffed to their beds to a couple of drunks who stabbed each other and then walked the halls arm-in-arm like best friends; anybody who didn't need intensive care could be assigned to B2100. Despite the long hours, nurses have to stay totally alert and focused on each patient--their mistakes can be fatal. It takes commitment, intelligence, and heart to be a good nurse. Ruth totally fit the bill.

Getting married and honeymooning at Sea Island took me away from coaching for two weeks, but the boys didn't stand around waiting for me. They were close to my goal for them: knowing how to coach themselves. By now I was just supervising their development. In early spring, when Willie Gibbons first rehired me after Nashboro Village, we had gone through our yearly exercise of coming up with a tournament schedule and as they finished the school year we prepared to train in earnest.

Like Jack Nicklaus, we favored events played on great courses. That year the U.S. Junior Amateur Championship was being played at the Ohio State Scarlet course in Columbus, a great old Donald Ross design. The year before, Bob Wolcott had missed qualifying by one shot. Since then his game had matured tremendously; he had gained length, finesse, and heart and was among the most highly recruited players in the country. Every college team wanted him. In July Bob headed to Ohio with a good chance at the national championship.

Bob finished second out of 150 competitors in the thirty-six hole stage that determines who advances to match play. This gave him a great placement in the brackets; sixty-four go into match play and Bob played the sixty-third seed--and lost. If it had been stroke play, maybe six players had the game to win. In match play, that number can be tripled. Bob knew this before making the trip. Congratulate the winner. Thank the officials. Get on the plane and count your blessings. Where do we play next?

I didn't tell Bob about my goal for many years. Matt King and Bob Wolcott were legitimate contestants; we just didn't get it done. Unable to see another horse in my stable that could do it, I wondered if the goal was too ambitious. They certainly had the heart for it. If these young men only knew how much I cared about them . . .

But they *did* know--that's why they played so hard. Trade for some others? No way. I got the players I needed. If we kept encouraging, showing our affection, and staying committed, I liked our chances. NEXT!

***

Mary Lu Jordan and Jim Campbell--another match made by Miriam--were getting married in Houston in August. The pro that Willie Gibbons learned from must have learned from someone else that nobody gets a weekend off. When I brought up the wedding two weeks beforehand, Willie told me, "Man, it's a weekend. Nobody in the golf business any good takes a Saturday or Sunday off."

I let him go through this tape, then told him, "It's Ruth's best friend." That's Ruth's friend. "No, she's *our* friend and Jim is our friend, too." We're talking about a summer weekend. "Yeah, it's August and 110 degrees in the shade." I knew Willie well enough to know the cards he had in his hand. "Willie, Ruth made our reservation some time back for the cheap rate. She'll really be hurt and disappointed if I have to tell her I can't go." Oh . . . long pause . . . *Ruth* already purchased tickets? "Yes, she has."

Willie hesitated. "OK, I suppose it will work. Let me know the dates you'll be off." I told him we were leaving on Wednesday, coming back on Sunday, and I could come in Monday if he wanted. "Just come in on Tuesday as usual," he said. "Mike will take Monday. We'll stay with the normal schedule." Willie had a big heart; he just liked to bluff with no cards.

I had gotten word to bring my clubs. To get us out of the way of the ladies on Thursday, George Jordan, Mary Lu's father, arranged for us to play golf at his club, River Oaks. Belle Meade isn't the slums, but as we drove down River Oaks Boulevard I stared at one gigantic mansion after another, built on what looked like two-acre lots. At Belle Meade the big ones sit on ten acres minimum--they don't hit you all at once like that.

On the way to the club Mr. Jordan told me they had just hired a new golf pro named Dick Harmon. I anticipated his next words: "Dick is Claude Harmon's son." Everyone in the golf business knew that name. Claude Harmon had placed close to fifty assistants in the best jobs in America. Willie Gibbons trained under Bob Moser, who had worked for one of them-- Jack Lumpkin, director of instruction at Sea Island. Therefore, Willie considered himself, and by extension Belle Meade as well, to be "in the Claude Harmon network."

At the club entrance we stopped for the security guard. The only other club where I'd been met by security was Augusta National. Caddies in white coveralls retrieved our bags in the parking lot. High, vaulted ceilings made the men's locker room look like a church sanctuary. Wood-paneled lockers, card tables, whirlpools, nap rooms, masseuse, barber, weight room, more service people than members . . . I had been in some great locker rooms, like Indian Creek in Miami, but this beat anything I had ever seen. Mr. Jordan told me the course was a Donald Ross design. Ross also designed the course at Belle Meade, but the club had hired Robert Trent Jones to tamper with it. I later found out River Oaks had succumbed to the same fad, with Joe Finger doing the redesign; these clubs are now paying architects to restore the Ross integrity. River Oaks was still a great course; Finger hadn't messed it up too badly.

The starter had us playing with Dr. Charlie Williams and his son. Around 10 a.m. our caddies were lined up. My caddie, Melvin, had a sense of humor. Warming up, I glanced at the sky to see dark clouds gathering and mentioned it to Melvin. "If you don't like Houston's weather," he said, "just wait fifteen minutes--it'll change." The thought of playing this great course had my adrenaline pumping. Number 1 was a short par-five with a slight dogleg right. I reached it in two and made birdie. After parring the second, I birdied the par-four third. "What's the course record?" I asked Melvin. "We're gunning for it!"

Laughing, he plucked a cigarette from his mouth. "I believe it's 64," he told me.

I clapped him on the shoulder. "Then let's shoot a 62 and have one to spare."

It never even started sprinkling to give us a warning. The thunder sounded like cannons going off all around us. It was raining sideways, with winds thirty or forty miles an hour. Growing up in the country I thought I'd seen everything, but never such a thunderstorm as this. As we took refuge under a rain shelter near the 4th tee, Mr. Jordan said, "They will come get us." Sure enough, seven or eight big vans came out and retrieved everyone. I had never known a club to have vans designated for this purpose, with drivers responding so quickly.

On the drive back in I winked at Melvin. "Don't you be running off on me--we need to shoot that 62."

He laughed. "I'm not going anywhere, Mr. McKeebles."

Mr. Jordan ushered me into the golf shop, where everyone else from the course was ending up. Full-length plate-glass windows made up the shop's entire front, so for almost an hour we watched it blowing and raining outside. This much water could make a course unplayable--it just can't drain fast enough. I was pretty sure a 62 wasn't in my bag, but I was still thinking about getting back out there when Mr. Jordan took me by the arm. "Bobby, I'd like to introduce you to our new pro I was telling you about, Dick Harmon."

Well-dressed and socially polished, Dick looked close to my age, twenty-nine. I told him about my indirect connection with his dad through Willie. Friendly and good at making idle chatter, he stood and watched it rain with me. "It may quit any time," Dick said, "and we could get back out."

Recalling that he had been on board six months, I said, "I assume you have your staff in place." It wasn't so much a question as an attempt to make small talk.

Dick looked at me. "No, both of my assistants are leaving the golf business. I will be hiring two assistants for the fall."

Pre-occupied with making chitchat, my conscious mind let those words fly right over. Around 12:30 the course was closed. Mr. Jordan and I had lunch and left without seeing Dick again. The next night the Jordans held Mary Lu and Jim's rehearsal dinner at the club--in the ladies locker room. But this was River Oaks: they could have hosted it in the boiler room. The wedding went off without a hitch. Many of the same Vanderbilt friends from Ruth's and my wedding were there, too, making the occasion feel like instant replay at a different location.

On the Sunday night flight back to Nashville I was sound asleep, uncommon for me on an airplane. Suddenly at 30,000 feet I opened my eyes and roused Ruth from her deep slumber. "Baby, Dick Harmon is looking for two assistants. He told me on Thursday--I don't know what I've been thinking. I've been at Belle Meade for six years, and my boys can make it without me now . . . I believe this is an opportunity worth chasing. What do you think?" Ruth told me she would support me whatever I pursued. Back home I immediately drafted a letter, put together a resume highlighting the records of my juniors, and mailed it to

Dick. Dick responded quickly, saying he was looking for some-one to be a leader in his junior program. That sounded good.

Then the waiting started. One week turned into two, which turned into three.

Working at Belle Meade I had met more than my share of heavy hitters. Tennessee Ernie Ford called to put in a good word for me. But Dick Harmon had been around Bob Hope and Gerald Ford--was Tennessee Ernie going to be a deal maker? Jess Neely had coached at Rice for decades. A member of the Football Hall of Fame, he was revered in Houston. Now in his eighties and a member at Belle Meade, Mr. Neely had coffee with me every day. He taught me how to watch a college football game. River Oaks member Vincent Buckley had played for Coach Neely at Rice. When Dick showed him Neely's letter, Mr. Buckley said, "If Coach Neely says a rooster can plow, hitch him up." Dick replied promptly, but another two weeks passed.

It was mid-October, two months since I applied, before Dick called and asked me to fly down for an interview. Now I had to let Willie Gibbons know of the job prospect, and my intention to accept it if offered. He understood. If Willie hadn't allowed me to make that first trip, I never would have had this opportunity.

Dick wanted to interview me with Jimmy Greenwood, a committee member whose two young sons had expressed an in-terest in playing golf. I didn't need notes to talk about junior golf or my coaching philosophy--training juniors was my game. Afterwards the three of us played nine holes. I had been in a lot of competitive games and tournaments, but when I teed it up my hand shook so much I thought I was going to have to use both hands.

Dick must have noticed. "Let's just play," he said. "We aren't worrying about the score." Breathing easier, I shot a 38 or 39.

Dick finally called to offer me the job late in October. I accepted immediately. He wanted to talk about compensation but I cut him off. "I will give you an honest day's work. I'm not worried about receiving an honest day's wage."

After some lovely going away parties, Ruth and I packed our two cars and headed to Houston. I was off to River Oaks--to join Dick's staff and get "Harmonized."

***

Many years later Dick Harmon told me this story: "I'm out on the course playing and George Jordan drives up. He's holding something in his hand. I see it's an envelope and he pulls out a letter. Mr. Jordan told me, 'I don't know Bobby McIver well. I met him at my daughter's wedding and he was a nice young man. But I'm holding a letter from my daughter, and I *do* know her. She speaks very highly of him. It's clear she thinks he is a person of substance, ability, and character. The fact that she would write me such a letter says something to me--it should say something to you. She was led to write this of her own free will.'"

Dick lowered his voice as he told the story. "I told Mr. Jordan, 'Bobby impressed me. His references spoke very highly of him and he can certainly coach junior golfers. There is only one problem I have with him, Mr. Jordan. His hair is too long.'"

George Jordan has a presence about him to this day. Dick said, "He took the letter and leafed through it and maintained an uncomfortable silence . . . and then he said 'Dick, the man my daughter is describing here will cut his hair any length you want it.'"

Dick continued, "I excused myself from my game and drove to the golf shop to call you. Mr. Jordan made me feel like, duh, what have I been thinking about. Hire the guy."

I didn't find out about Mary Lu's letter for a decade. What it said exactly, Ruth and I do not know. But Mary Lu's heartfelt message was the dealmaker--not Tennessee Ernie Ford. Not even Jess Neely. Mary Lu delivered the knockout punch, and we doubt she knows it. Because of Mary Lu, we connected with one of the greatest families in American golf. Because of Mary Lu, I met Claude Harmon, my main mentor. And because of Mary Lu, I came to coach a twelve-year-old boy from Dallas named Scott Verplank.

In back, l. to r.: Mike Keliher, Clay King, Matthew McIver, Matt King; in
front: Rett Crowder

River Oaks Golf Staff with guest Ben Hogan; l. to r. Dale Kahlden, Bobby
McIver, Hogan, Dick Harmon, John McNeely

April 23, 1977

Bobby with Tennessee Walking Horse Black Beauty

Sea Island Honeymoon

Scott Verplank, age 12, with Bobby McIver

Rett Crowder, age 9

{ 6 }

HARMONIZED

The man who has no imagination has no wings.

–Muhammed Ali

When addressing the ball, take dead aim.

– Harvey Penick

Nashville isn't a small town. Houston dwarfed it; a college friend who worked as an accountant for Shell Oil had a 90-minute commute twice a day. Ruth and I were lucky to rent a little house three blocks from Rice University, only a short drive to River Oaks. We arrived the first week in November and I showed up at the club on November 5.

Dick Harmon had mentioned hiring two new assistants when we first met during that thunderstorm. I met John McNeely for the first time in the hallway outside the River Oaks golf shop. From the outset, John's sociable personality impressed me. John had worked with Dick at Winged Foot and Thunderbird for Dick's father, Claude. Because Dick already knew he was going to hire John, I had actually been vying for one open position.

The Harmon name was already so prestigious that Dick could have had his choice of anyone in the country wanting to make a move. Claude Harmon was to golf what Vince Lombardi and John Wooden were to their sports. All four of his sons followed him into the game. Butch, the premier teaching professional in the world, has served as a personal coach to Tiger Woods, Greg Norman, and the King of Morocco. Craig is the long-time head professional at Oak Hill in Rochester. Dick was more than ready to step in as head pro at River Oaks after running Thunderbird for his dad for years. Billy, the youngest, is a teacher in Palm Springs.

All the Harmons got schooled in how to have fun. They shared this philosophy: if you can coach someone to *enjoy life*, you are providing a great service. Dick brought out the best in people with different strengths, assembling a staff that meshed perfectly. He gave me oversight of the junior program, and once I showed a knack for merchandising he put me in charge of buying menswear. Many said that River Oaks golf staff was the best in the country.

Shortly after I came to River Oaks, Claude Harmon retired to spend most of his time in Houston. Dick loved his father, but he suddenly found himself with a bored celebrity to entertain. His solution--hand him off to me--was possibly the biggest break of my life.

The last club pro to win the Masters (in 1948, the year I was born), Claude Harmon had served as head professional at Winged Foot in Mamaroneck, New York, in the summer and Seminole in Palm Beach, Florida, in the winter. Ben Hogan used to practice at Seminole for the month leading up to the Masters, and he and Claude became best friends; when Claude realized he could keep up with Hogan at Seminole, he knew he could compete with anyone at Augusta. The day *after* Seminole's big pro-am, which offered a purse larger than many tour events offered at that time, Claude Harmon shot a twelve-under 60 on the course. In the club's famous wood-paneled locker room hangs a big course layout that shows every shot Claude Harmon played in that round, as he set the course record that still stands.

Winged Foot consists of two courses, West and East, ranked among the toughest in America. Except for Fuzzy Zoeller's win in 1984, Winged Foot-hosted U.S. Opens have always been won with an over-par total. The renowned A. W. Tillinghast designed both courses, and neighboring Quaker Ridge, another Tillinghast design, features a similar level of difficulty. The course record for all three is a 61, shot by Claude Harmon.

Tillinghast courses share a trademark: extremely deep bunkers. Playing out of these hazards takes exceptional skill, and Claude Harmon was among the best bunker players the game has ever seen. In 1959 Claude finished third in the U.S. Open played on Winged Foot West; he also had several great finishes in the PGA championship when it was match play. He could hold his own with the PGA Tour players of that time, but elected to remain a club professional.

Claude Harmon was a great player, and an even greater teacher. It is the job of a professional to determine the root cause of a player's problem. Mr. Harmon had cultivated his eye for spotting "the gall stones" of a swing and making a quick diagnosis, with no need for a video camera. The golf swing is a link action: the problem you *see*--Claude Harmon called it "the hang nail"--is almost always caused by something earlier in the chain. Sitting with me on a bench on the range, Mr. Harmon would have me tell him what I saw as the core problems of various players on the tee. These drills helped me immensely when I was diagnosing swing flaws as a coach.

Excellence in coaching goes way beyond swing mechanics, however. Encouragement and kind words came from Mr. Harmon's nature. In this regard I resemble him; whether it is innate, learned early, or both, the "encourager" personality is simply a part of our makeup. A great coach nurtures a player without over-inflating his ego, fosters confidence without arrogance. As Claude Harmon said: "It is easier to make a golfer out of a gentleman than a gentleman out of a golfer." This is a fine-- and invisible--line, and a teacher must develop the sense to both detect and walk it with each student.

A thirty-minute lesson with Mr. Harmon usually involved less than five minutes of physical instruction. He spent the first ten minutes setting the student at ease, asking him what his problem might be, and making a diagnosis. He would then usually offer no more than one suggestion--the rest would be fifteen minutes of cheerleading.

In all my years around Claude Harmon, he only had one swing idea for me: a longer and slower waggle. My swing had a quick setting of the wrists, but rather than draw attention to what he saw as the problem, he looked for something I could do easily that would remedy it. Claude Harmon didn't like to call too much attention to the swing because he wanted to keep your focus on *making shots*. If you were working on your swing and didn't have a target, he would say you weren't practicing golf.

Winged Foot had no driving range. Lessons were given down the 18th fairway, with caddies shagging balls until the morning tee times were scheduled to play through. In the afternoon the golf staff found games with the members; Mr. Harmon hired office staff to cover the shop. He wanted his assistants to be GOLF professionals: playing and teaching came first. Some great players started out working for Claude at Winged Foot. Jack Burke, Dave Marr, and Dick Mayer all won major championships, and in the few years Mike Souchak served on Mr. Harmon's staff, he became one of the top PGA Tour players of his time.

Mr. Harmon always gave his assistants nicknames. Deciding I looked like New York Mets right fielder Rusty Staub, whom he knew from his Winged Foot days, Mr. Harmon called me "Rusty." With this group of people I am Rusty to this day.

***

The juniors at River Oaks were eager, there just weren't as many as at Belle Meade. I worked with brothers Cameron and Todd Greenwood; Cameron, quite the natural, became a good college player for the University of Texas.

Mark McMurrey showed up at River Oaks about the same time I did. At fifteen, Mark was getting a late start. Youngsters starting around age twelve have the best chance because the ego hasn't emerged yet and getting them to dream big is much easier. But Mark hung around us like a puppy dog, and a natural learner like him would soak it up just by osmosis.

I suggested he take one of those big baskets of range balls and hit nothing but two irons. My rationale: if he had confidence hitting his two iron, he would have it with every other club in the bag. To help him focus on a smaller target I had him hit through some thick pine trees at the far end of the range. This was the best fast track for his game I could imagine. Mark hit two to three hundred two irons a day; he also dedicated a lot of time to his short game, especially the sand wedge. His patience, commitment, and natural ability allowed Mark McMurrey to make up for that late start, and go on to play college golf for Wake Forest.

I'd forgotten about the two-iron deal until Mark brought it up recently. "The two iron is still my best club," he laughed. "I think of you every time I pull it out." How did a fifteen-year-old go from struggling to break 80 to a scratch handicap and a spot on the powerhouse Wake Forest golf team? It's the intangibles. You can't coach them. They are the qualities you try to *coax* out. Mark McMurrey already had the ability; sometimes it takes a helping hand, and someone who can supervise a player's learning the way Harvey Penick described.

Shortly after I arrived at River Oaks I got a call from a lady named Elizabeth Bybee. Her grandson, Robert, had seen River Oaks' announcement that I was joining Dick Harmon's staff. Having competed against Bob Wolcott, Robert knew who I was and wanted lessons. Mrs. Bybee continued, "Robert has a little brother who wants to take lessons from you, too. His name is Scott. He's twelve years old and weighs about ninety pounds, but he has a big heart. Oh," she added, "Their last name is Verplank."

Robert Verplank showed some game; he ended up playing for Houston Baptist. Scott Verplank was so small when he first started that I wondered whether he would ever get the necessary size and strength; Scott already knew he had juvenile (Type 1) diabetes. The Verplanks lived in Dallas, so Scott would fly to Houston for a weekend every four to six weeks. I gave him as much attention as I could during his visits. We focused, getting down to the essentials quickly. Before he returned to Dallas we would come up with a things-to-do list that allowed Scott to go home and learn to coach himself. I didn't have a chance to over-coach him.

***

The colts from Belle Meade came to Houston frequently. It was during this period that Ruth began calling them "Bobby's boys." Matt King received a full scholarship to Wake Forest two years ahead of Mark McMurrey; Matt visited two or three times a year, and during one of these visits I taught him Claude Harmon's famous "Lily Pad" bunker shot technique.

Mr. Harmon had developed the "Lily Pad" bunker shot at Winged Foot with its infamous ten-foot lips. When he set about teaching me on the River Oaks course, he placed a six-foot stepladder on the lip of the bunker, about four feet above the ball. The objective was to hit the ball over the stepladder.

To do this you have to find what Mr. Harmon called "*those air stairs*." The idea is to "throw the club head under the ball": weaken the grip to let the face be wide open at the top. The ball is way forward, creating maximum loft. The bounce prevents the club from digging, and distance is controlled by the speed of the swing: "long and lazy" and a full motion. Learning to hit the shot "high and soft enough to land and stay on a lily pad" makes anyone a better bunker player.

The ladder was intimidating, but Mr. Harmon helped me get the hang of it. He never over-coached, just supplied the essentials and left it to your inner artist to figure it out. Once I got it, he had me play the shot with the right hand only. "Let Me Get You Out of a Bunker with One Hand," Claude Harmon's 1972 cover article about the Lily Pad shot for *Golf Digest*, was recently rated one of the top ten articles in the magazine's history.

I had the privilege of learning the technique from the master, and then passing the lesson on to a receptive and lightning-quick student. Matt King's coach at Wake Forest, Jesse Haddock, said he never saw another player that good at the bunker shot.

Bob Wolcott still talks about seeing Vida Blue--then with the Giants--pitch a one-hitter in the Astrodome . . . and lose. Jay Hebert at The Champions Golf Club gave Bob some help with nuances of the game. Bob's ball striking was always superb, but the thrill of playing--and just talking--with a great former Tour player like Jay gave him some extra fuel to take home. Bob graduated from high school during my time in Houston. After being heavily recruited by the best college coaches, including Mike Holder at Oklahoma State, Bob made the tough decision to commit to Georgia.

In the spring of 1979 Jack Larkin showed up for a visit. After moving to Atlanta, Jack had kept up those 6 a.m. "sunrise service" practices on his own. Since being the youngest player on that Battle Ground Academy team, he had continued to improve, too, more than I fully perceived. Jack was about to hand me one of the biggest (and best) surprises of my career.

Mike Keliher missed his friends from home so much that he had transferred from Arizona and was now playing for Tennessee. Mike came to River Oaks while preparing for a U.S. Amateur qualifier in Nashville, one of those thirty-good-players-for-one-spot deals. Out on the course, I badgered him. "What is your play?" I asked over and over, in a variety of situations. Then came the Three Questions: *Can you see it? Do you have it? Do you need it?* I gradually escalated the pressure, throwing balls off the greens and challenging him to make the shot. Mike hit a towering six iron over a pine tree to within four feet of the hole. I threw another ball down. "Anybody can get lucky," I said. "Hit it again and show me you're *good.*"

I believed Mike could cover that shot, and he did. When we got up to the green and he pulled out his putter, I told him to put it back. "Mike," I said, "you're good--damn good. I've known it all along. I just wanted to make sure you do, too. You're ready."

You have to know your player to sense the right time for a tactic like this. I had been looking to affirm Mike Keliher when this situation presented itself. Not only did Mike go on to win the qualifier, he almost beat Bobby Clampett--the #1 college player in the country--in the U.S. Amateur at Plainfield Country Club in New Jersey.

***

The members of a Harmon golf staff always keep their games sharp, and mine started improving. There was another inducement: we all wanted to qualify for the 1978 PGA National Club Professional Championship.

Eighty players, including six former touring professionals, would be competing for six spots in the 36-hole qualifier at Austin Country Club. I drove to Austin two days before the event, arriving after dark. The next day I played an early round to get a look at the course, had lunch, and then went to the practice area. I was swinging okay, but the ball kept fading more than I wanted. While I worked, I noticed a frail old man driving a golf cart and picking up golf balls. As he piddled around on the range I realized I knew that frail figure: it was Harvey Penick.

He must have recognized me at about the same moment because he drove straight over. "Bobby, how are you? I saw your name on the list and knew you were coming. I'm glad to see you." It had been four years since he gave that three-day seminar in Nashville. I was surprised Mr. Penick even remembered me, when in fact he was looking for me. I was deeply honored. "How are you swinging?" he asked.

I shrugged. "I'm hitting it pretty solid and playing well, but my shots are fading to the right more than I'd like."

"Would you like me to take a look?" he asked. Would I! "Set up with a five iron," he said. "Take dead aim on that flag out there, about 175 yards." Following directions, I started from behind and set up, taking aim. He observed carefully.

"Let me suggest two things," he said, before I even hit a ball. "Without moving your left hand, put your thumb right center on the handle at 1:00 o'clock." Mr. Penick had told me he never liked to use the word grip because it seemed to always lead to greater tension in the arms and hands; he preferred the phrase "holding the club." Getting off his cart, he took my bag and laid it on the ground parallel to my target line. "Square up your alignment to your bag," he said. This necessitated moving my feet, hips, and shoulders counter-clockwise slightly. "Go ahead, let's see your swing now."

I hit one of the solidest five irons of my life. It flew straight over the flag and must have carried two hundred yards. "So, Bobby," he said in his soft voice, "do you think that will work?"

I had to laugh. "Thank you, Mr. Penick. That one will do, trust me."

The next day I started in one of the first groups. With a new confidence in my swing, knowing I had to push it to win a spot, I decided to play as aggressively as I could. I hadn't been hitting my driver very well so John McNeely let me use his, an old Mac-Gregor persimmon (this was back when woods were woods). The shaft was right for me and it just looked good sitting behind the ball. After shooting a 67 in the morning round, I didn't check the scoreboard during a short break for lunch; knowing other players' scores wouldn't help me.

Back out there for the afternoon round, to stay in the moment I was looking at the clouds between shots and saying to the sky, "Lord, let me keep making birdies." I shot a 69--eight under for a 36-hole qualifier, my lowest ever--and won by five or six shots. I never played as well in a 36-hole qualifier before or since.

Mr. Penick was waiting for me behind number 18. I don't know which one of us was more pleased. It felt like all I needed to do was set up and rip it--every bounce went my way. A one-ball lesson from a master and the magic not only shows up but stays with me for two rounds.

That October I traveled to Callaway Gardens in Georgia for the championship, missed the cut, and came home. The magic didn't show up. This is golf: some days you have it and some days you don't. As Claude Harmon told me, "If you're playing great, enjoy it. It won't be long before you can't hit it in a fifteen-acre field. If you're playing bad, that's a good sign! You're on your way to playing great again."

Dick Harmon and I won the Southern Texas Section PGA Pro-Assistants Championship, an 18-hole better-ball competition, twice. The first time we won easily. The second time, playing at River Oaks with Charlie Epps and one of his assistants, we had the wind howling into our faces, as it was known to do in

Houston on occasion. By the last hole--a par-four, 90-degree dogleg, with water in front and around the right side of the green--it looked like a par would do it. Playing first, Dick drove his ball into the water. I decided to hit a three wood down the left side, hoping to be in the fairway or at worst a few yards into the rough. The hole would play two or three clubs longer this way. This play wouldn't win the tournament, but I could lose it by following Dick into the water.

I found myself with a very difficult back-right pin location. With a nice gallery of River Oaks members following us, I decided to play a five iron and cut it into the wind. Dick said he liked it. "Now, Bobby," I told myself, "we need it *now*." The shot ended up six feet from the hole. I made the putt, giving us a 65 and a one-shot victory.

Dick was the better player, but he seized this opportunity to build my confidence and help me improve. "Bobby had a shot we needed," he told people, "and he delivered when the tournament was riding on it."

***

Shortly after the club-pro championship I learned Ruth was pregnant. Our first child was born on June 2, 1979. The night before, Ruth said it felt like he flipped; sure enough, he was breech and had to be delivered surgically. With Ruth still unconscious, the nurse cleaned up the baby, wrapped him in a small blanket, and handed him to me. We already had a boy's name picked out: I was holding Matthew Downing McIver, named for Matt King and a maternal grandfather. He looked me straight in the eye, as if to say, "Here I am. Are you ready?"

I stayed at the hospital all night, looking at him through the nursery window. When Ruth regained consciousness I got to see her hold him for the first time. The birth of a baby seems like a miracle, because it is: there on the hospital bed was the lady of my life holding our first child.

My first interview for a good head professional's job at the Metairie Country Club in New Orleans had gone very well. When Claude Harmon called the chairman of the selection committee on my behalf it was as if Bear Bryant had called to recommend me for a football-coaching job. The gentleman told Claude, "I believe Bobby already is our first choice. I think this call is the icing on the cake." They were flying me in on June 2 for a final interview.

After staying up all night I couldn't rest if I wanted to; my mind was at the hospital as I boarded a plane and got picked up at the airport. The chairman had scheduled me last of three candidates. I entered the club's boardroom expecting to meet with the five-man committee I had already gotten to know and saw instead a dozen board members I had never met. The chairman told them about our little boy showing up earlier in the day and how I'd had no sleep. Then the club president asked, "Why should we hire you as our golf professional?" I made my way through, but not hitting on all cylinders. Afterward, the chairman took me to my motel. "We should have a decision within an hour," he said. "Sit tight. I'll call you--I think everything will be okay." He made it clear I was still his #1 candidate. An hour passed. I drifted off to sleep.

The call came after midnight. "Bobby, it was close. The board labored over the decision. I'm sorry to tell you another candidate was selected." The guy they chose, David Mathews, later became a friend. Being a head professional at a major metropolitan club was one of the six long-term goals I'd set for myself in that development of human potential course; I had just missed accomplishing it, but I had a healthy son. Other positions would come up. I vowed that I would never again interview for a job unless I was totally prepared to give a presentation instead of waiting for questions.

***

About six weeks later I got pulled from the lesson tee at River Oaks to the phone in the golf shop--the caller had said it was urgent. On the other end was Bob Larkin, Big Jack's father. He got to the point quickly. "Bobby, our boy is in the finals."

Even after thinking for a second, I was at a loss. "Mr. Larkin, what finals are you talking about?"

"Bobby," he said, "Jack is playing in the finals of the U.S. Junior tomorrow."

During Jack's visit earlier that spring, Dick Harmon and I had adjusted his grip. Very much like Mr. Penick's tweak of mine, it was a minor change but it seemed to really kick-start Jack; about the time Matt was born he'd won the Southern Junior at Pinehurst. Jack Larkin had some game, but Dick and I felt he had a ways to go.

The next day they came and got me off the range again. I remember nothing from that second call except Mr. Larkin saying, "Our boy won."

I went into Dick's office to tell him. Before I got half a sentence out, I broke down crying. Dick knew what this meant to me. He jumped up and grabbed me in a hug.

It was actually Dick who'd suggested the grip change when Jack Larkin visited in the spring. I wanted to get Jack's ball flight down, but for the life of me I couldn't see where the problem was. That left thumb position is key. The thumb supports the club at the top. Jack had his thumb running down 12 noon, the way I had mine when Mr. Penick spotted it. Moving the thumb slightly to the right of center squares the clubface at the top. Otherwise, it is open. It makes a huge difference.

Dick put his arm on my shoulder. "Go! Celebrate with Ruth. I know how much of your heart and soul has gone into these kids, and Ruth was a big part of it. Go celebrate with her."

I had poured myself into getting Matt King and Bob Wolcott ready, fully believing they could win. Jack Larkin snuck up and got me when I wasn't looking. Ruth and I felt like our hearts might burst out of our chests. I walked the three miles around Rice University, carrying six-week-old Matt in my arms and crying most of the walk.

My thoughts returned to those 6 a.m. practice sessions with the BGA team. Jack Larkin had been the youngest, the weakest link. I kept telling him he was so cool under pressure that he had ice water running in his veins, because I *needed* Jack to have ice water in his veins. And Big Jack kept his cool when it counted. As Charles Price, the brilliant golf writer, described Jack's tournament demeanor: "Young Larkin accepted the loss of a hole like the Pope receiving a traffic ticket in the Vatican City."

Winning the U.S. Junior Amateur Championship, Jack Larkin displayed all the talent I had perceived, enhanced by the hard work he put in on his own after moving to Atlanta. Jack was realizing his potential, and he had developed self-reliance-- my goal for all my players.

That dedication, along with Jack's poise under pressure, meant I could now mark off my own national championship goal. Jack Larkin proceeded to join Bob Wolcott on the University of Georgia team; as my players earned college scholarships, our hard work was paying off. It felt like we were being swept along by the flow, as if forces of nature were moving us in the directions we wanted to go. I just had to keep them thinking *the best is yet to come.*

{ 7 }

OUT OF THE BUNKER
WITH BOTH HANDS

If you happen upon a turtle on a fence post,
know he didn't get there by himself.

-Armenian Proverb

In the spring of 1980 I learned that the professional at the
Country Club of Jackson (MS) was leaving. When I interviewed
with the CCJ committee, I had a presentation ready to forestall
the awkward question-and-answer session and let me make my
points. In addition, Claude Harmon had given me some coaching. "Nobody in the room knows the golf business and the game
as well as you do," he said. "Take charge of the meeting without
coming across as arrogant. They need to know what they want.
They don't know--so you tell them."

As I prepared for the second interview, Mr. Harmon provided
more specific suggestions. "Tell them you would like a one-year
contract, and if you can't do the job you will resign." The committee heard this pledge from me and I landed the head pro job

at a metropolitan club with over a thousand members: goal #3 from my list.

The first to leave River Oaks, I was ready to lead my own staff because Dick and Claude Harmon had taught by example how to treat your staff and others. "If you always take care of the little guy, he will take care of you," they liked to say. I learned this at home, but the Harmons' reinforcement helped build my confidence. River Oaks was graduate school for me: given a lot to learn quickly, I felt like I was leaving with a Masters degree.

There's also something about Texas. Maybe it's the sheer size of the state. Ruth and I got caught up in that "Can Do" Texas spirit: at River Oaks, nothing seemed impossible.

When I walked into the Country Club of Jackson on April 1, 1980, it had been pouring down rain for a week. The year before, a huge flood had topped the levee by twenty feet in some places. Homes had washed away; it was national news. The very first thing I did at CCJ was to check the levee with officers of the club. Seeing the water a foot from the top, I considered telling Dick Harmon I might need to return.

Then I recalled Columbia Military Academy basketball Coach Bill Wade barking out encouragement in our huddles. "We're ten down--what are we going to do? Are we going to quit and lay down? No, you guys have too much heart!"

I had longed to become a head professional, but I wasn't walking into River Oaks or Belle Meade. With 1,400 members and twenty-seven holes, the Country Club of Jackson was in trouble financially, the golf program almost non-existent. The course was in terrible shape: the driving range and the third nine had been renovated, but the 1979 flood had created serious problems. *What are we going to do? Quit or keep playing?* Overwhelmed, I just didn't know where to start.

Consulting with club officials, I finally developed a plan and went to work. The challenge was to organize myriad steps in the right sequence. A tournament golfer has to do the same thing: getting ready is an art form all to itself.

Learning to *think well* will help your game much more than striving for the non-existent perfect swing. When Scott Verplank was around fourteen I gave him a set of tapes called "The Psychology of Winning" by Dr. Dennis Waitley, a proponent of the human development field. Scott kept the tapes for a year and since he did everything else I asked him to do, I assume he listened to these messages once a day for one week.

What distinguishes a champion from a good player who has trouble winning? The difference lies in how you think-- specifically, how you perceive a challenge. Where winners visualize opportunities to succeed, losers can't see beyond the obstacles in front of them. If you want to accomplish some goals in your life, think and use the words *intend* or *intention* every chance you get. I had to use all these skills at the Country Club of Jackson. My *intention* was to bring this old club back. By the time I left eight years later, dramatic improvements had become a reality.

Being a head pro proved much more stressful than being an assistant: I was carrying the entire team. Lacking the budget of River Oaks, and thus forced to get by with fewer people, I really needed a good assistant.

John McNeely had left River Oaks to start a golf travel business. Shortly after that he was playing a pick-up basketball game when his Achilles tendon snapped. At the time of the injury John had no health insurance, but an orthopedic surgeon at River Oaks did the surgery at no cost and got John hobbling around with a cast. While he was recovering John came to Jackson for a visit. I hated to see him without a job, hauling around that cast that went up to his knee. One day on the driving range my heart told me to call him. "There really isn't a spot open," I said, explaining I could only pay him a modest salary, "but I'm confident we can do a good job and make that money back."

After John accepted I told him about a group of heavy hitters at CCJ who were building a Jack Nicklaus-designed course. John and I set out to rub some service on them they weren't used to at Jackson. My shop sales shot up, and when Walter Denny opened Annandale Golf Club in 1981, he made John McNeely head pro.

We also spent a lot of time teaching. Randy Watkins, at Ole Miss, was friends with Bob Wolcott and Jack Larkin; Doug and David Allen played for Mississippi State. I helped them with their games, but it's different when you've coached a player all along. The first time we held a junior clinic at CCJ sixty kids showed up, and one unexpectedly caught my eye. "I have a Thoroughbred race horse in this clinic," I told Ruth later. "His name is Rett Crowder, and he's only nine years old."

This is the only time I have ever seen something in a player so young. Along with control of the club, Rett Crowder had the hand-eye coordination that normally takes years to develop. I typically discourage parents from starting kids before eleven or twelve because the club is too heavy and they lack the strength and coordination to make consistent contact; I don't want them to get the idea they can't handle the game. Junior clubs are notoriously bad. One-size-fits-all doesn't suit anyone, and kids usually get stuck with clubs that are too long, forcing them to make a bad swing to hit a good shot.

The easiest way for me to help a player is to get them into the right set of clubs. After convincing his dad to pay for a really great set, I fitted Rett Crowder into a Hogan Special sand wedge with the proper lie angle, length, and amount of bounce. Rett got Claude Harmon's Lily Pad shot right away, soon proving to be a wizard out of the bunker. When Rett was twelve I suggested that he attend the PGA National Junior Camp in Boca Raton, Florida. He had been down there a couple of days when Gary Wiren, the camp director and a very good instructor, called me. "Bobby," he said, "Rett Crowder put on the most incredible bunker demonstration I have ever witnessed. When I saw him playing these shots I blew the whistle, assembled every kid in the camp, and for thirty minutes he played one shot after another. And when I say the best, I'm including Gary Player and Chi Chi Rodriguez." He asked what I had been teaching.

"Hey," I told him, "it's all Claude Harmon, the best bunker player in history. Rett's been Harmonized."

Scott Verplank was now driving to Jackson in his burnt-orange Oldsmobile. We got together every three or four months, but he stayed longer. Scott was starting to show some size and strength. After I told him, "If you can be great with the sand wedge you will have par for a partner," no player of mine ever worked on his short game so diligently, spending hours doing the practice drills I gave him. By the time he finished high school he had worn out the grooves of a second wedge, so I gave him a new one for a graduation gift.

The thing about Scott that I could not coach is willpower: the winner's mindset. Scott Verplank practiced with winning on his mind. He played every time out with winning on his mind. When he got to the tournament he just had to do what he was doing every day. I once sent him out to play with Steve Grantham, chairman of the CCJ selection committee that had interviewed and hired me. After the round Steve came back in to tell me, "Your boy Scott just shot an easy 67--he never missed a shot."

Scott Verplank's great-grandfather was a legendary University of Texas geology professor who had made a mark in the oil business. Scott's father had played baseball for Texas. Scott's role model was Ben Crenshaw, who first gained fame while still a Longhorn. The entire family was totally loyal to the University of Texas. Now that it was Scott's senior season, of course he wanted to go to Texas. But Texas golf coach Jimmy Clayton didn't recruit Scott. In fact, Clayton told Dick Harmon that Scott Verplank "can't play Southwest Conference golf."

In 1978 the American Junior Golf Association had established a national junior tour and an All-American team. Bob Wolcott was named to the inaugural AJGA Rolex All-American First Team. At an event in New Orleans in 1981, Scott got paired with AJGA Player of the Year Tommy Moore, by then a freshman at Oklahoma State, the premier college golf program. After playing nine holes with Scott, Moore ducked into the clubhouse and called his coach, Mike Holder. "Coach, you have to get this kid. Scott Verplank is a player. We need him." Like Texas coach Clayton, Holder had seen Scott--and was also going to pass on him. But then, he told me much later, "I went with Tommy's intuition . . . The rest is history."

Scott's game came along slowly and steadily. Even I had a hard time noticing the excellence he was starting to demonstrate; apparently Mike Holder wasn't seeing it either. Tommy Moore died from a rare blood disorder and I never got to ask him what it was he saw in Scott Verplank. I believe it had to be heart. How do you coach heart? I'm not sure you can. Scott learned to coach himself. By helping him with lists of what to do and encouraging him I may have gotten him to dream bigger, but he did the work.

The Country Club of Jackson was slated to host the 1982 Southern Junior, so I sent myself to the 1981 tournament--held at the North River Yacht and Country Club in Tuscaloosa, Alabama--to see what was involved. Despite playing well, Scott was having a hard time. The five-footers weren't falling. Struggling to hit his stride, Scott was behaving like every shot was life or death--missing putts, then dropping his putter and looking to the sky like 'why me, God?' I didn't say anything the whole day.

I was staying in a condo with Scott, his mother, Betty, and some other Dallas kids including Brian Watts, who lost the British Open to Mark O'Meara in 1998. That evening, as I'd expected, Scott asked me what I thought about his round.

"Scott," I said, "I couldn't tell if you were a golfer or an actor out there today. All those dramatics about a missed shot aren't helping you." If he couldn't control himself, his opponents would think they had control of the tournament. "When you miss a putt or a shot, 'Never let 'em see you sweat' tells the other guys by your body language that you can't be rattled."

I never had to tell Scott this again.

Scott Verplank was named AJGA First Team All American and Player of the Year in 1982. The best for that year, however, was yet to come. The week before the 1982 Southern Junior Scott won the Texas State Amateur. At the age of seventeen he beat four NCAA All Americans, including Mark Brooks, Billy Ray Brown, and Steve Elkington. The tournament was held at the Crown Colony Country Club in Lufkin, a very good course. This win was a shock--I didn't even know he was playing. Nothing he did later even surprised me.

The next week he finished second in the Southern Junior at Jackson. It was a fluke loss; I kept reminding him how significant the Texas win had truly been. Now I knew Scott could hold his own with anyone.

I have a picture of Scott at thirteen holding a trophy for his age group. Wearing a Hogan cap over his long blond hair, he hits me about at my shoulder. You can see intention in his eyes. Whatever I suggested, Scott would do the work. After I told him he needed to be great with his driver, putter, and sand wedge he wore out the grooves of his Titleist sand wedge in a year. His MacGregor VIP driver became an extension of his body. And he had the Ping Anser putter that he uses to this day. I didn't have to be present; any player hitting that many shots will figure it out naturally. We kept working together on a fairly regular basis until he went to Oklahoma State where, under the positive influence of coach Mike Holder, Scott just continued to improve. As Holder says, with the great ones it's hard to tell whether they hate to lose or love to win.

***

Bob Wolcott made a run in the 1982 U.S. Amateur before losing to the eventual winner, Nathaniel Crosby, in the quarterfinals. Bob looked rock-solid in every way and his record was better by far, but that means nothing in match play, and Nathaniel--Bing's son--was playing before a hometown crowd at San Francisco's Olympic Club.

That fall, checking in with the UGA boys, I found out from Jack Larkin that Bob had dropped out of school. His mother, Betty Lou, had suffered an aneurism. They weren't sure she would make it, and Bob had gone home.

Connie King later told me that when things were critical Bob had spent the night with his mother in the hospital. As sunlight was starting to fill the room in the morning, he had picked her up in his arms, carried her into the sun's rays, and said, "Lord, I need her." Bob stayed home all of 1983 as, defying all odds, she recovered. The NCAA let him defer his last year of eligibility. When the NCAA announced the First Team All Americans in the spring of 1984, Bob Wolcott was among them. Scott Verplank also made the list.

One day, maybe six months later, it dawned on me: I had my two First Team All Americans. I'd chosen this goal only because Harvey Penick proved it was possible with Ben Crenshaw and Tom Kite. Seeing Scott and Bob standing together to have their picture taken at a New York City gathering honoring the team, I felt blessed, and humbled. Hey, I didn't hit a shot--Bob Wolcott and Scott Verplank got it done.

***

Country clubs expect a head professional to promote golf. When the Country Club of Jackson hosted a Pro-Member in 1982, Claude Harmon, Dick Harmon, and Dave Marr all flew in from Houston and generated some excitement. With *Golf Digest* promoting their five-day schools, in 1983 I decided to host one of my own. I told Mr. Harmon I wanted to hold the Claude Harmon Golf School, and he actually sounded excited about it.

The week was supposed to start with a fifteen-minute 'greeting' from Mr. Harmon. "If you want to have this," Dick Harmon told me during the planning stage, "you better write his speech for him."

I picked Mr. Harmon up at the airport. "Rusty!" he exclaimed as he came off the plane, "I have my speech ready!"

What he had was a few notes scribbled on his boarding pass. When I handed him an outline, Mr. Harmon glanced at it and laughed, "You know my stories better than I do." It was true: he could say five words and I could finish the anecdote. All I had done was list about six points, indicating which story he needed to tell. To cue his closer, I just typed: "RACING MULES." Claude Harmon gave it the juice that night. "Men, we can't make a Thoroughbred racehorse out of a mule. But if you listen to what we tell you . . . Well, we may have some *racing mules* by the end of the week."

The good times continued for five days. We could all see Mr. Harmon coming to life, providing great instruction and--of course--stories. Mike Keliher, who had joined my staff, served during the first golf school. Some years later when Mike and I were sharing stories, he asked, "Do you remember Mr. Harmon talking about getting out of the sand with one hand? He holed the second shot and just threw up his arms, saying 'that's how it's done' and then walked out of the bunker." Claude Harmon had done this at Winged Foot every time he gave a clinic. Retirement didn't agree with Mr. Harmon; our golf school got him back in the game. I was hoping some of those assistants he had placed around the country would pick up on the idea and keep him busy, but only two got it.

I charged a premium, but it was far cheaper than the *Golf Digest* Schools. After expenses we had a $3,500 balance. I sent Mr. Harmon a check for $4,000, with a note: "The Golf Digest guys get $3,000 and none of them are in your league. Please accept this with my heartfelt thanks. I appreciate you more than you can ever know." Dick told me later his dad didn't open it until he was sitting in a recliner in the River Oaks golf shop. Not expecting anything near this amount, Claude Harmon was moved to tears.

When I repeated the school I arranged for all the scattered Harmons to reunite for another Pro-Member. Dick said they hadn't all been together since his mother died in 1970. They put on a clinic for my members that no amount of money could buy. The PR was priceless, too. I tried to do everything the Harmon way: with professionalism, class, and laughter. Want to play great golf? *You better enjoy it*--otherwise the game can be brutally hard. Never hurry so fast that you can't enjoy the company of others. Travel a little slower . . . you'll get there just as soon, in fewer strokes, and you'll have *fun.*

Mike Keliher did a fine job but returned to Nashville after a year, having decided the club-pro game just wasn't for him. David Cowger and Mark Danton, two young, enthusiastic assistants, came to me from River Oaks. We started identifying the more interested juniors and determining who should focus on whom.

David Cowger had a knack for picking up people's mannerisms, how we moved and talked. Finally, with a golf shop full of people, I got treated to his impersonation of me. Dave had me down cold. Mark Danton served as straight man, setting him up. The shop erupted in laughter. Being around Dick Harmon had reinforced Mark and Dave's sense of humor--taking oneself too seriously was *not* the Harmon way.

***

On January 11, 1982, Ruth gave birth to our second child, a girl. We named her Elizabeth Gale after my mother. Ruth's mom, Marty, was with us. Dr. Joel Payne, who went to Ole Miss with me, performed the surgery; in those days, once you had a C-section the rest would be also. Because Ruth didn't have to go under anesthesia, they handed the baby to her while I waited my turn. When I finally got to hold her, she gave me a look like Matthew did: Elizabeth was on her way to being Daddy's girl.

There had been a heavy snow, unusual for Mississippi. As I stared out the hospital window, my mind drifted in the blank whiteness.

Mississippi has no postcard mountain ranges like Colorado. Mississippi ranks #50 (or close to it) in about everything they rank: economics, education, health. But something sets Mississippians apart. Many of the country's greatest writers are from Mississippi. William Faulkner, Eudora Welty, and John Grisham take the southern penchant for storytelling to the level of art by using the Mississippian's trademark: a deep grasp and appreciation of human nature. Mississippians are a special breed.

In January, with nothing going on at the club, I usually took off with Buck Dearman, a friend I'd made at Jackson. We would head to Greasy Bayou Hunting Club, a big camp north of Vicksburg where Buck was a member, for weeks of duck hunting in the green timbers. In the spring he took me turkey hunting; when Buck died some years later his wife Barbara had him buried in his camouflage. Buck Dearman could really play golf, too, winning the Mississippi Senior Amateur Championship in 1982. He had used the same MacGregor Tommy Armour putter for forty years. "Come on, Tommy, we need this one," he always said when he played, and more times than not he would make the putt.

In the early 1990's Buck learned he had terminal colon cancer. I made a trip from Virginia to spend one last week with him. The morning I was leaving Buck said, "Wait a minute--I have something for you." He disappeared into the other room. When he came back, he handed me his putter. "Bobby," he said, "I want you to have Tommy." I got in the car and cried for the next two hours. If it weren't for friends like Buck Dearman I wouldn't have a reason to play golf: the game is about people and relationships.

I'd met Bob Travis briefly during my college years when I was playing the fried chicken circuit. Bob had graduated from Yale Law School but rather than practice law he taught it at his alma mater, Ole Miss. He still loved playing golf and he'd won the Mississippi State Amateur twice in the 1960's. We became close friends when I came to Jackson.

Ruth and I once joined Bob Travis and his wife Judy at Hilton Head, for what was supposed to be a weeklong vacation. The second night, one of my assistants back at Jackson called to tell me the cart barn was on fire. As he was describing the flames I suddenly remembered that the cart barn housed the bag-storage area too: over five hundred sets of clubs were in the process of being destroyed. I told Bob what was happening.

"The bad news is you need to fly back immediately," he said. "The good news is, if you handle this properly you'll make a pile of money." Bob drafted a letter for me to send out to those who'd lost clubs, and his way with words smoothed a calamity into an opportunity.

One Sunday morning I asked Bob to come along as I took Claude Harmon to the airport. Driving 30 miles per hour on the back roads, I pumped Mr. Harmon for the maximum number of stories. Bob knew I was making a thirty-minute drive take almost an hour. As soon as Mr. Harmon was on his plane headed back to Houston, he flashed his huge smile. "Bobby," he said, "I can't begin to tell you how much this meant to me--I've never been in the presence of a man with such an engaging personality. It's obvious now that this wonderful man has profoundly stamped you." I told him if I could be half the man Claude Harmon was, I'd feel I had done something. "Well, you have accomplished something," Bob said. "You're a chip off the block."

Cobby Ware was pastor of Trinity Presbyterian, the church Ruth and I chose when we arrived in Jackson. Very few people at the club knew that Cobby had been an NCAA Second Team All American at Georgia, on the same team as Bob Moser; I assumed this was in the early sixties but could never verify the time frame because Cobby kept the plaque in a drawer. He had a smooth, graceful swing with an ever-so-slight pause at the top. After seminary school Cobby became the first PGA Tour chaplain. In those days before players flew around in private jets, everyone drove from one site to another, and traveling with the tour brought Cobby close to many of game's greatest players.

At the grand opening of Annandale Golf Club, Cobby's son Mark got to caddy for Jack Nicklaus, the course's designer. Mark was standing near the first tee getting ready when Nicklaus turned and asked him, "Do you know how great a player your dad was?" Before Mark could answer, Nicklaus continued, "Cobby Ware could really play, and I doubt he ever told you this. I'm telling you now--your dad was a great player."

I learned by just observing Cobby. So calm and collected that simply being around him had a calming effect on me, Cobby was just always *there*. If he'd chosen a different path, he would have made a great coach.

One day Cobby called and asked me to play. He wanted me to meet someone, "a world-renowned theologian." *Theologian?* I pictured a guy with white hair climbing down from some ivory-tower think tank.

R.C. Sproul totally overturned my picture when he showed up, laughing, telling jokes, and displaying some real game. R.C. had a high-vibration energy field around him. He had gone to college on a football scholarship, playing quarterback. He grew up in Pittsburgh but he and his wife Vesta now lived in Orlando. He traveled all over the United States giving seminars, and each spring from 1984 to 1987 he taught at Reformed Theological Seminary in Jackson. He wanted lessons, so we were soon spending hours together every day.

R.C. acted like a twelve-year-old. I mean this in a positive way: he was child*like* without being child*ish*. Whenever I suggested a change, R.C. would ask "Why?" Then I would have to think hard in order to articulate some logical reason having to do with physics that I had never thought about before. I'd suggest something else, R.C. would ask "Why?" and this time it might be a logical explanation relating to biomechanics . . . that I had never thought about before. Yes, I was coaching him, but by challenging me in a friendly manner he was stretching my mind and I was learning--naturally.

R.C. Sproul routinely drew hundreds of listeners when he spoke publicly in Jackson, and he worked an audience like no one I had ever witnessed. R.C. relieved the serious moments by bringing in some humor. Since most of the audience knew me, I made a good target. R.C. mimicked the expressions I employed to put an exclamation point on my lessons, in a similar vein to David Cowger and Mark Danton, who made fun of my stories and animated coaching style in the stand-up routines that earned them local renown as 'Jackson's Abbott and Costello.' When David and Mark came up with an R.C. Sproul routine, it had all of us rolling on the floor--and no one loved it more than R.C.

I never made a major decision at the club without discussing it with Steve Grantham, the chairman of the Country Club of Jackson selection committee who had interviewed and hired me. Claude Harmon used to say, "A club professional has to be a public relations genius. You have a thousand members and their spouses. This is two thousand. Add 1.5 children and you are up to 3,500. With guests, you're pushing 4,500 . . . and the club pro has to make them *all* happy." Occasionally something would pop up--as I reminded my staff, members were hauling problems from their lives with them--but it takes two to fight and it's harder to get upset with us if we're friendly and respectful. Steve helped immeasurably in maintaining this tone.

Buck Dearman, Steve Grantham, Bob Travis, Cobby Ware and R.C. Sproul were my "private board of directors"--a board so private that none of them knew about it. I tell my children that you don't have to *be* a genius; you just have to know some, and be willing to solicit advice when needed. Decide ahead of time who you will listen to, remember that wisdom is harder to find than intellect, and always choose integrity.

***

My coaching philosophy owes a debt to the Hippocratic Oath, "First, do no harm." Don't suggest a change unless it will improve what a player already has. Rett Crowder was a low-maintenance natural, coming on strong by age fourteen--like Scott Verplank, on track to self-reliance. He didn't need much swing coaching, but getting him to think like a champion was a different matter.

One day I sent my assistant on the course with a message for Rett: "The pro needs to see you in his office." When he walked in I told him, "Close the door and pull up a chair," with a serious look. "Rett, God gave you an abundance of natural ability. You know how well Scott is playing?" He nodded. "You're playing better at fourteen than he was--you'll only be limited by how big you can let yourself dream. You get to *choose* how good a player you can become . . . I'll help you, but you have everything you need to be a champion."

His whole face opened up, not just his eyes. It was like I had removed the curtain concealing a whole new world out there. I was telling the truth: Rett Crowder *was* that good. I ended the meeting by giving him a hug, saying, "Rett, let me know how I can help your dreams come true." I had done this before--I call it anchoring. What kind of impact does a talk like this have on a young player? You'll have to ask them, but I believe it can do no harm.

The 1984 U.S. Amateur was being played at Oak Tree Golf Club, outside Oklahoma City. I had told Rett's parents that if Scott Verplank made it to the finals I wanted to take Rett to see it. Once the semi-finals concluded the table was set: Scott was playing Sam Randolph on Sunday in the finals, which would be broadcast to a national television audience. Catching a Saturday afternoon flight, Rett and I arrived in Oklahoma City about ten o'clock and stayed with Marty and Robert Margo, my sister- and brother-in-law. Tickets would be waiting for us, but we had to get up early; U.S. Amateur finals are thirty-six holes and the first match was scheduled for 8 a.m.

It rained all night. When we got to the course, around 7:30 a.m., play had been suspended. Scott was sitting with Mike Holder, the Oklahoma State coach and his caddie for the week, in an area roped off for players. He told officials to let us in, and we sat there talking for almost two hours while it rained. I tried to draw Rett into the conversation, but he was in awe and all ears. Coach Holder and I knew how to keep Scott loose. There is no secret: just relax and focus on the moment. The USGA would tell us when to warm up.

When play finally began, both players started out playing pretty well. Scott finished the front nine two down and Sam Randolph made several six- to eight-foot putts. After the players ate lunch in private Scott came over to the putting green. "How do you feel?" I asked him. He said he felt good. "Let me tell you how *I* feel," I said. "Randolph got all he could out of the first round. Your best round is coming. I like your chances and I believe you will win."

"You're reading it just like I am," Scott said calmly.

Rett and I had a problem: after that rain delay, we only had time to watch a few holes before we had to catch our plane. "We're not going to be able to see you win this thing," I told Scott, knowing we would be leaving before the front nine was over. "Let 'em see your smoke--rub it on him. Don't take any prisoners."

In a lounge area at the Oklahoma City airport, Rett and I watched Scott take control of the final match with great play and excellent putting. After Scott won, 4 & 3, we got to see him and Sam Randolph shake hands just moments before we boarded our plane.

I rarely go to events to watch my players. This is not because of jinxes or any of that superstitious stuff; I just believe the coach can show confidence by staying out of the way. This trip was primarily for Rett. "Now there are two national champions on the list," Rett said on the way home. I could see his mind working.

"What do you think?" I asked him. "When are you going to get that third one?" I pulled his head into my chest for a hug, feeling happy and proud simultaneously: it was pure joy.

***

Scott Verplank's 1984 U.S. Amateur win qualified him for the 1985 Masters and U.S. Open. I had attended many Masters, but this was my first with a player in the field. Mike Holder was caddying. Late Wednesday, the day before the first round, I walked inside the ropes and onto the practice tee. Mike was sitting on the ground, leaning against the bag. I stood behind Scott and watched him hit a few balls. "Man, I love those thin divots!" I exclaimed. After a few more: "You have to love those thin divots!"

By the third time, Mike--a brilliant student of the swing and an even more brilliant coach--couldn't stand it any longer. "*Why?*" he demanded as the practice concluded.

I had to think for a minute. "Mike, his divots are absolutely the same every swing. This means he's making contact with the same scoring line on the face . . . which gives him unbelievable distance control."

After Scott went into the locker room, Mike was still frowning, perplexed. I went over to him. "Coach," I said, "it's the day before the first round of the Masters. I'm going to like his divots no matter what depth they are." Mike shook his head, but now he was smiling--he got it. We were on the same wavelength.

Scott's final round at the 1985 Masters came on Friday when he missed the cut. Afterwards he walked over to me. "I would like you to caddie for me in the U.S. Open," he said. I wasn't expecting this. Oakland Hills in Detroit . . . Father's Day weekend . . . I couldn't stop thinking about it.

***

The annual Country Club of Jackson Intercollegiate Championship followed the Masters. Mississippi State was the official host and MSU coach Gary Meredith invited all the teams. Most of the SEC teams attended, plus some others; we attracted some really good teams, and many players went on to play on the PGA Tour. Nathaniel Crosby played in 1983 after winning the U.S. Amateur. The event didn't put anything in my cash register--in fact, it hurt my golf shop business--but showcasing college talent gave my juniors a glimpse of golf at another level.

When Mike Holder brought the Oklahoma State University Cowboys to town for the 1985 Intercollegiate Championship, they advertised the intangibles I coached: "Hey, straighten that back, tuck that chin in, and walk like a champion. If you want to be a champion, act like one! Have those shoes shined, your clothes fitting you good and freshly pressed." Some of my juniors even knew how to use an iron. Urging my players to acquire the best shoes and new spikes, I showed them how to lace their shoes like combat boots so the lacing wouldn't loosen and their feet would stay anchored to the ground. As Mr. Harmon used to say, "The big picture is nothing but the sum of all the details."

Other players stopped their practice to watch those OSU boys make their way to the course at Jackson, and when the team--especially Scott Verplank--walked in the dining room, everyone stopped eating and looked. But these Oklahoma State players calmly paid attention to business from the moment they showed up until they left. My juniors got the message: carry yourselves like champions--even in a fake-it-till-you-make-it manner--and you too will command respect.

The Jackson newspaper, The Clarion Ledger, came out to get a picture of me with Scott. Starting with the nice story they ran the next day and a few magazine articles, I sensed things changing for me, too, not just Scott. An extra charge of electricity surrounded our collegiate tournament. Ole Miss's great team--including Randy Watkins, Chip Sullivan, and Dave Peege, a first team All American--had won the SEC in 1984. Buddy Alexander's LSU team, with David Toms and Greg Lesher, was another strong contender. Oklahoma State defeated these powerhouses to win the team competition. Scott Verplank and Rob McNamara, a freshman on Buddy's squad, separated themselves from the pack contending for the individual title. Proving himself a fighter who would not quit, Rob prevailed.

Rob McNamara started driving from Baton Rouge for lessons, often bringing other players with him. US Junior Champion Greg Lesher had a lot of game, and I never met a nicer young man. When Rob showed up with David Toms, I observed David for about twenty minutes. "I don't need to be tampering with anything you're doing swing-wise," I told him. "If anybody tries to change your swing, pick up your clubs and run." David never showed up for another lesson. He didn't need one.

I gave Buddy Alexander, the LSU coach, a lesson once. He could play, so I was reluctant to change anything. A few years later he won the U.S. Amateur at Shoal Creek in Birmingham. All these gurus--or magazine poster boys, as I call them-- couldn't caddie for Buddy Alexander and Mike Holder. College coaches have to win or they don't have a job, and they know much more about developing winners than the swing-concept stars. Anybody who knows golf understands what I'm talking about.

I was running six miles three times a week to get in shape for the U.S. Open. As the U.S. Amateur champion, Scott Verplank would be paired with the 1984 British Open and U.S. Open champions, Seve Ballesteros and Fuzzy Zoeller. Planning to meet Scott at the course, I boarded a plane for Detroit unpre- pared for *cold* weather; where I come from, June means summer, not winter. One day's practice rounds got rained out. The Oak- land Hills course was tough, with lots of subtleties, and yardage books weren't as good back then. We needed local knowledge.

Al Mengert, the veteran pro at Oakland Hills, had been an assistant under Claude Harmon. Late Wednesday afternoon I approached him. Explaining my own connection with the Har- mons, I said we needed some help. Mr. Mengert studied me be- fore inviting us into his office. There he proceeded to annotate my yardage book: "The grain always runs towards that street." "This hole plays half a club longer than the yardage." "This putt looks straight and it breaks six inches to the left." These "local knowledge notes" would prove invaluable.

Scott asked me to get the yardage for him. We would read the putts together. Finally he said, "I'll ask you for advice when I'm uncertain." What he didn't need to say: keep your mouth closed otherwise.

Wednesday night, after stretching out on the bed in the hotel room we were sharing, I sat up. "Scott, I didn't come all the way up here for a walk in the park--I could do that in Jackson. I came up here because I believe you can win."

He looked at me and said, "I'm glad, because I feel the same way." I had a warm feeling inside my chest. Scott and I started together in 1977 when he weighed less than a hundred pounds. Eight years later he's playing for the U.S. Open Championship and I'm on the bag.

I had never seen anything like the crowd that greeted us when we walked on that practice green the next morning. For the forty yards to the first tee, two police officers walked ahead with ropes, parting the throngs. My heart was pounding. It felt like we were entering an arena for a prizefight. "Come on, Scotty, let 'em see it!" "Go, Scott, we're behind you!"

I felt fans patting me on the back but kept my shoulders square and said nothing. Scott handed me Seve's scorecard. I put my arm on his shoulder and stage-whispered, "Let's have some fun."

A few holes in I realized Scott was out-driving Ballesteros. Walking the yardage from the sprinklers I knew I was on the money, but when I heard Seve's caddie give him his yardage he was calling it six or seven yards shorter, so I kept stepping it off again. After Scott hit his second shot to the sixth, Seve's caddie walked over to me and said, "Hey, man, we're in meters." Oh--I got it now.

Scott played very solidly. I read a few putts well and got his yardages right--with one exception. On #16 in the second round, Scott hit his ball in the left rough. The pin was on the front with a pond guarding the green. Without a sprinkler head near, I had to triangulate a yardage, and after walking it twice I gave him a number. When he played a great eight-iron shot that came up a yard short, I felt like I'd let him down. "Shake it off," Scott said. "Let's get it up and down for a bogie." After doing just that, he proceeded to make par on number 17.

We weren't talking about it, but we both had the feeling we were on the cut line. Number 18 was a long dogleg-right par-five that they had turned into a par-four. The fairway sloped left and there was a bunker out on the right. 275 would carry the bunker, making the hole much easier, but it was a gamble. Scott hit a perfect shot. After walking off the yardage, I said, "Par, big man--a par will do it."

"No," Scott said. "We need a birdie." He hit it four feet from the hole. Rolled in his birdie . . . and he was right: that birdie let him play the weekend.

The last thirty-six holes are a blur now. Scott just kept playing stronger; he finished as Low Amateur. Elizabeth Bybee, Scott's grandmother, had told me he had heart, and these ladies really do know. The local paper in Jackson had asked me to keep a journal, and my piece filled up an entire page in the sports section. *Dreams come true*, I wrote, *for those willing to stake their claim.* Scott Verplank had arrived.

In the 1985 Western Open, a month later, Scott took the lead in the first round and never relinquished it. Jim Thorpe caught him on the last hole, but Scott won the playoff. I can still hear the roars in the 19th hole at the Country Club of Jackson from everyone crowded around the television. Scott had visited the club enough that our members staked a claim on him, too.

After Scott identified me as his coach in press conferences I received phone calls from the L.A. Times, New York Post, Chicago Tribune, U.S.A. Today, and many more. All of them asked me the same question: "Are you surprised?" I'd been amazed when Scott won the 1982 Texas Amateur as a senior in high school, I said, but since then nothing surprised me. Besides, I told them, "Scott has the heart of a champion." They could write that down.

People wondered how Scott could make such a move so quickly. The short answer: it's a mindset and a state of being-- winning is a foundational, building-block deal. The distance between Dallas and Houston, then Dallas and Jackson, meant nobody was messing with Scott much. He came to see me, got four or five weeks of homework, and in the process became self-reliant. Lessons upon lessons are not the secret; *no* instruction is better than too much.

And nothing helps a player win like winning. Scott knew he beat a good field in the 1982 Texas Amateur. Mike Holder thinks about and talks about one thing: winning. Yet not every player coming through OSU accomplishes these things. Champions have an entirely different perception of the world: failure never enters their minds. Scott Verplank radiates calm, an indication of inner peace, but he's one of the greatest closers you'll ever see. Some players go through the motions, hoping it's good enough. With Scott, winning is everything.

***

On August 15, 1985, Robert Edwin McIver, Jr. made his entrance. Just like his siblings, Rob eyeballed me when we first met, checking me out pretty good. I think he was saying, "Hold on, I'm coming." Matt McIver's personality matches Matt King's--focused and steady--while Rob and I are just alike: both redheads (one current, one former) with a flashpoint. Matt was six and Elizabeth three when Rob came on the scene.

When they got a little older, Ruth once asked why three were such a challenge. I told her they took us out of a man-to-man and forced us into a zone--basketball players will get it.

***

In 1986 the Country Club of Jackson adopted a new business concept, hiring a "strong general manager" who would have control over everything. This was supposed to simplify things by giving authority to one man. But when the man doesn't know the golf business because he's really a food and beverage guy, he can't pull the trigger.

The new G.M. wanted to cut my staff by one person. "The board thinks there are too many people on staff," he told me. But the board didn't know my personnel needs--nobody had talked with me--and we were already running lean. A couple more Claude Harmon Golf Schools had worked like shots of adrenaline: rounds of golf had never been higher and the club was doing better as a result. CCJ officials couldn't attribute it to the golf operation, but having kept up with numbers and activity levels, *I* sure could--as lesson income grew, so did shop sales and 19th Hole revenues.

And stress. About twice a year now, I was becoming exhausted. First the doctor called it burnout, later mild bio-chemical depression.

Nobody was forcing me to do anything. At River Oaks Dick Harmon and John McNeely had called me a "grinder." They knew I was like a duck on water: calm on the surface while my feet worked frantically underneath.

I kept hearing about other guys getting hired to coach full-time. A head pro has a lot of hats to wear and things to juggle, whereas a director of instruction can focus on coaching. Coaching young players gave me the buzz. Running the Ladies' Valentine's Day Scramble was starting to wear me out.

Bobby McIver with Scott Verplank in 1985

THE ONLY CONSTANT IS CHANGE

Imagination is more important than knowledge.
For knowledge is limited to all we know, while
imagination embraces the entire world, and all
there ever will be to know and understand.

–Albert Einstein

Scott Verplank's Western Open victory had earned him a berth in the1986 Masters. With Mike Holder on the bag, he'd missed the cut. I joked with Mike, "If you have any honor, you will lay the bag down--we've seen who can caddy!" We had a good laugh.

Scott asked me to caddy again for his pro debut, the 1986 U.S. Open at Shinnecock Hills. At the eastern end of Long Island, Shinnecock had not hosted a major championship since the second U.S. Open back in 1896--ninety years--due to concerns about limited road access. In 1984, traffic jams around mainland Winged Foot had forced players to jump the fences and run to the clubhouse to make their times. They got the traffic figured out at Shinnecock, but not the weather: for the first round on Thursday it rained sideways.

Ahead of us on number 10 Jack Nicklaus lost a ball. This is nearly impossible for a superstar with the galleries following him; he must have hit it seventy-five yards off-line. That cold wind blew harder and harder, and I was in charge of keeping up with the wind direction. You could see the clubhouse flag from every hole; that flag was the size of Rhode Island. I stepped yardages and read putts. Scott would do the same, and then ask what I had if he was uncertain. Scott finished Thursday's round with a 75, but low was a 72. With a 67 on Friday, he put himself in contention. We were in the flow.

The wind changed directions every day. One hole on the back nine of this notoriously difficult course has a small pond about sixty yards short of the green. It was a six-iron on Friday. On Saturday, with the wind in our face, Scott had the ball in the left rough. Looking at that pond, I didn't like the lie.

Our understanding was that I spoke only if Scott solicited my advice. He pulled out a four wood and stood pondering. With the snarly lie, that four wood didn't have the club-head weight to go through it. Staring down the fairway, I pulled the six iron about eighteen inches out of the bag. Scott frowned. "Don't . . . "

He didn't finish the sentence. Instead he set the four wood behind the ball, came over, and got the six iron. He played the shot and got it up and down for a par. I breathed a sigh of relief.

I waited until that evening, after he had time to unwind, to bring it up. "Scotty, the deal is for me not to say anything. I never said a word . . . I was just adjusting the six iron in the bag." Realizing I was making a joke, he laughed. Scott could get it up and down three out of four times. I didn't want him in that pond, and taking it out of play with the six iron worked.

On Sunday he was within striking distance, in the fourth from last pairing. Raymond Floyd and Payne Stewart were directly behind us. With a twenty-footer on number 1, Scott asked me what I saw. I scanned the terrain around us. These contours looked like the surface of the primeval ocean that once covered this island. Background slopes going in every direction can give you a "gravity hill" effect: you think it's sloping one way when it's the opposite. I thought it would break two feet to the right, and Scott agreed. The putt broke three feet left.

Normally you can't make a mistake like this, but there's always a lot of backing up in a U.S. Open--you have to just hang tough. I still have the 1986 U.S. Open yardage book. It brings back memories of every shot. Scott kept making pars until we came to the par-5 fifth hole. It was reachable in two and he played a great two-iron shot. But the pin was on the right side of a ridge in the center of the green, and Scott's shot caught the left side of the ridge by two feet, rolling about fifty feet from the hole. Had it caught the other side he likely would have had an easy eagle putt. As it was, Scott made one of his few three-putts for a bogie.

Thirteen holes to go. Scott parred the par-3 number six hole. The USGA has the toughest rough of any major and they hadn't cut it since the event began. That "Yankee" grass lies in whichever direction the mower was headed: if you hit it where the mower was pointed toward the green you can play the shot, but if you catch it with the grass leaning away from the green all you can do is take a short and dig it out. It played out that way on numbers 7 and 8. Scott turned three over for the round, seven or eight shots back.

Behind us the gallery was roaring: Raymond Floyd was lighting it up. I'd sensed this hardened veteran could bring it on Sunday, while Greg Norman, who had the lead, seemed like he was going to fold like a cheap tent.

Finishing in the top 15 would get Scott back in the Masters and the U.S. Open again. Continuing to grind, he played a great back nine. On the walk to the number 18 tee I let him go ahead so I could check out the board: Floyd had taken the lead, Norman had gone south, and Scott was three over for the round-- right on the bubble to make the top fifteen.

At the tee I set the bag down eight or ten yards farther away than usual. Scott had to walk over to where I was standing. As I handed him his driver I said, "Par, big man, we need a par." A good drive gave Scott a four-iron to the pin. His ball wound up pin-high in the bunker on the right side, but with about sixty feet to the pin he played a shot to within one foot, then tapped in for a par.

The caddie of the player putting last always replaces the flag in the hole. I was standing to the side of the green. Scott came over and handed me his putter and we hugged. "It's been an honor caddying for you," I told him. After he checked and signed his card, Scott and I walked to the scorers' tent, way above the number 18 green. There we got to watch Raymond Floyd hole out for a 66 and the title. At age forty-three, he became the oldest U.S. Open Champion to date. Many times the U.S. Open turns into a battle for survival--with players dropping back on the board, the last one standing wins by default--

but a 66 on that course, that Sunday, was an unbelievable round. Raymond Floyd deserved his championship.

Ever since Scott Verplank won the 1985 Western Open, his professional debut had been highly anticipated. After Shinnecock, Scott joined the PGA Tour full-time. Then he started struggling. The PGA Tour wants their players accessible to journalists. At press conferences before events, sports writers--the same people who had dubbed him "the next Nicklaus" when he joined the tour--started asking Scott why he was missing cuts, and calling him "Kerplunk."

Lanny Wadkins suggested that Scott get in touch with his first teacher--not knowing who it was--and Scott asked me to meet him in Florida. After observing for three or four days, I told him there wasn't anything wrong with his swing, but I noticed he was taking four or five looks at the target in his pre-shot routine. Scott played his best with two looks at the target before the swing. Rhythm and timing starts when you step toward the ball from behind, so the pre-shot routine has a rhythm and timing that blends into the swing. Scott's extra looks indicated he was trying too hard and disrupted the flow of everything.

Nothing technical, no swing changes, just take two looks and swing. Jackson to Florida was a trek . . . add three days together . . . and this is all I saw. The gurus would have messed with his swing. *Know your players*--there's no substitute.

***

For the 1985 Masters Scott had been partnered with Gary Player, who always goes out of his way to encourage the young guys. Filling out the foursome were Seve Ballesteros and Mac O'Grady. Mike Holder was on the bag. I was walking with them during a practice round when Player remarked to Scott, "You're playing with the best player, and the player with the best swing, in the world." Ballesteros was #1 in the world rankings, and I agreed with Player--O'Grady had as good a swing as I ever saw.

But as we were walking to number 18, Ballesteros made an unsolicited comment: "Scott," he'd said with his Spanish accent, "if you are looking for longevity, you need to lengthen your swing--your three-quarter backswing will only get shorter as you age." I followed, silent, hoping Scott hadn't let that register.

Scott asked me to caddie for him again at the 1987 U.S. Open, held at the Olympic Club in San Francisco. Although he now had a semi-full-time tour caddie, for the Open, he said, "The chemistry is right." When I met him in San Francisco, I saw it immediately: Scott had in fact attempted to lengthen his swing. The resulting tension in his backswing was causing his right knee to pop out, setting him off balance. The three-quarter swing that Ballesteros had told Scott to lengthen already included a full shoulder turn, so he *was* fully loaded. When Butch Harmon began working with Tiger Woods, he wanted a shorter arm swing and fuller turn: Butch was working Tiger *toward* the same swing Seve had labeled as too short.

Kneeling behind Scott, I grabbed his right knee to keep it braced. You hear "keep your head still," but that's nonsense-- the head swivels and moves with the coiling motion of the swing. The only thing that does not move on the backswing, ideally, is the right knee. Scott had gotten away from his winning swing, and by now he had hit enough balls with the popping-out that it had become grooved. He's such a competitor that he could still bring it--nothing had popped out in his heart--and I hoped he could get his game back at Olympic, but a U.S. Open is tough enough without a swing change. He missed the cut by a couple.

1987 was my third and last U.S. Open with Scott. I no longer coach Scott Verplank. He's told me he hadn't had a lesson, looked at a magazine article, or read a golf book in twenty-five years. Self-reliance was our goal. His caddie, Scott Tway, stands behind him in practice rounds and monitors his alignment. That's it. I like to grab Scott's bag and tell Scott Tway, who is Bob Tway's brother, "You have my bag--I want it back!" This ritual gives us a laugh.

I call the two Scotts "Scott Squared." Their first week together, in 2001, Scott Verplank won at Lake Tahoe. At the 2007 Arnold Palmer Bay Hill Classic, during my annual visit, I hung back walking down the fairway to ask Scott Tway a question. "OK, you guys win your first time together--there must have been something magical going on. Before we finish today, I want you to remember . . . what was the magic?" Tway had never been asked this, never thought about it. He walked about fifty yards, turned, and came back to me.

"I don't have to think anymore," he said. "Before we played, we said our goal was to have as much fun as possible." There it is: the magic lies in *having fun.* It doesn't hurt to be childlike and a little playful--if you aren't twelve years old anymore, you can pretend you are. Remember, it's just a game. Keep smiling, keep playing, and *enjoy yourself,* no matter what.

***

The USGA formally recognizes the youngest qualifier for the U.S. Amateur. In 1987 Rett Crowder, 17, became the third player of mine to accomplish this feat, after Matt King and Jack Larkin. Rett's father asked me to caddy for him. The tournament was held at Jupiter Hills in south Florida, a great 36-hole course built by some wealthy industrialists. Near the Atlantic Ocean, Jupiter Hills has such huge sand dunes that if you didn't know, you would think you were in North Carolina.

A precocious player, Rett Crowder already displayed many of the attributes that would distinguish his adult game. Rett is built small, with a low center of gravity, so the club just orbits around his body in a perfect circle. His swing has minimum wobbles; less can go wrong when the swing is this efficient. Rett has soft hands around the green, which means he has great touch. His excellent bunker play would serve as a good building block. Rett lacked the experience to win against this field, so my private goal was making the 36-hole cut and qualifying for match play; he played well but failed to qualify by several shots.

Rett played in the morning of the first round. That afternoon we found Rob McNamara on the course, carrying his own bag. After making sure there was no rule against caddying for two players, I carried Rob's bag the last nine holes. He qualified easily. Rett and I were leaving, so I called Rob off to the side and rubbed it on him loud enough for Rett to hear, too. Rob had qualified for the U.S. Open at Oakmont in Pittsburgh as a six-teen-year-old--he was capable of winning any amateur event, and he made it to the quarterfinals at Jupiter Hills.

During the event, several players I didn't know asked me to look at them.

Who was Bobby McIver to them? Scott Verplank's coach.

***

I told R.C. Sproul about my frustration with the "strong manager" concept CCJ had implemented. Then I asked how he thought I might achieve my goal of teaching full-time. R.C.

suggested writing a book. I had a strong regional reputation; getting a book published was the best way to gain national exposure (and this *had* been one of my original goals). Mike Holder was reading *The Golfing Machine*, by an engineer named Homer Kelley. The book was so technical and densely written that it was like studying the game in a foreign language. I had to take it sentence by sentence to digest it. If Holder and R.C. hadn't been into it, I would've put it down. I definitely wasn't using it on the lesson tee, except with R.C., but when he suggested that I translate it into my farm-boy, common-sense language, I began working on a manuscript.

In September of 1987 Ruth and I took off for a few days. The Grand Hotel in Point Clear, AL, where my career in golf had begun, was like a smaller version of The Cloister at Sea Island. The resort now featured a bar in the middle of their swimming pool; Oliver North was testifying at the Iran-Contra hearings on television as Ruth and I talked over drinks in our swimsuits. I said I'd had my fill of the Country Club of Jackson. She knew I wanted to teach full-time, but it was hard to find a position that paid what we were used to. "I just wish I could have a six-month sabbatical to sort things out," I told her, but it was just a wish. I knew I had to make the best of a situation I no longer found fun.

Early in 1988 the new manager fired a waitress in the mixed grill. I found out about this when her husband Frank Ward, one of our locker-room guys, told me the manager had invited her back--with a condition: he wanted Mahalia to spy on her fellow employees and report her findings to him. I went up to the manager's office and confronted him. He denied it all, never getting up from his desk. Mahalia had turned down his request and every black employee in the club knew it along with me. The next week the manager called me in on Saturday morning and asked for my resignation.

Country clubs are minefields. If I resigned, gossip would spread that I'd been caught with someone's wife, or stealing, or whatever they might come up with. After consulting with my "board of directors," I decided to make the club fire me. With two weeks of vacation coming to me, I planned on dropping a letter off at the club at 3:59 on Monday, saying I was leaving town for two weeks to think it over. I waited until the last minute to drop off my letter. Then we rushed to pack, picked up Matthew from school, and headed to the vacation house Ruth's parents had built on Lake Rayburn in east Texas.

While we were in Texas, Ruth and I drove to Houston to see Claude Harmon. His health was failing, but when I walked in his bedroom, he got up and wrapped his arms around me. Dick had told him about my situation at Jackson. "Rusty," he said, "I'm proud of you. You stood up for the little guy. You won this deal . . . You can never go wrong trying to do right."

As always, he was utterly genuine. This proved to be the last time I would see him. Mr. Harmon died several months later, following heart surgery.

When the news of my firing by CCJ first leaked, Hal Busching, president of the new Annandale Golf Club, had called to offer me a position for six months selling memberships. Hal said he wanted to provide me a base of operations--I could work for them while pursuing another head pro job. I decided to wear a tie to work and not talk with anyone about the events at The Country Club of Jackson. For the third time I was teamed with John McNeely. I worked hard, selling memberships, having prospects out to play, and writing my book at home. But when people asked for lessons, I declined; that was John's turf.

In three months I sold about thirty memberships at Annandale. With food service limited to a 19th hole and no evening meals or social functions to speak of, Annandale was strictly a golf club. Its Nicklaus-designed course and pure golf focus made it a luxury item for the golf lover and a status symbol, but it wasn't for everyone. Knowing the people at CCJ, I chose legitimate candidates who could afford Annandale. Memberships still weren't easy to sell.

Despite working the phones hard, I had spare time to work on my game and my book. Now titled *Swing More Efficiently and Play More Effectively*, it was my "translation" of *The Golfing Machine*. Homer Kelley's book was getting a lot of publicity, but few could understand the technical language; I articulated similar ideas using common sense terms. Any player pursuing excellence could benefit, I thought at the time.

Not knowing of any openings, I hadn't applied for another job when Will Brewer called in June. I'd coached Will when he was in college in Nashville. Now Director of Golf at The Golf Club of Tennessee, Will had heard that Farmington Country Club in Charlottesville, Virginia, was taking applications for their head professional's post. I had never been there, but Will said Farmington was a special place, and folks from Belle Meade were non-resident members. Through the PGA, I learned the club had forty guest rooms, 1,000 resident members, and 1,400 non-residents, an unusual mix. I quickly put a letter together and fired it off with my resume.

Attorneys in Jackson who had gone to UVA's law school started getting calls from Peter Low, the associate dean of the law school. He was also chairman of Farmington's selection committee. Farmington was being very methodical and professional in their search. This was a coveted job up that way and there had been over a hundred applicants, including some big-name club professionals. When Peter Low finally talked to Bob Travis, Travis immediately called me afterwards, elated. This was "more than our lucky day," he said. Within a week, Mr. Low called me. The selection committee wanted to interview me on a Tuesday morning in early July, but he asked me to arrive on Sunday because he wanted some time with me alone.

Mr. Low arranged for me to stay in one of the club's "sleeping rooms." This is a "Mr. Jefferson says" deal; in Charlottesville they talk about Thomas Jefferson in the present tense.

Before dinner with Peter Low Sunday night, I strolled the club and grounds. Farmington was the most beautiful club I'd ever seen, not brassy or glitzy but just incomparably elegant. From a terrace on one side of the main building you could see the Blue Ridge Mountains rippling away, shading lighter and lighter with distance, from indigo blue to pale gray.

Peter Low put me at ease right away with his gracious manner. He showed me the club's jewel, the Jefferson Room. Designed by Thomas Jefferson himself, this exquisite octagonal room was filled with a golden glow. It seemed to retain centuries of sunlight even long after dark.

After cocktails in the dining room Peter finally said, "Bobby, we liked your resume, but we couldn't figure out your last move. I called a man at the Country Club of Jackson and he told me you were the biggest S.O.B. east of the Mississippi River."

I almost dropped my fork, but managed to set it down.

"I didn't like his answer," Peter continued, "so I decided to investigate it fully. I determined who the S.O.B. was. If it were you, we wouldn't be having this meal. I got out our alumni directory. Fourteen graduates all gave me the same story--you turned the club around and were caught in a bad deal." He added, "Bob Travis and I talked for almost an hour. I've never met him and I feel like he's my friend." I couldn't suppress a smile: Travis always had that effect on people.

"One other thing," he said. "That first guy said there was some talk that you are bi-polar. The committee is sophisticated--one of the members is female and this runs in her family."

I told him I would freely discuss both topics. As we left the dining room, I said I'd prepared a presentation and some handout material (I'd learned my lesson at Metairie).

Peter Low didn't have to bring me in a day early or fill me in on sensitive topics. He told me the attorney in him took over after the manager at the Country Club of Jackson fired that shot my way. In the legal profession everyone is innocent until proven guilty, and there are always two sides. I was grateful--for being declared innocent, of course, but maybe even more for the fact that Peter Low had taken it upon himself to investigate.

***

The interview was scheduled for 9 a.m. I woke up at 5:30, 4:30 a.m. central time. Normally not an early riser, I'd gotten an internal wake-up call. I put on casual clothes to walk the course as the sun rose, stopping several times to take it in. It was like getting ready to compete: put your conscious mind in neutral, focus on your breathing, just observe without thinking . . . This is meditation on foot. I took my time to appreciate the flowers. The exquisite natural beauty gave the place a spiritual feel. I get the same feeling whenever I'm at Pebble Beach: there is something mystical about the Seventeen Mile Drive along the Pacific Ocean.

Back in my room I took a shower and put on my gray suit. Moving in slow motion, doing everything very deliberately while breathing deeply, I got ready for the meeting. After a nice breakfast at the 19th hole I returned to my room and looked over my notes without thinking much. Then I stretched out on the bed, relaxed, and let my mind become quiet, exactly what I would do before a tournament. The principles of peak performance apply to everything. Your mind and body can give it to you when you need it, if you know the process. Nobody in the interview room would know the golf business better than I did. I reminded myself that I wasn't afraid to tell the truth--it's the way I was raised. Six friends had promised to send up prayers on my behalf on Tuesday morning.

When I arrived at the designated meeting room fifteen minutes early I felt totally at peace. I was ready. It was time. As Bob Travis always said on the course when I needed to make a hard shot: "Now, Bobby, NOW!"

My presentation was about how to run a golf program the Claude Harmon way. At River Oaks and the Country Club of Jackson the golf staff was turned loose to teach instead of tied down in the shop, but golf shop sales doubled within two years at both places. The reason? We had tripled lesson income. Many people use rounds of golf as the barometer of a program's health, but enthusiasm for the game develops on the lesson tee. From what I knew, once Farmington installed a team that could teach and play, they could anticipate rounds of golf increasing by 30 to 40%, bringing up cart and driving range income as well as food and beverage sales. Jim Brackens, the GM, gave me a big nod of affirmation.

Claude Harmon, the master communicator, taught never to lose eye contact with your audience. I had my outline, but I knew it so well I looked every one of them in the eye. I didn't overdo it, but someone with two national champions, multiple college scholarships, and All Americans could surely deliver with both juniors and members. I closed by describing the revitalized golf programs at *three* clubs, including Belle Meade, where Willie was proud to follow in "the Harmon line."

After I finished, Peter Low announced a five-minute break. I knew the tough questions were coming when we reconvened. Al Clements, a bank president, requested an explanation for the committee of what happened at the Country Club of Jackson. I said there had already been tension between that Jackson manager and me; perhaps my confrontation was too aggressive, but I told the committee I wouldn't change a thing.

Steve McLean, the club president, leaned forward. "From my standpoint," he said, "this was a noble act." Robbye Youel, a teacher and the only woman on the committee, nodded.

They didn't ask about my termination after the first question. When Peter Low brought up the bi-polar issue, I was prepared. "I don't know that I am bi-polar. I may be what they call uni-polar--I'm a very intense person and hard worker. Dick Harmon described me as a grinder. About twice a year I just feel very tired, not sad or hopeless. But I am treated with an antidepressant which resolves the condition, and I've never missed a day of work." I said that I had done some confidential one-on-one counseling at the request of my doctor, helping others with similar conditions if they wanted someone to talk to, and would be more than happy to do this again, if the situation presented itself.

When the meeting ended I was overwhelmed with gratitude. A positive spirit had filled that room. The issues Peter was concerned about had worked in my favor. The Big Man upstairs had been with me: I could sense His presence. It looked like I might get a second chance.

They wanted to see me give a couple of lessons: first Dick Funk, a committee member, then Robbye's daughter, who was fourteen and a beginner.

Mr. Funk was already loosening up on the lesson tee. From the shots I saw he appeared to be a low-80's player, and visibly nervous. First I asked him to step back so I could get between him and his balls. Claude Harmon taught me this; you're trying to make a point while your student is focusing on getting another ball from his pile. I spent ten minutes just talking with Mr. Funk to get him to relax. When I asked him what he felt his problem was, he mentioned a troublesome slice. He was hitting a seven iron. After teeing the ball up, I had him relax his grip and close his stance a bit, and he hit a nice shot with a slight draw. "Next!" I joked.

The correction was that simple: the tight grip was part of his personality, and aiming left is natural for a slicer. For twenty minutes I let him swing some other clubs. He was drilling it and I was cheerleading, big time. A coach should focus on building up the student's self-esteem and helping them have positive expectations. Swing changes are secondary--usually a minor change will do. When I pronounced Mr. Funk "healed," we all laughed.

I found out later that Robbye Youel had won numerous state amateurs, and as a teacher herself she was well equipped to assess my instructional style. Her daughter Ellen was a true beginner. A shy young lady, Ellen seemed scared, keeping her pretty face downcast. I don't think she wanted to be there.

I told Ellen my goal was to get her making a motion. We could forget balls for now--the golf ball will paralyze a beginner quicker than anything. When I'm working with a newcomer, I want to give them some feel. Ellen had a decent grip that only required a minor change. From there I got her into a good posture, the feet under the shoulders and no wider. I wanted her to flex her knees and tilt forward, letting the hands just drop under the shoulders. We went through it a few times, with me focusing her attention on her feel and balance. She got it quickly.

I teach the finish before the back swing, so I next told Ellen I was going to hurl her into a balanced finish. Taking a club by the club-head end, I let her know what was coming, put the grip on the backswing side of the shaft, and hurled the club around. Her body responded naturally--no technical analysis needed. I did this ten or twelve times, aiming each time to get her standing up in balance on her front foot and making sure her hands and the club were where I wanted them. I was using the natural learning process without saying so. What does a teenager care about jargon? Then, without telling her beforehand, I switched the grip to the other side, gave her a hurl, and said, "Go to your finish."

Ellen had just made a better than decent golf swing.

After doing this for ten minutes I placed her arms at the 4 o'clock position on the finish side and asked her to swing back on her own and make a good finish. She was getting it and her confidence was soaring. A big smile bloomed on her shy face, replacing the fearful look. Once she was swinging a seven iron in balance, making a good, tension-free motion, I put a ball on a rather high tee. "Okay, Ellen, give me a good finish--forget the ball."

Ellen hit a beautiful shot. She was so happy and proud. I looked at Robbye and called out "Next!" We both shook our heads. I told Ellen to keep smiling and keep it fun.

They had my clubs on a golf cart: Farmington wanted to see a little of my game. I would play four holes, numbers 10 through 13, with Peter Low and Wayne Hall, the assistant manager, before departing to catch my flight. On the cart with Peter, I took out the scorecard to see what these holes looked like. Number 10 was about 210 yards from the white tees, a good par 3. Except that they drove me to the blue tee.

Past a little street, way back there at 255 yards, it was the hardest shot you could imagine, out of bounds all along the street on the left. I'd expected to have a chance to loosen up-- your body cringes when you ask it to make a full swing without warming up--but found myself forced to get the kinks out the best I could while visualizing my target. *Can you see it? Do you have it? Do you need it?*

Mr. Harmon used to say, "You have to have a bread-and-butter shot--when you have to put groceries on the table, you need a shot. It has to be one that will work any time you need it." I decided upon a prevent-left shot. This is an Arnold Palmer tactic: tee the ball very low with the driver, aim left, and intentionally play the shot off the heel of the club--balls struck on the heel always fade, they never go left. I had it, I just didn't know if

I was loose enough. But it was my turn. I pictured the shot, trusted it, and swung.

It was perfect: the ball faded, ending up in the center of the green. Trying not to look surprised, I pranced off the tee like Lanny Wadkins with his "no problem" swagger. We played those holes in about an hour, and I parred them all.

Robbye Youell had ridden around without playing. When I asked if she saw what I was doing with Ellen, she nodded and smiled. The two of us had hit it off immediately. Peter Low told me they would be back in touch in a couple of weeks. When I got in after midnight and gave Ruth a play-by-play, she could tell just from my voice how well things had gone. We were going to make it. It might not be Farmington, but something was out there for sure.

The next day, Wednesday, I was exhausted. Interviewing when you need a job is intense. Back at Annandale, John McNeely and I took a ride on the cart; I was telling him all about the Farmington interview when he stopped. "There's something you need to know," John said. "I was up there interviewing last week." I stared--John and I never held anything back. "Rusty," he said, "we're going after the same jobs." John was friendly with Allan Strange, Curtis's twin brother, who lived in Richmond. Allan had given John a heads-up about the opening and called a few people on his behalf. John is a charming, good-looking guy whose pedigree was the same as mine. If I couldn't get it I hoped John would.

Seven or eight years later, in Houston for the Claude Harmon Pro-Am, I got to talk to Dick Harmon. When John McNeely was in the running for Farmington, he had called Dick; explaining how he and I were both in the hunt for the same position, John had asked Dick what he should do. Dick said he didn't hesitate. "Withdraw your name," he told John. "You don't want to be going up against Rusty--there's too much at stake." John never once said a word to me about sacrificing his own shot at Farmington, or Dick Harmon's advice.

***

The entire U.S.G.A. admired Scott Verplank. Bob Travis advised me to hold Scott for the end, to "let him bring the last punch at the right time." The time had come, and Scott was happy to call. Two weeks passed before Peter Low called to invite me back. And this time, he said, "bring your wife."

I told Ruth to go buy the prettiest dress in Jackson. She did. It was red: her color.

Friday evening they held a dinner party across the street at the famous Boar's Head Inn--to get out of sight of the wait staff, Mr. Brackens told us. Fourteen of us sat at a long table in a private dining room. Place cards put Ruth at one end and me at the other: my wife was indeed being interviewed.

Ruth could always draw out even the shyest wallflower. Every time I glanced down at her end, she had all the guests in her area engaged in lively conversation. Ruth knew exactly what they were doing. She just needed to be herself. It was another home run--a walk-off grand slam, this time--for Ruthie.

On Saturday we'd gotten dressed for another dinner party when Mr. Brackens called, asking to see me in his office. On the walk over it occurred to me that I had been asked to resign at Jackson the second Saturday in February. It was now the second Saturday in August.

Mr. Brackens asked me to have a seat. "Bobby," he said, "our selection committee made a unanimous decision. We would like to offer you the position here." The board would ratify the committee's action Monday morning, but he told me that was just a formality. "We have to keep it quiet at dinner out of respect for the board, but we want you to meet with Ruth in the Jefferson Room, to inform her."

In the loveliest room in Virginia I just hugged my bride and wouldn't let go. I couldn't even open my mouth. Six months to the day: the closest thing to a miracle I had ever experienced.

LEWIS CHITENGWA AT THE EAST LONDON GOLF CLUB IN EAST LONDON,
DURING THE SOUTH AFRICAN AMATEUR. WON SA.
EVENT IN DRAMATIC FASHION IN APRIL 1992 AT 1, 10

Lewis Chitengwa playing in South African Amateur

{9}

'THAT GUY' FROM HARARE

If you can envision it, you can accomplish it.
If you can imagine it, you can reach the heavens.

–Zimbabwean Proverb

We arrived in Charlottesville the week before Labor Day. Realtor Steve McLean from Farmington's selection committee had persuaded a developer to let us rent a new three-bedroom house for a year; this way we could get to know the town and make a good decision when we bought a home. Farmington's general manager Jim Brackens told me to take all the time I needed moving in, but I was excited to get started at the club the week after our arrival.

The average age of Farmington members was over sixty-- about a dozen kids showed up for the first junior clinic. The golf shop was also overdue for a renovation. If I wanted to coach, everything else had to be running smoothly. Achieving that would require a strong staff. Following Mr. Harmon's training, I recruited gentlemen and ladies with character and social skills

who were also very strong players. My guys should be winning
state opens and gaining standing within the Middle Atlantic
PGA--what confidence would a membership have in an assistant
or head pro who couldn't break 80? If they could play better
than I could, so what?

My first hire was Mike West. A University of North Carolina
graduate, he had finished in the Top 10 in the Memphis Open
but grown tired of trying to play the PGA Tour after a year.
Pete Mathews, a first-team AJGA All American in 1981, called
me from South Africa where he had been playing on the South
African Tour; Pete was tired of the grind, too. Having seen him
as a junior, I knew he was classy. When Libby McClure, a holdo-
ver from the previous staff who had played at Wake Forest, left
to get married, Kandi Comer--a seasoned tournament veteran
who had made the U.S.G.A.'s 1986 Curtis Cup team, the
equivalent of the Walker Cup for men--came on board. Members of our staff were playing at the major section events, kicking butt and taking names. By the early 90's, Farmington's golf
staff could rival any club's.

Farmington's large non-resident membership included famous and powerful figures in all walks of life: Supreme Court
Justice Sandra Day O'Connor; Lawrence Eagleburger, the sec-
retary of state under George H.W. Bush; Marvin Bush, George
W.'s brother; and many others. But a study we did showed that
of the total rounds of golf, only 5% were non-residents. This
suggested an opportunity: why not promote golf schools? The
resident members were eager to get good instruction, while the
non-residents were looking for a reason to come to Farmington.
Not only did they attend, they brought guests to the schools we
started. We set a twenty-four-player limit in order to have a

six-to-one student-teacher ratio and everyone ate together for four days, concluding with a nice dinner in the Tap Room with semi-formal attire.

I set out to nurture Farmington's junior program. Mike Moraghan, UVA's golf coach, would send members of the team who were struggling to me. Younger athletes (including my son Matthew) kept picking up a lacrosse stick--that game's popularity in this region gave other sports strong competition. Mustering enough sense to avoid the father-son dynamic, I gave Matt to Pete Mathews for golf instruction and watched from a distance. Matt was just reaching adolescence with the self-conscious ego showing up. When he played well he heard "What do you expect--his father is a pro." When he played poorly: "Can you believe his score? His father is a pro." I told Matt this would continue until he whipped their butts. And since critical comments are a reflection of the source, we can't let them get to us.

I coached Matt's YMCA basketball team. Not too many 14-year-olds in Charlottesville had played basketball, including Matt. I told them we wouldn't win by focusing on scoring; our best chance lay in limiting the opponent's score with aggressive defense. I based our full-court pressure defense on John Wooden's famous full-court zone. Coach Wooden had what he called "a center fielder." In this role for us, Matthew set up behind mid court. Our two guys up front would make our opponents pick up the dribble, back away, and throw a long pass; Matthew's job was to anticipate and intercept that pass. With just a couple of skilled players, we won with a plan nobody else used, and our kids learned something.

They knew the other teams were better, yet through aggressive defense we could win. *You can make up for a weakness by developing a strength*: this has applications to golf and life. I pretty much let them play, signaling subtle changes in the defense either by calling a time out or shouting a color (red, blue, green). I got so immersed in the action I would coach unconsciously. Matt showed up on the bench once near the end of a game. I didn't see him until he was right next to me. When I asked, "What are you doing over here?" he replied, "Dad, I fouled out!"

***

I had been working on that book R.C. suggested for several years. My detailed attempt to make common sense out of *The Golfing Machine*, I thought it was pretty good. Homer Kelley's book had gained popularity when Bobby Clampett, who endorsed and adhered to his system, was the best player in college golf. Oklahoma State University golf coach Mike Holder made several trips just to talk with Kelley directly.

An engineer who decided to figure out the golf swing, Kelley declared that there are 24 components to the golf swing--not 23 or 25, but *24*. I never would have read this book if I didn't know Holder was using it, or written my own version if it weren't for R.C. Sproul's belief that it could help propel me into a full-time teaching position. After spending two years reading it sentence by sentence with a dictionary close by, I actually learned a lot about how the swing works. Everything comes under Newton's laws of motion--for every action there is an equal and opposite reaction.

Now I had a job that I wouldn't trade with anyone, but just before leaving Mississippi I had finished a draft of the book. I sent the manuscript out to three readers: Mike Holder, Buddy

Alexander, and Dick Harmon. College coaches have to produce winners--I think they know more about playing than anyone--and there was no one in the club business I respected more than Dick. These guys would find any spots that were unclear, or even wrong.

Dick thought I had succeeded in making Kelley's ideas more accessible. Buddy Alexander wrote, "This book has the potential to be the best golf book ever written." I appreciated his comments, knowing Buddy had read the manuscript very carefully, pondering every sentence and paragraph. Then came Holder's response. With a teacher's red pen he had written: "You are describing a golf swing, perhaps the ideal swing, but there are many ways to swing a club."

Mike's one sentence in red ink stopped my book in its tracks. There are no perfect swings out there. It is very hard to really change a player's natural move, and trying to make major changes never works. *The goal is to produce lower scores*. To accomplish this, work with a player's natural move and emphasize doing the right things to get better. A technical focus on the golf swing usually does more harm than good.

I finally let go of trying to get my book published. I still have several copies of the manuscript around the house, but Mike Holder was right. It is the antithesis of everything I believe about playing great.

The winner is the guy with the most heart, every time.

***

In Texas, where Dick Harmon and I had won the Pro-Assistant tournament, a head pro could play with two assistants. For the Middle Atlantic Pro-Assistant, however, we could only field one team. In 1989 Mike West and I were scheduled for the

Virginia Chapter qualifier at the Salisbury Country Club in Richmond, which neither of us had ever seen.

The weekend before that event Ruth and I made a trip to Philadelphia with Peter Low and his wife. Our host was a member of Pine Valley and Merion. After eating some rich food in fancy restaurants, by Monday morning I was experiencing persistent, uncomfortable indigestion. I had gained some weight and Ruth, the nurse, was worried about my heart. I told her Mike and I had business to take care of in Richmond, with or without indigestion. She extracted a promise: if I experienced any further discomfort in my chest area, I had to get Mike to haul me to a hospital.

As soon as Mike picked me up at the airport I started in on my motivational chatter. "Are we ready? You know we're ready. Can they handle us? You know they can't handle us." You get the idea--I had Mike pumped. I told him, "Par is a bogie for us. It's pedal to the metal!"

"Hey . . . by the way," I said as we warmed up. "I've been having chest pains. I promised Ruth if they got any worse I would get you to take me to a hospital." When Mike looked at me I could tell it shook him a little. "I'll try to make it until we finish," I added, smiling.

The motivation worked. We got to our finishing hole, the toughest par four they had, tied for the lead and needing a birdie to prevent a playoff. We both hit good drives. The pin was tucked. Electing to avoid the trouble, I put it about twenty feet away. "Okay, Mike," I said. "Let 'em see what you've got." The shot required a fade and Mike had a natural draw. But he didn't mull it over--just set up, pulled the trigger, and hit a beautiful four iron with a fade, six feet out. I miss, he makes, we win.

The section championship took place a couple of weeks later at an historic club named Woodholme in Pikesville, Maryland. We were paired with the winners of the Maryland chapter, the defending champions and experienced players. Again we played no practice round, although we got there the day before. Mike and I had heard that Woodholme was a great old course, with quick greens and some length. We noticed that par was a 73-- they had five par 5's and three par 3's or something like that-- which is highly unusual; I've never seen it before or since. As winners of the two chapters, we had the premier pairing and went off last.

The guys from Maryland shot seven under, or a 66. It was good enough for second place. Mike West and I shot 13 under-- with 2 bogies, one par, and an amazing 15 birdies--for a 60 on a par-73 course. When they signed our card the head pro said, "We should have had to pay for an admission ticket to see this."

Early in the round we had encountered an especially tough par three. The green sloped severely from the back to where the pin was tucked in the front. Mike had hit first all day; he buried his shot in a bunker, left and short of the pin. I had mine about forty feet directly above the hole. "Mike," I said, "this thing is so greasy fast I'll either make it or it'll roll off the green." It was too fast to tap it so I stepped up, took dead aim, and just nudged it--the ball hit the back of the hole dead center, popped up in the air, and fell in. That magic sustained us the whole round.

How did we play so great? Mike West and I had a relationship with no baggage. We didn't have to say a word, expressing how much we cared for each other using male code. All we had to do was keep smiling, keep playing, and keep making birdies.

That round is etched in my subconscious. I can see many of the holes, the blue sky . . . I was looking up there a lot, asking The Big Man for it. Woodholme was a very tough course, but we felt like we were being carried along on a wave. Dialed in, connected with nature, our awareness increased. Highly focused and completely relaxed at the same time, we felt love for each other and our fellow competitors. Locked into the moment, we played every shot we needed, boldly. It was spiritual golf coming directly through our hearts.

That indigestion I'd experienced? It had died down since the qualifier in Richmond--Mike never had to haul me to the ER after all.

It was a pretty good drive from Baltimore back to Charlottesville. We were quiet as the miles passed by. Finally I looked over at Mike. "Did you have any idea five over would win this deal?" Mike just shook his head, and we laughed.

***

After having too easy a time in middle school, our son Matthew was headed to Woodberry Forest School, a renowned private boarding school 35 miles away. He would be starting as a freshman in the fall of 1993. In June of 1993 Ruth and I decided that we would like to host a foreign exchange student. We hadn't contacted anyone or taken any action, however, when the phone rang one day in August.

It was Wally Armstrong, R.C. Sproul's Orlando golf coach. A great player for many years, Wally had tied for fifth place in the Masters back in 1978. I had come to know Wally by reputation, through R.C. Sproul, and Cobby Ware knew Wally from his days as PGA Tour chaplain. My mother was an Armstrong, and the first time I saw Wally's picture the resemblance struck me.

Scots who had lived in northern Ireland for decades (hence the term Scots-Irish), the Armstrongs came to America in the 1700's, entering the port in Philadelphia on rickety ships. My ancestors headed to South Carolina. Others went west; Wally Armstrong grew up in Indiana, not far from Wapakoneta, Ohio, where astronaut Neil Armstrong was born.

"Cousin Wally" was calling us that August day to ask a favor.

Nick Price had introduced Wally to a group of junior golfers from Zimbabwe, Price's home country. They were in the United States to compete in the Orange Bowl World Junior Championship in Miami. After the event they went to Orlando to visit Disney World, and Nick had asked Wally to find them housing.

"Bobby," Wally said, "there's this young man who just won that World Junior--he beat Tiger Woods. But he did something *historic* just this March." Even by Wally Armstrong standards he sounded excited. "Bobby, this kid went into South Africa, with apartheid and all this going on, and he won the South African Amateur! Eighteen years old, and he's the first black to ever win it. His name is Lewis Chitengwa. This kid is *special*."

Wally told me more of Lewis's story. After the University of Virginia offered him a golf scholarship, their dean of admissions had said that in order to be accepted he had to do well in fifteen hours of core courses. Lewis was enrolling in Piedmont Community College in Charlottesville. UVA couldn't help him since this would constitute an NCAA violation. "So," Wally wound up, "would you go to your church and find a family to sponsor him?"

Wally does a lot of speaking for the Fellowship of Christian Athletes. Before I could answer he said, "I think the Lord has His hand on his should--"

"Wally!" I finally had to interrupt him. "We don't need to go to our church--he can stay here. It's done! When will he be coming?"

As we pondered later, a lot of homes lay between Charlottesville and Zimbabwe. How did this young man end up on our doorstep? When he had to make his own arrangements in Orlando, Lewis Chitengwa only knew one person to call--Wally Armstrong. Wally only knew one person in Charlottesville. This began a saga that would change all of our lives. Lewis wasn't going to stay with us for three or four months--we were in it together for the long haul.

***

I tried to focus on the clinic I was giving at a Woodberry Forest School summer sports camp in late August, but my mind kept drifting. Lewis Chitengwa was arriving that night.

I left everyone at home when I went to the airport. It took Lewis forty-eight hours to get here and it was close to midnight when his plane landed. I spotted him immediately, a thin young man with a handsome, boyish face. He had perfect manners. After I introduced myself, he told me that he couldn't sleep on an airplane. Neither can I, so I knew how tired he must be. He had his clubs, in a worn travel cover, and just one big bag for his belongings.

Lewis spoke with a soft voice and melodious accent, but he hardly said a word unless he was answering a question. Not knowing anything except that Zimbabwe bordered South Africa on the north, I asked where exactly he was from. "Harare," he told me. "Harare, Zimbabwe."

We rolled in to find everyone wide-awake, waiting to meet Lewis. Ruth asked if she could fix him a peanut butter and jelly sandwich with a glass of milk. He took her up on the offer and then headed to bed, exhausted.

I had a hard time falling asleep. This wasn't unusual. Ruth can be asleep in five minutes--some nights I wished I could do this in the worst way. That night I couldn't get Lewis off my mind. He'd been Zimbabwe Amateur Champion three straight years, and this little country produces some great players--including Nick Price, then ranked #1 in the world. Tiger Woods hadn't intimidated him. Lewis beat Tiger head to head in Florida. But when Lewis Chitengwa won the South African Amateur it was a Jackie Robinson event. Historic. *Monumental.*

A world-class player had moved in with us. Unable to sleep, I went downstairs for a glass of milk.

There, in their travel-worn bag, were Lewis's clubs.

Golf pros are this way--I needed to know what clubs Lewis was playing. Opening the bag I found an old Ben Hogan set of irons with a regular shaft. From what I had heard about Lewis's tremendous power and length, I was stunned to see those regular shafts. His woods were OK, but the copper wedge he had was almost worn out. That wedge's grooves reminded me of another player: Scott Verplank used to wear his grooves down every two years. I kept staring at those clubs. I was already in awe of Lewis' game, and I'd just met him.

Early the next morning Ruth woke Lewis so he could register for classes at the junior college. Still getting over the jet lag, he started out very quiet and reserved.

I knew his father was his golf pro. Wanting to understand his game and what his dad emphasized, I asked him about that. Lewis said, "My dad told me before I left to always keep it natural. He told me not to tinker with my swing."

These are the words of a wise man. I echoed them, further instructing Lewis to stay away from this pro in Orlando who would do everything *but* keep it natural. At some point I knew Lewis would be pressured to see the guy. He met my gaze and nodded. He knew who I meant. He also seemed to grasp why I was putting so much the emphasis on this point.

I was eager to get Lewis fitted into a great set of clubs. Club fitting was my specialty--the easiest way to help a player find his natural swing is a good fit. He needed extra-stiff irons, which didn't surprise me. Bob Wolcott had helped me get a pair of three woods made inside a Taylormade van at the Kemper Open. Both were set up strong, meaning 13 degrees loft instead of 15. Lewis looked at those clubs for quite a while, then took each club and vigorously shook the club-head, feeling the spring of the shafts--I had never seen this done. He finally chose the smaller-headed club with weight on the sole (bottom), and he was a magician with that club.

For the first time in his life Lewis Chitengwa was well equipped. I still hadn't seen him play when Ruth took Matthew and Lewis to play Meadowcreek, Charlottesville's short and fairly easy municipal course. Matt got to witness golf like he'd never seen before: Lewis drove two par fours that were close to 350 yards and reached two par fives in two. Matt went up to Bill Heron, the pro, and said, "Lewis just shot a 64. What's the course record?" When Heron told him it was a 63, Matt grinned and announced, "We'll be back." Notice the *we'll* part? Matt felt a part of that round, as indeed he was.

Lewis and Matt were playing the muni because the NCAA compliance officer at UVA couldn't make a determination as to whether Lewis could play at Farmington. Ruth and I had gone to see her with Lewis and UVA Golf Coach Mike Moraghan; in her office I got a peek at the massive NCAA rulebook. She said she had to check with the Atlantic Coast Conference. A week and another meeting later she still hadn't made a decision.

When we got the same thing a third time, I spoke up. "Lewis isn't a student at UVA yet, he's a foreign student who Farmington Country Club considers a dependent as long as he lives with us. We have nothing to do with UVA. We didn't take him in because of his golf. And Mike Moraghan did nothing to arrange this." The compliance officer was really nice, merely cautious. I asked her when she got off work. Five-thirty, she said, looking puzzled. I told her, "If I don't hear from you by 5:30 today, Lewis will have a scholarship somewhere else by the time you get here tomorrow. I can make a few calls and we can solve this problem for UVA."

We walked into the hall. Lewis looked confused, and the blood had drained out of Coach Moraghan's face. Neither had ever seen me pull something like this. Ruth just shook her head. "You have to know when to hold them and know when to fold them," I said. "I just called her hand--this lady will fold before 5:30." Everyone laughed. At about 4:45 I received a call from the compliance officer: Lewis was free to use Farmington. Her decision wasn't that tough after all.

Shortly after Lewis came to live with us, he was invited to play in the Middle Atlantic Amateur Championship. One of the oldest amateur tournaments in the country, it drew lots of good players. In 1993 it was held in Maryland on Swan Pointe, a tough Bob Cupp course on the Potomac River where the wind blew hard. I was caddying for Lewis.

A number of the participants had played in the Kenridge Cup at Farmington in late April. These guys kept looking at us. Pat Tallent--a great all-around athlete and onetime draftee of the NBA's Washington Bullets--had won our tournament. Finally Pat came over. "Bobby, where in the world did you come up with this guy?"

"Pat," I replied, "you are paired with 'this guy.' You need to go to the locker room and get your ankles taped. 'This guy' is going to rub something on you." I smiled and Pat got a laugh. "While you're at it you should tighten your jock strap, too."

This was my first chance to see Lewis with the bit in his mouth--when he put his game face on I saw pure *specialness*. At no more than 150 pounds, he could carry the ball fifty or sixty yards past these other guys, including Tallent, and he could do anything with that copper sand wedge. Now I knew he was the real deal--I had assumed he was, but I still needed to see. I knew what I was looking at. Pat Tallent's raised eyebrows told me he did, too.

Lewis got this kind of reaction wherever he played. There seems to be an energy field or something around the great ones. Lewis Chitengwa was going to teach *me* some new things--it wouldn't be the other way around.

{ 10 }

KNOW YOUR ALL STARS

In the middle of difficulty lies opportunity.

–Albert Einstein

Woodberry Forest School's nine-hole Ross course naturally appealed to boys who liked golf. The team had fifteen or sixteen with experience, and several were really good. Used to playing (and winning against) the UVA junior varsity, Woodberry's best players were destined for college golf. The first parents' weekend I met Matthew's classmate Miguel Coles and his parents, from Caracas, Venezuela. Miguel went on to play for Vanderbilt, where he got an undergraduate degree and later his MBA. Josh Points, a year ahead of Matt, has a golf academy in Raleigh, NC. I started giving clinics on the Woodberry campus.

With *The Golfing Machine* shelved I could focus on coaching. Lewis Chitengwa's UVA teammates sometimes needed tune-ups. I worked with Simon and Tim Cooke, Max Rein from Germany, and Andrea Brotto from Italy, focusing on what they already had and following Harvey Penick's advice: "Only give them one aspirin at a time." Or, as Claude Harmon put it, "Use an eyedropper." I was still working with some of the originals from Belle Meade; when Jack Larkin gave professional golf a run, he would visit. After Greg Lesher got his PGA Tour card, he came to Farmington and shot a 62 with perfect nonchalance--maintaining an even keel lets you stay in the flow.

The PGA held three events close to Charlottesville: the Greensboro Open, the Kemper Open in Washington, D.C., and the Anheuser Busch at Kingsmill in Williamsburg, Virginia. They gave me a great chance to catch up with Bob Wolcott and Scott Verplank.

Both played great in the early rounds of the 1990 Williamsburg tournament. With Bob and Scott in the top five or six, Saturday I loaded my Farmington juniors in our van and headed for Williamsburg. Jeff Fleischman, head of marketing for the Kingsmill Resort, had gotten me a parking pass for the players' lot, so I just walked out onto the tee where the players were warming up. Scott was by himself getting ready. He never wanted any last-minute motivation--he had all he needed. Bob, however, could always use some extra juice.

The two Virginia veterans, Curtis Strange and Lanny Wadkins, were warming up within ten yards on either side. Approaching as close as I could get to Bob's side without getting hit with a club, I leaned towards his ball. "Big Man," I said, "it's time for you to let 'em know who you are. These boys are too old! Lanny and Curtis can't handle you if you bring all you've got." Bob was soaking this in. He wasn't nervous, but the adrenaline was running high.

Bob's caddie played professional hockey and many of his teeth had been knocked out. He was one sturdy hombre. "I'm glad to see you," he told me. "Every time you show up I make a good check." These guys work on commission. Bob did tend to play well when I was around; so did Scott. When Scott walked down to wish Bob good luck I stepped back to tell him, "I can feel Bob needs me near him today. He hasn't won--"

"Hey, I understand," Scott cut me off. "I really do understand. If I can't win, I hope it will be Bob."

Lanny Wadkins, paired with Scott, won the tournament. Larry Mize birdied the last hole to finish second. Scott and Bob tied for third. Good. But I would have given anything if they had tied for the win and gone into a playoff.

At the 1991 Greensboro Open I hooked up with Bob again. Rob McNamara joined us that week. A great college player, Rob had won the Southern Amateur twice in a row. Bob and Rob had competed many times; Rob even caddied for Bob a time or two. The weather had turned cold and lots of rain made a very long course play even longer. We knew Bob's greatest strength was his length, but he tended to play safe, not using that length to his advantage. We double-teamed Bob with our strongest motivational tactics. Then, late Wednesday, I announced, "Big Bob, you're playing great and you know what you need to do. I'll just be in your way, so I'm going home. You're ready--just let 'em see your heart."

I felt like my leaving would give Bob confidence, when he realized he didn't need me to get the job done. Bob opened with a 67. Playing great, he held the lead going into the final round. That day Mark Brooks shot an unbelievable 64.

Bob didn't lose. Passed by with one of those fluke rounds, he finished third, the closest he ever came to winning on the Tour. Rob, Bob, and I had chemistry and affection that ran deep. Bob Wolcott is very spiritual and can sense a need in others. I've asked him what made that week different. He gave this answer: we were all helping each other in our own ways.

About a year later Bob told me to bring my clubs to play a practice round at the Kemper. He assured me there would be no problem; I could park with the players and had all the credentials I needed, except a player's badge. Since Bob had lined up a caddie, I decided what the heck, this could be fun. The day brought beautiful weather. There were no glitches as we warmed up. At the first tee, however, a security guard stood holding a list of players.

"Just keep walking," Bob told me. I heard him say to the guard, "Oh, he's a Middle Atlantic Section Alternate--he won't be on your list." They do have sectional qualifying for these events. There are indeed alternates, and if someone cannot play, the alternate gets the spot.

But an imposter had just gotten caught representing himself as a contestant at all these prestigious events. My hands were shaking. I hit my first tee shot fifty yards off line. All I could think about was getting caught and the Washington Post running a story.

Finally, thinking I was off the hook, I settled down. Another security guy was waiting at the 10th tee. Walking past I overheard my caddie saying, "I can't pronounce his name--he's a Middle Atlantic Section alternate." I hit as quickly as I could and made my way.

PGA Tour pros I knew kept congratulating me for qualifying. When I finished playing I told Bob, "Don't be putting me through this much stress again! I can't handle it."

Bob might have known what I would run up against. Hmm . . . the old Middle-Atlantic-Section-alternate trick? I wouldn't put it past Bob; he was getting a kick out of seeing me sweat. They do call it *playing* golf. And he could use the break: one year Bob Wolcott was the "Iron Man" on tour, the guy who plays the most events. Scott Verplank has always played a more limited schedule and only courses he likes. The PGA Tour is a grind. I used to plead with Bob to play three weeks and take one off, or play four and take two off, but he was relentless.

***

Sergio Garcia made his United States debut in the 1998 U.S. Amateur, held at Oak Hill in Rochester, NY, where Craig Harmon was head pro. The entire golf world was focusing on the charismatic and talented young Garcia. Except for me. The day before the semi-finals, I called Craig. "I'm taking McKnight," I told him. "I'll let you have all you want." Craig laughed; it's unprofessional to bet on something like this, so he knew it was all in fun. "Sergio will not beat Tom McKnight tomorrow," I insisted. And sure enough, Tom beat Sergio.

Tom McKnight had two boys at Woodberry Forest School while my son Matt was there. I started working with him after we put on a clinic together at Woodberry. Tom lost the finals of the 1998 U.S. Amateur to Hank Kuehne, but his runner-up finish earned him an invitation to the 1999 Masters.

I had just one piece of advice: knowing those slopes and the lightning speed of the greens at the Augusta National course, I told Tom to really practice his lob shots. He would have tight lies where he had to have this shot; high and with a soft landing, it's the most difficult to play. Tom did something brilliant: he practiced the shot off hardpan. He had such great hands he could hit the shot off concrete if he had to.

Tom McKnight made the cut at Augusta, quite an accomplishment for an amateur or a first-time pro given the adrenaline and intimidation of a first Masters appearance. The last day of the tournament Tom had the ball to the left and way below the number 10 green, with the pin back left. Facing a fiendishly difficult shot, he took that lob wedge and hit within a foot of the hole. Watching him, I smiled inside.

The famed sports psychologist Bob Rotella was a Farmington member and soon became a friend. We pooled our skills, teaming up to work with Bob Wolcott, Jack Larkin, Greg Lesher, Rett Crowder, and others who came to Charlottesville for consultations.

By the time Ian Baker-Finch arrived, many--including Ian himself, perhaps--had given up on his playing career. After Baker-Finch won the 1991 British Open, something went haywire. It got to where he couldn't drive it anywhere near where he was aiming. At St. Andrews in 1995, he hit a ball out of bounds over 100 yards to the left, where nobody in history had likely hit it. When Ian visited Farmington, I found him to be a very nice guy. I observed his motion. He had beautiful rhythm with his irons, hitting it solidly, and I told him he had a great swing.

Bob Rotella took Ian out to see what was going on with the driver. Out of earshot of me, Ian commented, "Your pro doesn't know what he's doing. He's telling me I have a great swing."

"Bobby McIver is an accomplished coach," Bob told Ian. "He helped Scott Verplank develop into the great player he is. There's a steady stream of great players looking for his help. If he tells you your swing is great, take it as the compliment it is."

Rob McNamara, by then my assistant at Farmington, played with them that day. "It was unbelievable," he said. Ian Baker-Finch hit everything pure, but he'd hit one drive sixty yards left and then sixty right. So Rob and Bob drew up a plan for Ian to come in monthly for four days. I felt that Ian's problem was 100% mental. He obviously had a picture of his ball flying anywhere with the driver: he was having a mental spasm with one club. Because it had absolutely nothing to do with his swing, Bob Rotella could help him.

After agreeing on this plan with Bob, however, Ian called. One of the magazine poster boys had given *his* diagnosis, and Ian had decided to work with this guy . . . on his swing.

Our choices have consequences. All we can do is make the best decision possible given the information at the time. Ian never got it back, but he's a broadcaster in the tower with a major network and enjoying life. If Bob and I could have double-teamed him--and brought in Rob--I believe we could have helped him.

***

My reputation with Scott Verplank, Jack Larkin, Rett Crowder and the others had preceded me when I moved to Charlottesville, and my peers in the Middle Atlantic Section named me Teacher of the Year in 1991. The award was presented at a black-tie banquet outside Washington, DC. Ruth's parents touched my heart by flying in from Louisiana. Reflecting on my career, I wondered if I had done my best coaching when I was young and knew the least, before magazine articles and concept books like *The Golfing Machine* had been on my radar.

In 1995, *GOLF Magazine* named me a TOP 100 Teacher in the United States. Recognized teachers throughout the country vote on new inductees. I contributed to an article on curing the slice, but my advice--soften the hands as you grip the club; it'll work almost every time--was really Harvey Penick and Claude Harmon's. I remained on *GOLF Magazine's* Top 100 Teachers list for six years, until I exited the club pro game and fell out of sight. Being recognized by my peers had been one of my six long-term goals way back in the 1970's. I was deeply humbled by these honors.

In 1993 both Mike West and Pete Mathews got good head pro jobs--Mike at the Country Club of Virginia, Pete at the New Orleans Country Club. Both bore out Claude Harmon's philosophy: recruit gentlemen and ladies who can play and let them learn the business. Mr. Harmon used to say, "Your reputation is all you leave behind, so don't do anything to tarnish it." In about five years with me, Mike and Pete had earned a good reputation. I told Mike, "I hope you enjoyed winning all those tournaments. When you get strapped down with more responsibility things will change." He and I have laughed about the truth in those words; these guys can still play, but your lick is freed up a little more when you are an assistant.

Rob McNamara had married and gotten a very good job in California. But after an earthquake scared his wife--and Rob himself--he accepted my invitation to join my staff. Rob could really play, he had a great personality, and we had a long history together. College players who can't quite make the tour tend to be good prospects. Rett Crowder, who was playing professionally after graduating from LSU, recommended his college roommate William Lanier and I quickly saw he was a perfect fit.

Rob, William, and Rob's wife, Carrie, all did a great job at Farmington. Kandi Comer left to take the reins of a club her dad developed, a move I had long known was inevitable; I replaced her with hires from the Greenbriar resort hotel. Betsy Sinsel came first, followed by Sarah Neville.

A sweet young lady and a very good player who wanted to go somewhere with it, Sarah was eager to get my coaching. The two of us resumed the sunrise service, meeting at 6 a.m. and working until 7:30, when we changed into clean clothes to begin the day officially. There is something mystical about the early morning: in the peace and quiet you connect with nature, but for me the magic lies in the fact that the noise of human life hasn't started yet. Every player in any game needs silence and solitude to quiet their minds. Leaving to compete after about a year, Sarah Neville turned pro in 1993.

***

I cannot stand crowds--we left Virginia Beach one year because of the chaos. After requesting recommendations from Steve McLean we made two trips to Bald Head Island, just south of Wilmington, N.C.

My mother went with us the second time. After we got onto the island late, Ruth's mother phoned to say a hurricane was headed directly toward us. When Ruth called the security office it became obvious they had no evacuation plan. We left the island and drove a hundred miles inland, winding up in a tired and worn-out place near some military base. We let the hurricane miss Bald Head Island before we returned.

Mother was around 75 back then. When she couldn't remember details of a story, she kept saying, "I'm getting old."

Finally I smiled and told her, "Mother, I'm *getting* old. You have already arrived."

***

Friends invited us to stay at their cottage in Montreat, NC, a historic Presbyterian mountain retreat near Asheville. As soon as we got there it started raining and kept raining--it does this in the mountains. Trapped in a small cottage with three energetic young ones, we decided to make the daylong drive to Columbia and my family's farm.

Once we got there, as always I went into our house to speak to my mother. Then, before sitting down, I proceeded to the Gordons' house.

There I found Lillian Gordon, Horace's wife, very sick. I pulled up a chair. As we talked I learned that she had pneumonia. The next morning her doctor admitted her to the hospital. There, tests revealed that she also had leukemia that had gone undiagnosed.

When I went to the hospital to visit her in the evening, Lillian was asleep. Curtis Johnson, her granddaughter's husband, was in the room. We had never met. He was obviously wondering who I was, but as soon as he heard the name Bobby he knew. I went over to Lillian's bed and stroked her hand. Curtis was ready to wake her. "No, let her sleep," I said. "Just tell her I came by when she awakens."

That night the phone rang at 4 a.m. It was Curtis, asking for me. As Ruth handed me the telephone I thought to myself, this isn't good. "Mama Lillian just passed," Curtis said. Her grandchildren always called her Mama Lillian. My heart sank, but I wasn't surprised.

My mother had always been the one who held up everyone else in the family when someone died. The next morning she looked out the window of our family room at Lillian's house, tears streaming down her face like I had never witnessed before.

"Lillian was my best friend," she said. "There was nothing we wouldn't share." It had been a fifty-year partnership, with a good bit of that time spent raising me.

The church bulletin called her funeral service "The Homegoing of Lillian Gordon." Leland Webster, the pastor, had worked on the farm. We hadn't seen each other in around thirty-five years. His message was passionate and on the mark when he told the congregation what a fine lady Lillian was. I remembered her understanding my ups and downs, holding me in her arms. How sweet it had been to be loved by Lillian.

As Leland walked out in the processional, he saw me. "Is that you, Bobby?" He came over and gave me a bear hug. These folks had loved me so much. They were better to me than I had been to myself.

On the way to the cemetery, Curtis said Lillian had woken up after I visited. He told her I'd come to see her, and that I hadn't wanted to disturb her. When she heard about this, Curtis told me, "she smiled, and held it a long time."

***

Those years in Charlottesville defined our family. In many ways, Ruth and I were at our best. I was forty-five and Ruth forty in 1993. Matthew had hit his teens, with Elizabeth and Rob three and six years behind. Our children all had different needs but Ruth intuitively knew what to do; she could play unconsciously, too. Peak state isn't reserved for athletes; a good mother and wife can get there every day.

Knowing your players is essential to good coaching--and parenting. Every child is different. They have different gifts and passions from the beginning. You cannot handle them all alike. Children will make up their own minds what they are interested in; some parents and coaches don't get this. I've always trusted my heart and intuition when dealing with young people. They say the eyes are the windows to the soul, and I literally believe this. If you want to know what a kid is thinking or feeling, look them in the eyes and let your soul read what is going on with theirs. This is a spirit deal, not some conscious-thinking process. That's why manuals will never work, and good coaches have no use for them.

A group of boys Rob's age showed up at the same time in Charlottesville and grew really close. If you asked any of these seven who their best friends were, they would call off every name. In the fall of 1995, as YMCA basketball was about to get started, Erika Reynolds, one of the mothers, asked me to coach the twelve-year-olds. The proposed team was our son Rob, Tim Reynolds, and that band of best friends.

For a coach, the challenge lay in the rules: every kid got equal playing time. For the single hour of practice we were allowed per week, we were assigned to Meriwether Lewis Elementary School. We didn't even get the tiny gym to ourselves--we had to share it with another team. The other team's coach was an attorney who went to our church and had two older daughters who were really into basketball. Practicing alongside his team, I noticed that he only had seven players. They looked like an all-star team. I gave him a stare--at this level, it's far easier to coach with fewer players, especially when you know they can play. When I asked him what happened to the other three, he said they'd "decided not to play."

Two boys on my team knew something about basketball, and I had some good athletes who played soccer and lacrosse but lacked a goal or a ball. That first practice I held the ball. Instead

I walked them around, explaining the floor to them. "Guys, this is the base line. This is the free throw line. This is what's called the lane, and these large painted blocks are what we call blocks." Frank Cox, a father and friend, was assisting me, but it was so noisy in that small gym I couldn't hear myself think. I had them do some dribbling and passing drills.

With thirty minutes left, I went to the coach of the other team and said, "Let's scrimmage." His kids fully backed up the impression they had made; our team couldn't even make a successful pass, much less a basket. That night I vowed to myself, "We're going to beat this team before it's over."

We started out losing more than we won. On Wednesday nights, as soon as we came into the gym: "Hey coach, let's scrimmage." My team was just having fun, but with each scrimmage my guys were improving. If twelve-year-olds can see it, they will mimic, and learn quickly: *the all-star team was coaching my players.* I knew about twelve-year-olds and the natural learning process. This is the ideal age to teach a kid to play anything--there's no ego to detach and they just want to play. Winning or losing is something for the parents to fuss about.

While I am happy to sit down and tell parents what I am seeing regarding their children, I ask them not to attend practice. Nowadays parents can turn kids' practices into spectator affairs. They like to think they are supporting them, standing on the sidelines hollering instructions like they know what they are doing. Relatives interfere plenty during games. I ask my basketball parents to "get behind our team" during games--cheer after they make a good play--but too often parents get *ahead* of the team, yelling as their child goes to the free throw line. It's worst with baseball. I've gone up in the stands when I was coaching third base, to stop some obnoxious *grand*parents from being a nuisance to their child, and to me, too.

Late in the season Rob fractured his elbow playing dodge ball. It wasn't a severe break, but he was out for the rest of the YMCA basketball schedule. My team kept playing every Saturday, one player short now.

Coach Wade at CMA believed that winning started with good defense. With Matthew's team of 14-year-olds we could full-court press, soften the pressure, and then trap as the guard crossed the line. We had options. With the 12 year-olds, however, there was a "no full-court pressure" rule. The other teams settled into zone defenses, but I believe the kids can learn more playing man-to-man.

While my guys were making progress, that team we shared the gym with was on a winning streak. We were scheduled to play them in the last game. Trying to determine a way to beat those all stars and finish with a win, I kept hammering away at the problem mentally, but nothing gelled.

I wasn't even going to be there for the big game. Dick Harmon and I were doing a teaching seminar at Sea Island, Georgia. One of our players was going to be out of town, another had come down with the flu, and with Rob out, too, we were down to seven players ourselves. But those seven were athletic; my post or #5 player, Bo Carrington, later played lacrosse at Duke on a full scholarship. At the close of our final Wednesday practice I called the team together to tell them to pay attention to Coach Cox.

Friday morning around 3, I sat straight up in bed and grabbed a notebook. Our British guard, Joby Howlett, would be waiting for their guards with serious pressure at half court;

Joby would make their point guard pick up the dribble after taking one step over mid court. Then every player would get in front of his man. Joby would soften his pressure and back up--to allow the pass, and also to keep from getting in foul trouble. I hoped this new strategy would surprise our opponents; caught off-guard, they would start making ill-advised long passes. As soon as the pass left their point guard's hands, Cabell Cox--Frank's son, our ball handler and scorer--and Timmy Reynolds would break for our basket, so that when our guys grabbed their passes, Timmy and Cabell would be there for a layup.

I went over and over this plan, then called Frank Cox Friday morning. "We can't use full-court pressure," I said, "but nobody said anything about *half-court* pressure." I told him to get the players to the gym an hour early so he could explain the new plan. They would get it and be able to execute it.

Ruth went with me to Sea Island. By the time we checked in-to our room after dark, the game would have been over for hours. I called Frank. "Bobby," he said, "you aren't going to be-lieve it--our plan totally surprised them. Their coaches couldn't come up with a counter. We kept stealing the ball and just hurl-ing it down the floor. We beat these guys by ten points!" I pumped my fist and looked up. Frank went on, "Their coaches didn't take it well. They had ordered 'Undefeated' jackets, and their kids were sitting on the floor dejected."

I hung up. Tears formed in my eyes. Ruth was wondering if someone got hurt. I looked at her and smiled. "Our kids won by ten. We whipped their butts. Lord have mercy, we won!"

When people ask me for my best coaching story, they get this one--hands down, the most memorable team and game.

"I do my best coaching when I'm not there." I make a point of saying this whenever the subject comes up. People chuckle, but I'm serious. I missed Scott Verplank's last 18 in the U.S. Amateur, and didn't even know Jack Larkin was playing in the U.S. Junior until the final round.

These days, pros have their gurus follow them around on the tour. I heard one coach whose players talked about needing to get with their professor in mid-tournament. In his "On Tour" blog for Gear Effect Golf, Steve Pike recently observed that with the exception of Bubba Watson, today's younger PGA pros haul around personal swing coaches who scrutinize their every shot on the Tour.

Pike did offer one dissenting voice. "'He taught me to be able to make my own changes, make my own adjustments, work on the things I needed to work on so I could concentrate and I could understand how to play the game,'" Jack Nicklaus said of his long-time coach, Jack Grout. "'That was the important thing, that I knew how to play the game.'"

But kids see this handholding and think this is the way to do it. My guys have always taken care of business without me. It may be a new world, but I question whether anyone knows a better way. Self-reliance--it worked for this Hall of Fame pair of Jacks, and it works for me.

{ 11 }

CHASING SEVENS

*Courage is the first of human qualities because it is
the quality which guarantees the others.*

–Winston Churchill

After qualifying in the chapter, in the 1996 Middle Atlantic
Section Pro-Assistant Championship, Rob McNamara and I
found ourselves paired with the same men from Maryland that
Mike West and I had played seven years earlier. The tournament was held at Williamsburg National Golf Club, a Jack Nicklaus course in Williamsburg, Virginia. Making a few birdies, we
were still chasing our playing partners. These guys from Maryland were true gentlemen and excellent players. Even without
leader boards, I knew they were still likely the team to beat.

With four to go they were at seven under while we were at
five under. I called Rob aside, wrapped my arm around his neck,
and said, "Big man, the time is now--we have four holes and we
need to birdie them all . . . Let's run off and leave these guys."
Rob hit first with a five iron and put it thirty feet away. I hit the
six twenty feet out. After everyone missed I stepped up and hit

it dead center. On the next hole, a par five, Rob made a twelve-footer. I could pick up my six-footer--it was better ball of two. But since they made birdie too we were still one behind them.

We all parred the seventeenth, a tough par four. The 18th was a fairly long par four; the fairway and green sloped to the right and the pin was on the left. I told Rob to get it in the fairway so I could rip it down the left side. Rob hit a six on the green. "I have the shot," I told him. "It's an eight iron with a slight fade." The ball hit six feet short and above the hole, checked up, and bounced towards the hole, leaving me with a four-footer--a hard putt, all speed breaking left to right. I held my picture until the finish and the putt rolled in. We had tied the Maryland men with a 64. Third was several shots back.

In all my years in golf I had never been in a playoff. Rob took charge at that point, telling me to hit my Callaway three wood, which I could hit straight and as long as Rob could hit his driver. On the first Rob missed the green to the right and couldn't get it close. Pin-high and about six feet off to the left, I took a nine iron, bumped it on the green and let it run towards the hole. They had their pars. I had a three-footer to tie or halve the hole. Feeling some pressure, I made it.

On the second playoff hole I hit that three wood again and killed it. I was out in front of everyone. Rob drove it in the fairway and hit his second on the green, twenty feet away. Our opponents were about the same distance. I drove the ball past the fairway into some light rough. Rob, now caddying, advised me to take the safe play. "Hit a low sand wedge. It should hit and let it release forward."

Once you give your subconscious a clear picture without any inner chatter, it's better to be committed than right. The perfect shot doesn't exist, so trust your game: play the shot you *see*, know you *have* and *need* at the time. Playing the shot we pictured, I wound up six feet away. Our opponents both missed from outside twenty feet. I was visualizing my putt toppling in the hole when Rob stepped up and rolled his twenty-footer right in the heart. We raised our arms in triumph and gave each other a hug.

Nobody wins by thinking about coming in second. Winning this tournament with Rob was different than it had been with Mike West. Mike and I got in the flow and just ran off and left everyone, whereas Rob and I had to reach down and find the will to win. Knowing what we had to do, we got the job done, birdying four out of six holes at the end.

I met Rob McNamara in 1985, when he was the LSU freshman who won that college event in Jackson against the favorite, Scott Verplank. Twelve years later Rob had become my playing partner, my colleague, and my friend. We may not have run away with this championship, but we knew we had earned it together.

These tournaments were fun, but they never really captured my imagination. I never lay in bed imagining myself winning these individual titles; I was thinking about my boys winning *their* championships. Albert Einstein said imagination is more important than knowledge, and he should know. Imagination is where it all starts, whether a goal or an action plan. I was a coach first and my goals always reflected this. I wanted to know how big my *players* could dream.

***

Meriwether Lewis School had just paved a little walking path behind the school when my YMCA team started practicing in their gym. Less than a quarter of a mile from our house, it made a perfect walking destination, and one beautiful late-fall day the family headed up there to check it out. Rob and Elizabeth took their bikes and Babe, my Labrador retriever, came with us. The paved path, rather than being shaped like a track, zigged and zagged some. "Rob," I said when we reached it, "I wonder how fast you can get around this thing three times."

That's all it took--he was off. I was shocked at how fast he could ride. Even that young, he loved speed. As Rob made the first lap I started waving him down and hollering for him to stop. He kept going.

When he ignored me again on lap two, I started praying that this deal could end safely. On his third turn Rob was flying. And that last turn was downhill. He was picking up speed when his rear wheel hit some loose gravel on the pavement and spun out from under him. Rob instinctively planted his foot, and the torque snapped his femur like a stick of peppermint candy.

At the hospital the orthopedic surgeon showed us the x-ray, the largest bone in his body in two pieces. After surgery to set the bone, Rob would be equipped with what they called an external fixator device, which would keep him in a wheelchair for about three months. When the rush of EMT's and the consultations were over, it hit me: I had challenged Rob to three laps as fast as he could go . . . he just wanted to please me. I broke. The tears just kept flowing.

We had to set up a hospital bed in the living room. The first day Rob was home, Ruth called me at work. "You have to come home--Rob lost his balance and it scared him to death. He's wanting you." When I got there Rob was in his bed crying. I stretched out with him on his bed and started singing.

I used to sing "Swing Low, Sweet Chariot" to them all as a lullaby. Lillian and Mama Grace had sung it to me when I was small and I never forgot the words. As I reached the verse about "A band of angels coming after me, coming for to carry me home," Rob broke in: "I don't want you to go . . . I don't want you to die." My kids had all had their stitches and little injuries, but this one was different. I couldn't wave him down--he was trying to impress his father.

***

College golf provided Lewis Chitengwa with some stiff competition, but he capped his first season by being named ACC Freshman of the Year.

The father of Jeremy Julie, one of his UVA teammates, bought a large condominium where six team members moved in together, including Lewis. When they were on break he stayed with us. Lewis was always thinking of things to do for our kids. He liked to take Rob to UVA football games; they sat on a hillside behind an end zone with the college students. Since Rob was only eleven or twelve, this was major league stuff for him.

Tiger Woods turned pro during Lewis's junior year at the University of Virginia. Those close to him in Zimbabwe thought this was a signal for Lewis to do the same, but I took him aside and told him he wasn't ready--Tiger's game was his game. I didn't know it, but Lewis was actually suffering from depression. Zimbabwe's weather is warm and sunny; our winters got to him, and he was also struggling with some hard courses he took as electives.

Every spring UVA hosted the Cavalier Classic, a tournament that attracted some good teams. That year for the first time Lewis was in position to win the individual title. For the final round, however, the weather turned cold and damp and he shot a 76 or 77. After he signed his card, I watched him walk about fifty yards away to sit alone on a stone wall.

I went over to him and pointed at the scoreboard. "Lewis, those numbers by your name don't mean anything to me. I would've liked to see you play well today, but those are just numbers . . . We don't cherish and treasure you because of numbers." I put my fist against his chest. "This is what we love about you--it's your heart. Do you understand this? What makes you a champion is your heart."

Mike Moraghan had come up and heard all of this, but he remained silent as I used one of Mr. Harmon's lines. "If you are playing great, enjoy it--it won't be long before you can't hit it in a fifteen acre field. If you are playing poorly, that's good--you'll be playing great soon."

As we walked off, Mike said, "Bobby, I doubt that Lewis ever heard that before."

Lewis's dad was a ferocious competitor who drove Lewis hard. My encourager kind of coaching wasn't his way. As Lewis was packing to leave for a big tournament, Lewis, Sr. had asked what he hoped to accomplish in the event. When Lewis told him he wanted to finish in the Top Ten, his dad responded, "Well then, just withdraw! If you aren't playing to win, stay home." He also told Lewis: "Always play like you are chasing sevens." I think the idea was to play as if seven players were ahead of him and he was seven shots back; I never saw a more aggressive player than Lewis in my life.

Lewis Chitengwa learned to play by the natural learning process. He had never gotten all locked up with swing keys, which is why I wanted him to stay away from the swing guru in Orlando. We understood each other on this. When I told him, "Lewis, don't you dare let me hear about you seeing the professor," he knew who I meant. Lewis was very visual--if he could see the shot in his mind's eye, his body would give him what he needed without mental chatter about form and technique.

Lewis's uniqueness lay in his ability to visualize shots that had never been executed--his daring to dream outside the box. A benefactor gave the land for UVA's Birdwood golf course, with one condition: her nephew was breaking into the golf course architecture business and she insisted they use him. The 4th hole at Birdwood is a vexatious par 3, with water in front and a large green with far too much slope from back to front.

The team was practicing one day when Ryan Hall, Lewis's teammate and fellow countryman from Zimbabwe, hit his ball left and above that number 4 hole. Ryan slammed his bag down. "This putt is impossible!" he declared--with the hole on the front, he assumed his putt would roll off the green into the water hazard. Max Rein, a teammate from Germany, told me this story, because of what happened next.

"Anything is possible," Lewis said to Ryan. "Nothing is impossible." He got his putter and placed a ball on Ryan's spot. Then he walked around, eyeing the green and the shot with a gaze as focused as an eagle's.

"Lewis putted the ball about sixty-five feet *away* from the hole, to the rear fringe," Max continued. "Here the ball almost gets hung up in the fringe. Then it started rolling, one revolution at a time. It gained a little speed, rolled about seventy-five feet, and stopped--one foot past the hole." Looking at Ryan and Max as he picked up his bag, Lewis made his point again, softly but emphatically: "*Anything* is possible . . . Nothing is impossible."

Max said that was the moment he realized Lewis's brilliance: nobody else he knew would even dream up that shot.

Eagles don't flock. Lewis was set apart. His father helped him develop that brilliant imagination; if you are seven shots back and chasing seven players, you have to learn to see things differently. Where did it come from, his belief that anything was possible?

Our view of reality is just that: ours. Lewis grew up in a modest concrete-block building--formerly the pool house at the club where his father was the pro--such close quarters that he shared a double bed with his two brothers. But the sleeping arrangements didn't give Lewis his heart or soul.

One of the ancient Greeks said we are the sum of our experiences. I have heard it called a Spiritual Law of Expectation: as our expectations grow, our reality expands. Lewis was able to really see the world in a way that very few young people do. Starting when he was fourteen, golf had taken him to North America, Japan, Australia, and Ireland--he had played on five continents. He made friends everywhere he went and sustained these friendships, mostly through letters and postcards. Never mind how many brothers shared a bed. Lewis had big dreams because his reality was expanded.

I agree with Wally Armstrong: Lewis did seem to be part of a bigger plan, and somehow he seemed to know it, too. This explained why he was so humble. People were naturally attracted to his beautiful smile and the twinkle in his eyes. Even far away from home Lewis touched people--really touched them--with that smile and his eyes at first, then with his heart and soul.

***

After Rob broke his leg Lewis was there for him in ways so subtle they cannot be recalled. In many respects we became a family then: we started acting as a team. Rob knew he was cherished and we weren't going anywhere. One Sunday we went out to Keswick Country Club, where The Cavalier Classic had been moved, to see Lewis play. Still in his wheelchair, Rob was self-conscious; at first he didn't want to go. No sooner had we rounded the corner than the Florida State coach saw Rob and gave him a golf ball, and he got his players who were handy to speak to him. I didn't know that coach, but his compassion told me he was a winner.

Lewis and the team did well. Andrea Brotto played great, too, finishing second or third in the individual competition. Noticing that Andrea's eyes were completely blood shot, I went over and asked him what the problem was. "Bobby," he told me, "the girl I love called and broke up with me yesterday and I can't stop crying." These Italians are a different breed of cat.

"Now I know how to get you to play," I laughed. Later, before a tournament, I would call and ask Andrea for the phone number of his girlfriend at the time. "I'll get her to break up with you, and you will win." He always laughed. An Academic All American and excellent player, Andrea led the UVA team with Lewis after Simon Cooke graduated.

Simon and Lewis had been the one-two punch for UVA, and it was Simon who helped Lewis when he was down. Lewis had found out he was allergic to United States grass and the pine tree pollen that coats cars and pavement every spring. During serious attacks his windpipe closed off and he couldn't breathe. After going on for three years it was kicking in again his final season. Lewis was struggling, playing at a little over half speed. His body literally couldn't get the oxygen he needed; Mike Moraghan once saw Lewis lying down in the bus and took him to an emergency room. But being Lewis, he never complained.

I had talked with the doctor and knew this situation was coming in the spring. Going over to Lewis's condo with him, I discovered that his roommates were saving on their electricity bill by keeping the windows open. They were all seated around the television watching something. "I don't know how the university would let five guys in as stupid as you," I said. "We have an All American here with allergies to pine pollen. What do you geniuses do? Raise all the damn windows!" From bedroom to bedroom we went. I slammed them shut as hard as I could. "Lewis, let me know if they raise them up again and I'll come right over." My voice was loud so the others could hear me. BAM. BAM! "We have a first team All American and these fools have their windows up!" BAM! The windowpanes shuddered--I thought some might break.

The window in the living area was up. I walked over and BAM slammed it shut, then   looked at the five roommates. "Are you guys just stupid or are you crazy? Lewis has gone to the hospital four or five times in bad shape and you geniuses are trying to save ten dollars!" I grabbed one of the guys, Jeremy Julie, a super kid from Canada whose dad owned the condo. "Where are the air filters for this AC unit?" He had to think for a while--bad news in itself. Sure enough, the filters hadn't been changed in years. I pulled one out and threw it on the floor. The dust went everywhere when it hit. "Just look at that . . . We have an All American and a world class player with allergy problems living here. You geniuses don't have enough sense to use new filters *and* you have the windows up." I addressed Jeremy. "Get in your car and get six new filters--*right now*. Change them every thirty days until we are out of this spring pollen season. The rest of you, get the vacuum and dust cloths and get the pollen out of here right NOW!"

On the way out I said, "Lewis, if these windows go up to save on the electricity bill, you call me." I turned to the others. "Don't make me come over here again."

These young men clearly felt badly. I really liked them, but at this age their minds seem to sleep day and night sometimes. Lewis had never seen me quite like this. I told him later that my tirade had been an act, to make my point, but it may have frightened him; he seemed to bring a spirit of peace wherever he went. At least he didn't have to go to the emergency room again, unable to breathe.

***

Our pastor Skip Ryan started a men's group in 1988. When Skip moved on, John Hall came in to replace him. Going deep seems easier for females; males will talk about weather and sports, then up go the guards. Eight of us met every Friday morning at 6:30 to talk, whether our children did something stupid or one of us confronted a life-changing decision. We supported each other through serious illnesses, including one group member's battle with prostate cancer. The combined intelligence of eight men far exceeds the sum of the eight individuals.

One of our main purposes was to serve as an accountability check for a group of guys who naturally were independent. When I was later recruited by a club in South Carolina, David Turner rebuked me for not bringing it before the group, and I knew I had made a mistake.

I did discuss the difficulty Ruth and I were having finding the right school for our daughter. When Elizabeth was a toddler Ruth called her name over and over only to find Elizabeth searching for her. As a nurse she knew what this meant: deaf in one ear, Elizabeth couldn't determine the source of sound. Experts in children with learning differences diagnosed Elizabeth with Attention Deficit Disorder--in the process I realized I had it, too--and several medical issues that had delayed her development. We attempted to send Elizabeth to a private school that didn't specialize in LD kids, but children who are out of synch with those their own biological age can get teased unmercifully.

When Elizabeth reached middle school, the Einstein School for special-needs children seemed like the perfect fit. In January of her eighth-grade year, however, the headmaster told us that Einstein could not accommodate her for high school. Out of options in Charlottesville, we found ourselves at a loss. Elizabeth had started working weekends behind the counter in my golf shop, and she did an excellent job, hinting at the kind of work she does as an adult with great skill. She needed a place that would affirm her many strengths.

Ruth found an education consultant who specialized in assessing a child's needs and matching them with the right school. She had us visiting schools in Florida, Connecticut, and New York, but none felt right. Finally we landed at the Riverview School on Cape Cod in Massachusetts. I remained silent to let Ruth come to her own conclusion, but I knew within fifteen minutes that Riverview would be Elizabeth's school. Our challenge? The tuition and living expenses were on the level with some other private schools up that way--Harvard, Princeton, and Yale--and Riverview offered no financial aid like Woodberry provided.

Back at Farmington I started getting distracted thinking of ways to increase my income. A pharmaceutical company paid me $1,500 to teach and entertain a group of twenty surgeons at the Homestead, a luxury hotel in Hot Springs; maybe I could do more of those. Farmington was undertaking an $8 million renovation, which would give me a new shop. I had backed this plan--it passed by a close margin--but now I would be operating out of a house trailer for two years. And my sales would be impacted: you need room to display merchandise.

Earlier that year Congressional Country Club, just outside D.C., had invited me to interview for the head job up there. It paid quite a bit more than Farmington and they were hosting a U.S. Open, which would boost shop sales. This 36-hole club had lots of play: every member of Congress had an honorary membership and some real heavyweights belonged to the club. The pro would own the golf shop, with sales more than double Farmington's. Of course, the cost of living in the D.C. area was much higher.

The club didn't advertise the job, instead inviting a handful of candidates to talk with them. These clubs always want a good teacher, and my meeting with their committee lasted several hours. Afterwards, however, I had heard an inner voice saying, "This isn't for you." This job would require administrative skills, which were not my strong suit. After discussing it back home, Ruth and I had agreed that I should withdraw my name.

When Elizabeth's school became an issue soon afterward, we questioned whether we had made the right decision--but it was done. We still loved Farmington. We would somehow find a way.

Lewis, Rob, Elizabeth, and Matthew

Bob Rotella and Bobby McIver at Farmington CC

Lewis Chitengwa on UVA campus

Nobody had a more balanced finish than Mike Keliher.

12

"ASK THE UNDERDOG"

*The virtue in most request is conformity. Self-reliance is
its aversion. It loves not realities and creators, but names
and customs. Whoso would be a man, must be a nonconformist.
He who would gather immortal palms must not be hindered
by the name of goodness. Nothing is at last sacred but the
integrity of your own mind.*

–Ralph Waldo Emerson

A friend who was a member of the Honors Course in Chattanooga called one spring. "I like all those pro friends of yours,"
he said. "Why don't you call three of them and have them bring
a foursome?" So sixteen guys, basically strangers, gathered in
Chattanooga. By switching the pairings every day, we all got to
know each other. We did this every April for several years; golf
fosters such arrangements. Mark McMurrey believes that golf is
unequaled in affording people chances to meet and get to know
others from very different social worlds.

John McNeely had left Annandale to become the head pro at
Grandfather Golf and Country Club in North Carolina. John

brought Gunn Murphy from Greenville, South Carolina, and Gunn and I quickly struck up a friendship.

Not long after I'd withdrawn my name from Congressional in 1997, Gunn phoned. "I'm calling to get you to come be the director of golf at the Greenville Country Club," he said. I wasn't interested but thanked him for thinking of me. A month (and three more calls) later, Ruth and I decided it wouldn't hurt anything to check it out, so in early June I arranged to fly down and meet with the selection committee. I kept my trip secret.

After picking me up at the airport, Gunn Murphy gave me a tour. Greenville Country Club consisted of two courses with a couple of miles and a main road between them. The crown jewel was Chanticleer, a Robert Trent Jones design that was always listed among the Top 100 courses in the country. Despite a modest clubhouse and turn house, it was indeed a great layout. The primary club facilities were at the other course, Riverside.

I was compiling a mental checklist. The distance between the courses would present management challenges. The golf shops at both places needed a complete renovation. But I saw a bunch of juniors, and Gunn said the membership here was younger. Midway between Charlotte and Atlanta, Greenville had become a boomtown when Michelin and BMW built big plants there. The local economy was newly vibrant and getting stronger.

I didn't want to get involved with a club that wasn't a fit. I used my presentation to level with the Greenville Country Club selection committee. They needed to know exactly who I was. Strong at teaching and promoting golf, I'd always hired staff to cover administrative duties for me. When I asked them what qualifications they were looking for in a director of golf, Johnny

Dennis, club president and club champion, spoke for the group: "We want Bobby McIver to be our next director of golf."

It had never worked this way before--not for me. According to the committee, the club wanted to make major changes and have first-class service all the way. Going first-class wouldn't be cheap, I warned. Was the club financially strong enough to get it done? They assured me it was. I told them I needed to discuss it with my wife. On the way back to the airport Gunn Murphy said, "Just let me know what financial package it would take to get you to make a move."

Robbye Youel was being inducted into the Virginia Sports Hall of Fame, in Virginia Beach. Ruth and I used the drive to really talk about the Greenville offer. Turning it over to God, we asked that His will be done in the matter, and came home to work up a financial package. Instead of owning the two shops, I wanted a good salary plus percentages of every revenue source. I knew the revenue from the golf shops and driving ranges and guest fees from both courses would increase dramatically at first and then level out, but as the club raised fees my terms ensured a raise for me. I was asking for the sun, the moon, and the stars.

Subconsciously I probably didn't want Greenville to accept my terms. I was fully expecting a counter offer when I gave my proposal to Gunn Murphy over the phone. He said he had to take it to the other decision makers. Twenty minutes later, when he called back to tell me they had agreed, it was a done deal. Based upon what we knew at the time, it was also our best play. Ruth and I decided this was part of the master plan to let us cover Elizabeth's tuition. I made a good living at Farmington, but the package with the Greenville Country Club would be substantially greater. All things work together for good, as they say.

It was now mid-June. Gunn understood that I couldn't leave Farmington in the middle of the season. Both clubs agreed: after my last event, the Farmington Ladies Invitational in mid-August, I would start at Greenville.

***

On our fifth move, we were accustomed to the challenges of relocating. When we went to Greenville to look for a house, Ruth found exactly what she wanted the first day, about a mile from the club in a gated development. Everything fell into place. August 1 came quickly.

With Ruth, the kids, and our entire household already moved to South Carolina, I made arrangements to spend two weeks alone in a friend's cabin outside Lexington. I had never taken a retreat by myself. This experience set a precedent. Without it, I might never have sought out the circumstances that allowed me to write the book you are reading.

My last official task as head professional at Farmington Country Club was Robbye Youel's Ladies Invitational. I had stayed the extra two weeks solely for Robbye. Ladies came from all over to play this three-day tournament and I had gotten to know many of them. Wearing a coat and tie, I served as starter, and Robbye always had me award the prizes at their concluding luncheon. During my parting comments, I said the world might know Robbye as a great player, but her friends cherished a wonderful lady. Then Robbye--not the emotional type--rose to address the group. As she attempted to tell them I was leaving, she got half a sentence out and choked up. Once she composed herself, she said our friendship had deep significance for her as well. These words were coming from her heart. With nothing left to say, we ended up hugging.

Ruth and the children made the trip back from South Carolina for the club's farewell party. The whole family stayed in one of Mr. Jefferson's "sleeping rooms." Waking up very early the day of the party, just like the morning when they interviewed me for the job, I decided to take the same walk. The first time, I'd been quieting my mind. This time I lingered, stopping to take in the Blue Ridge Mountains in the distance. On the course, I observed each hole once more. Farmington was known for the beautiful landscaping, and I took the time to notice the flowers. The sun was coming up. In the absence of human noise the birds provided a symphony. I just breathed in that air.

This club chose me after I got fired from Jackson. This club chose me, knowing I dealt with clinical depression. Farmington gave me the job, and this job had given Ruth and me the best years of our marriage. I was filled with gratitude.

Officials and staff gathered in Farmington's main dining room that afternoon for the farewell party. Peter Low initiated the testimonials, saying "I liked Bobby from the first time we met, and I respect and like him more now."

David Carr had been on the selection committee. "Bobby," he said, "you did many things for us, but what I will remember is you brought together the best golf staffs we ever had."

Ruth and the children were standing with me. My heart was in my throat as people kept saying nice things. When my turn finally came, I described those two walks, the first one when I was interviewing and the other that very morning. "If anyone doesn't believe in God after seeing this, something is wrong with them."

As I gave my closing remarks for Ruth and the children, I could see my assistant, Rob McNamara, crying. Rob was always sentimental; I used to laugh when he cried during movies. Rob came up afterwards to tell me that many people were crying. "And you were one of them," I had the presence to say, hiding my own emotion. We hugged. My Farmington days were over.

The club chose Rob McNamara to replace me. A great team as golf partners--winning that Middle Atlantic Pro-Assistant the year before--we could count on each other off the course, too. I was leaving Farmington in very good hands.

**

We wouldn't be abandoning the Charlottesville area. Matthew had another year at Woodberry Forest, and Lewis had one more season at UVA. Golfers miss so many classes that many take five years to complete degree requirements, but Lewis intended to do it in four, taking summer school courses in order to graduate on schedule.

Matthew hadn't applied to UVA. The reason, he told Ruth: "I don't want to go to college in the same city that y'all live." What college had he chosen? Furman University . . . in Greenville, South Carolina. Going to Greenville ahead of us on a scouting expedition, Matthew called to say he loved the Chanticleer course. He also told me there were some kids waiting for me; one of Farmington's only drawbacks had been the lack of junior players.

Accustomed to working with a highly ethical management team and board, I assumed my new job included bringing these principles with me to Greenville. I had adopted the servant leadership model--with the leader on the bottom, the weakest team member gets the most encouragement and attention--which I had learned about from General John Grinalds, headmaster at Woodberry Forest. John, who had become a friend, had just been hired as president of the Citadel, so we were moving to South Carolina at the same time.

Ruth and Elizabeth drove to Greenville together. Matthew picked up Rob from a friend's house and told me later that Rob, who was leaving that close group of friends, cried for a hundred miles. I stayed behind to wrap some things up. My agreement with Farmington stipulated that I be paid in full for my inventory; after receiving a check from the club, I went to the bank to pay off a large business loan. That $8 million renovation would have disrupted my cash flow, and I had been worried about servicing the debt.

Driving to Greenville by myself gave me time to think. My health issues now included elevated cholesterol and high blood pressure. I came to Charlottesville at 190 pounds and was leaving at about 230. After we went on a retreat together, a physician friend told me he thought I had sleep apnea, but I hadn't checked it out. Back when I was caddying for Scott Verplank in those U.S. Opens, I ran six miles three times a week. In Charlottesville I'd worked out during the winter at the UVA athletic department facilities, but when we got busy at the club workouts fell by the wayside. I would have to make an effort to get into shape.

***

After I accepted the Greenville Country Club position they had invited me down early in the summer to finalize discussions and meet with the staff. During this visit the GCC manager and president asked me to retain the current personnel, for a while at least. I had agreed to this unusual request, telling myself I'd always pulled teams together--surely this would work out.

I had seen enough on my interview and this visit to start coming up with a plan. The facilities had to be addressed first. I didn't want to get too far ahead of myself, but my charge with the selection committee was clear: they wanted to go first-class. The prospect of a challenge energized and engaged me.

When I arrived in Greenville to stay, my first order of business was to call a staff meeting. Describing the concept of servant leadership, I assured them we would be a team and I was behind them. I said I liked to make as many decisions ahead of time as possible: come up with a plan and work the plan. This also makes a strategy for playing tournament golf--you don't have to think so much, just execute. We would have a staff manual that everyone would need to know. Finally, one thing was non-negotiable: everyone was expected to behave in an ethical and morally acceptable manner. "With me," I explained, "lying, stealing, cheating, or insubordination will result in immediate dismissal." If everyone knows the rules, behavior should follow. I closed the meeting by telling them to carry on as they had while I evaluated things and made recommendations.

Over the next three months, as I assessed both Chanticleer and Riverside, I made a habit of eating lunch with my employees, hoping to persuade them that I was there to help them.

In October Ruth and I attended a parents' weekend at Riverview. Upon my return, the manager at Greenville called me into the office. Members were complaining, he told me, some unhappy about my trip to Massachusetts right after starting to work. He said he knew why I was eating with my staff, but suggested having lunch in the 19th hole with the members instead.

The club had been foolish to ask me to retain everyone, and I had been a fool for agreeing to it. That dissatisfaction the manager was talking about? It was being fed to the members--by my staff.

I had my long-term plan completed by the first of November. It opened with an evaluation of current facilities and staffing, using photos to show where improvements were needed. Chanticleer didn't even have an acceptable entrance gate, and the golf shop and locker room were seriously sub-standard, with no place to store the clubs. In fact, *truly* getting to first class would require a major renovation of the Chanticleer course. Aware for ten years that the greens needed rebuilding, Greenville had hired golf course superintendent Fred Biggers, with Biggers understanding that the club was going to take care of these greens. It never happened. The greens would deteriorate and almost die during the hot summer months.

I suggested numerous changes at Riverside, too. We needed more staff at both places. The selection committee had charged me with elevating the club to first class. This document told them how we could accomplish that. I mailed out copies. At the club's annual past presidents meeting several former presidents recommended that we implement it. One board member, a CPA, said, "Bobby, you are our Moses. We need you to take us to the Promised Land." I shook my head. I was no Moses, and the membership ultimately has to pay for changes: first class comes with a price tag.

The golf staff met at my home on Thursday mornings. Shortly after the past presidents meeting, one of my Chanticleer assistants missed a staff meeting and didn't show up at the club the entire weekend. His co-worker told me the assistant had gone to an NFL football game with his wife; when he came back Tuesday and told me he had been sick, he was lying. I had already given this young man two private talks about his attitude and being professional. Asking for his keys, I tried to handle it with compassion, but word soon got back to me that the rest of the staff was on pins and needles over the termination. This group was too settled into the wrong ways.

My long-range plan would require the right staff to succeed. Chip Sullivan had worked for me at the Country Club of Jackson, I had coached Clark Sisson for several years, and Robbie Bradshaw would be entry level. Service at Chanticleer needed to be improved immediately so I put all three over there. After two problem employees resigned, all that remained of the prior staff was a trio of assistants; I believed these three wanted to be part of the team.

Everyone thought the long-range plan was brilliant--except about 50% of the membership. They had a chance to air their concerns at the annual stockholders meeting in January of 1998, five months after my arrival. Greenville was an old textile mill town whose economic fortunes had improved dramatically. Some club members had managed to prosper with the recent boom in the local economy, but among those who did not want to spend the money were retirees on fixed incomes who just couldn't afford it.

At the meeting I explained that the long-range plan was what the club had charged me to do. Once I described how the facilities had deteriorated, the membership came to understand and finally accept my recommendations. We started making changes, renovating both golf shops and making club fitting an integral part of the teaching program. I was named a *GOLF*

Magazine Top 100 teacher again, and giving a lot of lessons--the Greenville juniors were a breath of fresh air.

In Greenville I started walking every morning. This helped with the stress at the club. Vincent van Gogh said, "Great things are done by a series of small things brought together." Life, like golf, is about breaking things into manageable pieces.

Lewis Chitengwa graduated from UVA in May of 1998. We all returned to Charlottesville to witness the tradition of the graduates walking the lawn--Lewis strolling with his friends, proud and happy. After graduating he came to live with us while playing professionally; the Greenville Country Club gave him an honorary membership.

***

We were starting to have episodes of member misconduct, usually when one of my new golf staff tried to enforce a club rule. At my other clubs it was our job to diplomatically enforce the club rules. Farmington members would receive a six-month suspension for such transgressions, and if it happened again they would be expelled.

Fifteen or twenty GCC members, one a former club president, were causing all the problems. The current president called a secret meeting with the selection committee and a handful of board members to confront these guys and plead for them to respond appropriately; when only two showed it demonstrated that the problem wasn't imaginary. A suspension or two for just cause and everyone would have gotten the message. But the Greenville Country Club had started out as one of those small-town clubs where nobody wants to upset anyone. Despite its growth in size and sophistication, that mentality persisted. As I was learning, South Carolina had some social peculiarities.

In October 1998 Titleist invited fifty professionals from around the country to visit the company's old and new plants. We would be entertained for several days, play the Newport Country Club in Rhode Island, and tour Titleist's Research and Development facility.

The main reason for our presence, however, was to witness the unveiling of a new ball. The old wound golf balls were about to give way to the high-tech Titleist Pro V1--this ball that nobody knew about would revolutionize the game of golf, and we were getting a preview. With platoons of security and everyone dressed in white, the new plant looked like a scene from a science fiction movie.

Since I was in New England anyway for the Titleist event, I decided to extend my stay two days to see Elizabeth. I was in the neighborhood--when we visited Riverview, Ruth and I would fly into Providence, Rhode Island, and drive to Cape Cod. I loved that school. Every visit left me in awe of the job they were doing building up these children. When they're in classes parents have to get out of the way, so I stopped at her dorm before they all went to class.

The Atlantic Ocean wasn't far from Riverview. Giving me directions, Elizabeth told me you couldn't see it until you walked over a sand dune. The smell of the ocean is unmistakable, however. With the cool air hitting me in my face, I stared at the water without seeing it.

With the whole day to do whatever I wanted, I drove all the way out to the end of Cape Cod. It was a classic New England fall day; filtered by the salt water in the air, the light makes certain things look almost unbearably intense. Small stones kept catching my eye. Instead of the white sand we have in the south, beaches along the Atlantic coast up north have little round stones that we might call pea gravel. Most of them were shades of brown. But as I was looking at these stones, thinking about the creation of the earth and all this beauty, I saw one about as big around as a quarter and a shiny jet black. Scanning the beach, I found two more black ones.

With nothing else to do, a long way from all that nonsense at the Greenville Country Club, I had shut down my conscious mind. When I came upon what looked like the only solid white rock, I picked it up and put it in my pocket with the three black ones.

Visiting the school again after class, I took Elizabeth and some friends out for dinner. Things might have seemed tough at the Greenville Country Club, but those children at Riverview put everything into perspective. They had been dealt a tough hand.

I was down in Greenville messing around with "normal" fools who think the world revolves around them. There were at least 6 billion *other* people who couldn't give a damn about Chanticleer's greens. I headed back with a new perspective: I never would look at this (or any other) club the same way again. And I still had lots to be thankful for.

***

My son Matthew made the golf team at Furman University and played one season. College golf takes a lot of time, Furman was very challenging academically, and Matt had also pledged SAE, my fraternity. After his first year he came to me. "Dad, I can do two, but it's not possible to handle all three. I have to do the schoolwork, so that leaves golf and fraternity. My social life wasn't much at Woodberry . . . I want to go with the fraternity and give up college golf." He had clearly given it some thought.

Not long after that I got to participate in his initiation and put the SAE pin on his chest. Matthew went on to be elected vice president of his chapter--in SAE language, the Eminent Deputy Archon--and receive The True Gentleman Award, an honor reserved for an active member and voted on by the pledges.

***

Whether it was due to stress at work or my own habits, my health was suffering. A sleep study confirmed apnea, and its toll: I was getting the equivalent of two-and-a-half hours sleep a night. My weight had gone up to 245. Excess weight, high blood pressure, elevated cholesterol, and sleep apnea: these four "co-morbid conditions" made a heart attack that much more likely. My doctor in Charlottesville had been on my case, but I was too hardheaded to listen. In Greenville daily walks helped with the stress, but the weight wasn't coming off.

My mother had developed Alzheimer's. Unable to live independently on the farm, she was now in a nursing home in Columbia, Tennessee. Looking after her from South Carolina, I kept an eye on Horace Gordon and his family, too.

Horace's brother William had been murdered during the Columbia Race Riots of 1946 while Horace was locked in the jail room next door. They went to town for a haircut and got caught in this big mess. The next day my mother, thirty years old at the time, called her uncle, a Tennessee Supreme Court Justice; she asked him to go with her to get Horace out of jail. When he tried to discourage her from going, Mother cut him off. "I asked if you would go with me," she told him. "I'm going with or without you."

They got Horace home to safety, but that event affected everyone--even me, and I wasn't born for two more years. Nobody talked about it. I didn't find out until I was twelve years old.

Horace never liked to leave home after dark. He slept most of the time with a light on. He didn't like any strangers on the farm. Our family lived in the larger white house that stood closer to the road; the driveway continued to the Gordons' smaller white house. I was beginning to realize that Horace and his family felt safe--protected--when our family was home. With Mother in a nursing home, I just sensed his uneasiness. Nothing was said, but I felt it.

My mother kept everyone laughing and had a lighthearted spirit, but even while she was joking around she was scanning and surveying the situation. Sneaky smart and very perceptive, she could read character in a person better than anyone I ever knew.

I once asked her how she did it. She had to think for a minute before she said, "Watch their eyes. Look at their eyes. You can tell what's going on. If they have shifty eyes, watch 'em close. They will try to get slick on you. Also--this is important!--pay attention to how they treat the underdog. If that doesn't work, go ask the underdog."

Greenville Country Club was going to vote on a big assessment to pay for some things in the long-range plan. The most expensive remaining priority was rebuilding Chanticleer's greens. Fred Biggers--the most competent golf course superintendent I had ever known—would oversee this project. One afternoon Fred told me he was on his way to a meeting with the club manager and GCC's new president, who had been elected just the night before.

The next day I asked Fred about the meeting. "They asked for my resignation," he told me. When I called Jim Cassidy, the past president, to find out what was going on, Jim didn't have a clue--Fred's resignation had been engineered without the board's approval. It was supposed to be a forced resignation with confidentiality, but if I knew, it wasn't confidential.

I had planned to visit the PGA Merchandise Show, held every winter in Orlando. Ruth drove with me so we could talk. We were going to consult with R.C. Sproul about the situation, then head back up through Charleston to get advice from John Grinalds. Unaware of each other's guidance, both arrived at the same conclusion: the only honorable choice for me was to resign. We needed to trust in the master plan going forward. Did I have the guts to ditch this plane and then free-fall to . . . who knows where?

Back in Greenville I found out that Art Doty from Jackson, Mississippi was in town on business and wanted to have breakfast. Art had been on the Country Club of Jackson executive committee that asked for my resignation. After the pleasantries, I confessed that I'd held a grudge against him since that ordeal. I related what happened with Mahalia and my confronting the manager, and then asked if he knew any of this. The manager had claimed there were irreconcilable differences regarding my contract, Art replied. He had never heard my side of my story and he said he believed me. I told Art I was totally fed up with the golf business and planned to take a year off. He looked at me. "Consider making it two," he said.

After breakfast with Art I went to tell the new chairman of the golf committee that I could no longer serve at Greenville Country Club. A meeting was hastily arranged for 3:00 that afternoon. Five men attended. The club president asked, "Is there anything we can say to change your mind?"

"You hired a golf coach," I said; this job, I told them, was all about administration. "My suggestion is, find an administrator," I said. "I hope the plan helps you, but my decision is final."

The weight of the world lifted off my shoulders. Lord have mercy, I was happy to see Ruth. We just held each other, knowing we did the right thing. People back home were depending on us, and I finally had to admit my health needed attention. Maybe we were getting out of town just in time.

Exhausted, I told Ruth I wanted to drive around alone for a while. As I got in the car a fellow named Chuck Swindoll was concluding a radio message: "If you don't have the gift of administration, quit--let somebody else have the job. Plug into your gifts."

Word spread in Greenville, leaving people in disbelief. Gunn Murphy felt terrible. I told him to forget about it; he had done nothing wrong. The club had a small going away party and gave us a nice gift. Like that, my Greenville years were over.

I wouldn't realize it for some time, but that send-off back at Farmington had essentially marked the end of my career.

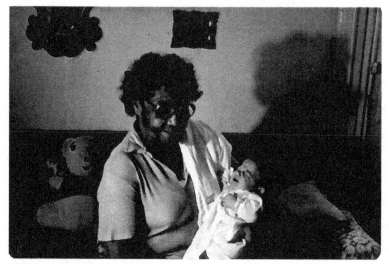

Lillian Gordon holding Matthew McIver, 1979

13

DOUBLE EAGLE

There are two ways to live: you can live as if nothing is a miracle; you can live as if everything is a miracle.

–Albert Einstein

Anything is possible. Nothing is impossible.

–Lewis Chitengwa

My maternal ancestors, the Armstrongs, were among the first wave of Scots-Irish Presbyterians to set sail for the new world, settling in Kingstree, South Carolina, in the early 1700's. At the apex of the Revolutionary War, George Washington sent General Nathanael Greene, a Rhode Island native, to take command of a southern army full of Scots-Irish troops spurred by the memory of centuries of English oppression. When these rebels engaged the Red Coats in the Carolinas, British General Cornwallis reported to Parliament: "We are fighting the bloody Scots again."

After my great-great-great-grandfather, James Armstrong, contributed to the upstarts' victory, in 1804 he joined a party of men venturing westward. Seeking land to relocate families from

Kingstree and seeing 100-foot tulip poplar trees in what is now Maury County, Tennessee, they knew the topsoil must be deep and fertile. Once Thomas Jefferson signed the 1807 treaty that opened up western territory for Europeans, they established a settlement in what is now Columbia. James Armstrong's sons each purchased part of their father's original tract. Armsdale Farm, where we live, is a 175-acre parcel that has been in my family since 1807--the only farm still inhabited by descendants of the original settlers. Our roots run really deep here.

Like our Kingstree predecessors, we were trading South Carolina for a life on this farm. Like my ancestors, we were trusting Providence going forward. I had never been in this position before: flying blind, without a job waiting. When Lewis Chitengwa asked, "What are you going to do?" I stood on one leg, spread out my arms, and said, "I don't know . . . We'll soar like eagles and figure something out." If I'd had any conception of what it would actually entail, however, I might never have followed the advice of R.C. Sproul and General Grinalds.

After we got back to Tennessee my mother started fading fast. On August 4 a call came from the nursing home: they were taking her to the emergency room. When I got there they escorted me to the waiting room. I knew what that meant.

She was dead on arrival, the doctor explained. He took me back to where her body was lying on a gurney. With Alzheimer's you grieve over a period of years as they slowly die before your eyes. Now Mother was finally at peace. She had been an icon in the community. She was beloved. She lived a good life. It was now my turn to step up.

The Gordon family's house had stood almost ninety years. When Horace's granddaughter called back in January to say that it needed repairs, Ruth and I had decided the old building wasn't worth repairing. Instead we had found some plans for a small three-bedroom house, located a trustworthy contractor, and told him to get started. The new little white house was almost finished when we got back home in June. I was able to take Mother to see it before she died, and on some level I believe she understood.

Mother had leased part of the farm acreage to a farmer. I asked him if he wanted more until I could come up with a plan. I bought some registered Belted Galloway cattle, thinking I could make a little more raising purebred livestock than with the typical cow-calf operation.

Will Brewer, head professional at the exclusive Golf Club of Tennessee, extended an offer for me to teach there. There were plenty of lessons to give; the problem was the commute. Fifty-five miles (one way), it was all back roads. It took forever.

In 2000 the First Tee Program was just getting started in Nashville under the auspices of the Tennessee Golf House. A converted mansion, The Golf House contained the offices of the Golf Course Superintendents of America, Tennessee Junior Golf, First Tee, and The Tennessee PGA. It was Dick Horton, now executive director of the TPGA, who had asked me to accompany Harvey Penick in 1973. The Tennessee Golf House property was maintained by the adjoining Vanderbilt Legends Club, which featured a 36-hole course, a fifteen-acre driving range, a small 9-hole par 3 around the facility, and a huge putting green with a bunker.

The Legends Club leased a large building on their practice area to the Golf Academy, a school run by two well-regarded female professionals. To make it clear that we had no designs on the Golf Academy's adult clientele, the Golf House had an oral agreement with the Legends, allowing us to promote *junior* golf as much as we wanted. We could teach the adults but they had to be walk-ups, so to speak. Players were lining up for lessons. Before long people were driving 150 miles from Chattanooga. But the Golf House wanted to keep lesson fees low; even with a good group of players, I couldn't make a living there.

My first wave of players included some sons of my original Belle Meade group: Matthew King, John Rowland Burch, Jimmy Ward. Bringing them for their lessons one day, John Rowland's grandfather came over beaming. "Who would have ever thought you would be back and teaching these boys?" he said. "History is repeating itself!"

***

Lewis Chitengwa made it to the finals of the PGA Tour qualifier in the fall of 1999. He didn't get his tour card, but he did make it onto the smaller Nike tour, which offered some good prize money and a regular schedule. In 2000 Lewis again reached the finals of the qualifying but played poorly. I had been on him for years to work with a physical trainer; he was so thin he looked like a distance runner, and he needed a flexibility program. Back in Charlottesville I'd found him a very competent trainer to work with at UVA, but he had resisted it. I used to tell Ruth that Lewis had her fooled into thinking he was easy-going when he was really hardheaded and stubborn. We all got a good laugh.

One summer day in 2000 Lewis called, asking for directions to our house. I gave them to him, wondering how he could forget. About three hours later he called again. "I just passed a sign saying I am 60 miles from Memphis," he said.

"How in the world did you get on the wrong interstate? You're a hundred miles from where you are supposed to be!" Incredulous, I had just finished giving him the directions again when he walked in, still talking to me on his cell phone.

"I got you!" he laughed. Lewis was always joking around like that. Enchanted by his playful, loving spirit, people overlooked the recalcitrant streak he occasionally revealed.

A few months later, on a cold afternoon in November, Lewis approached me to discuss his future. After the 2000 PGA Tour School and his second failure to qualify, Lewis's father had finally given his blessing for Lewis to ask me to be his coach. We sat on a bench and talked for at least an hour, until sundown.

I knew how to coach Lewis. I had been waiting for seven years. "First," I said, "you need to pay attention to what the guys are doing that you intend to beat. These guys are lifting weights. They have trainers--look at Tiger."

He was listening—maybe even hearing me, finally. Lewis's Nike Tour stats told me that he wasn't playing the par 5's well, and distance control with the wedges was the problem. "Lewis, you don't need anyone to teach you how to play, just someone to supervise your practices. Everyone gets sloppy when they practice. You think your short game is sharp if you're getting the third ball close, but when you compete you have to get the *first* one close."

Lewis nodded. "My dad told me to tell you to kick my butt and get me going."

"One more thing," I said. "Do you remember me telling you to stay away from that guru in Orlando?" Lewis nodded. "If you want to keep it natural, Orlando is the last place you need to go. You have my business card--if anyone approaches you, about

this or any other thing, tell them I am your manager and everything goes through me."

Lewis was such a gentle soul that people fell in love with him
immediately. I had seen what a hard time he had saying no to
people. Agents, endorsements, hangers-on--none of that had
happened yet, but when it did it would happen quickly. Good
looks, an irresistible and genuine personality, and an imagina-
tive, powerful game: Lewis Chitengwa would be highly market-
able. He needed a buffer to protect him.

We came up with the name Double Eagle Golf Group. My
main goal at the beginning was to protect Lewis from the
agents. When there is money to be made, they show up like buz-
zards, and the most ethical of the bunch can't be trusted. Lewis
didn't need an agent at that time, but we were laying the
groundwork. I wanted to surround him with a team of honorable men. They would be paid for their time and service--no
agent taking 20% off the top.

**

Everyone was home for Christmas in 2000. Previously Lewis's routine had been to go back to Zimbabwe, but this year he
spent the holiday with us. Finding small boxes for those shiny
stones I had picked up on the beach in Cape Cod, I put a card in
each box, with a note: "Keep this small stone in your pocket.
When things get rough just rub it knowing I love you." I gave
my kids the shiny black ones. Lewis was visibly touched to receive the smooth white one. After seven-plus years now, he was
one of us, and we loved him like he was our own.

I had gotten the idea of developing a learning center on the
farm. Seeking a business consultant to help sort through the
pros and cons of such a project, I heard from Wally Armstrong

and several others that Mark Arnold was very good. Ruth and I were soon making trips to his office at Charter Resource Group in Nashville to brainstorm ideas with Mark and his partner, Price Carney. Andy Banfield, a senior golf course designer with Tom Fazio's firm, came out to the farm and proposed a lake and a 350-yard fairway on the same exact site I'd envisioned.

It was not until we got to talking price--into the $400,000 range--that I stopped and reconsidered. My health had not improved. I still weighed 240 pounds with those other co-morbid conditions. We would need a loan to build a facility that wouldn't add a dollar of value to the farm, and if I dropped dead Ruth would be left with the debt. It made no sense now.

With their kindness and integrity, Mark Arnold and Price Carney provided an invaluable foundation for the team I was assembling to serve Lewis. Lewis needed a roommate and a social life. Mark and Price found the perfect match in Jason Corley, who took Lewis in and became his best friend in Nashville. Jason knew a good trainer for Lewis and helped get that going, too. Lewis started seeing a difference, and it would only get better.

PGA Tour qualifying poses a harsh test: if you are just a tad off, you will not advance. Lewis failed to get any kind of PGA card for 2001, but he did qualify for the Canadian Tour.

David Abell, a teammate of Matt King's at Wake Forest, was Nick Price's executive director. Since Nick was from Zimbabwe, I thought he might get Lewis into some PGA Tour events on a sponsor's exemption. When David succeeded in getting Lewis an exemption into the 1999 Memphis Open, I sent the Memphis Open officials a listing of his credentials, knowing this would get to the press. When Lewis appeared on television the broadcaster was clearly relying on the information in my packet as he recited Lewis's accomplishments. He mentioned Lewis's close relationship with Nick Price, who was also interviewed. Price said he hoped Lewis would eventually take his place representing Zimbabwe on the Tour.

***

I attended the grand opening of The First Tee. The Tennessee Golf Association then sent me to an annual meeting in Florida and later to a national camp at Kansas State University. This was all fun; it just didn't generate enough money.

The other four First Tee teachers were all counselors in the school system. They knew a little golf, but I was the only experienced golf instructor. Groups like the Police Athletic League sponsored the kids at The First Tee. John Drake, a former pro football player, led the PAL group. They were from needy homes, but well-behaved and fun to coach. In the clubhouse I would ask the kids if they wanted to be winners. Guess what? They all wanted to be winners. I started off by having them sit up and pay attention; when they slouched I'd lie down on the floor to get their attention. Then we'd practice walking like a champion to the tee--anything I could think of to build up their self-esteem.

Other groups came in for a couple of weeks at a time. One group of teenaged boys came from a home for physically abused children. Removed from their families by court order, they were wards of the state. They told us these kids had been beaten so badly that we needed to stand at least ten feet away.

I took that as a challenge: when I taught I knelt, making sure I was below them--a non-threatening position. I would talk softly to them and compliment a good shot. Each day I moved a little closer. On the third day we were on the putting green. When one of the boys holed a putt, I put my hand out--didn't make a big deal about a high five, just put my hand out--and this young man reached and touched me. As I kept praising them they were all slapping my hand. I merely observed them and acted on instinct. The man from their home witnessed all of this. On the fourth day, I came out of my kneeling position: they had gotten used to me and I had gotten inside the so-called bubble.

The fifth day was their last. When we wrapped it up, I held out my arms to one boy who was responding well. He came over and got a hug. I looked at their driver and winked.

"Don't let anybody get within ten feet." Says who? On auto-pilot the whole time, I just paid attention to their eyes. By the end of the week they were coming over to give me a hug. I had never before (to my knowledge) coached any kids who had been beaten. Although I know it is far more serious than this, on some level they just needed a little love and understanding.

John Drake had his PAL kids there, too. Noticing what I was doing, he watched closely. When the kids from the home for abused children left, I told John I thought I'd gotten inside that barrier by making myself familiar. "No," John said. "You cared. They felt your compassion."

***

"Did you know Lewis went to see him?" Mark Arnold asked me. It was April of 2001. I gave him a puzzled look. When he named the "professor" in Orlando--the guru Lewis promised me he would stay away from--I didn't say a word. Mark had no idea how strongly I felt about this because I had never mentioned it to him.

There was no misunderstanding. When Lewis first related his father's instruction to keep it natural, I said this was wise advice. I had told him to stay clear of this guy two weeks after he arrived in 1993, and again after he asked me to coach him in November, 2000. He knew.

I wondered who had put Lewis up to it. Whoever it was, somebody had pressured him into it--somebody with influence, authority, someone he couldn't refuse.

Lewis had never disobeyed me or kept secrets. I always gave him his space. I never stood over him when he practiced, and we stayed in touch by talking once a week. Feeling hurt and shut out, I decided that the way to handle this was to wait and let him get in touch with me.

A month went by. Jason Corley told me Lewis didn't know what to do. When he informed Lewis "Bobby knows where you went," Jason said Lewis had responded as if this was very bad news. He had seen me get angry before, but never at him.

The 2001 U.S. Open was being played at Southern Hills in Tulsa. Lewis had planned to qualify for it in Memphis. The Saturday before the qualifying he called Ruth and asked if he could come for lunch. I was in the pasture, digging holes for fence posts, when Ruth came out to tell me Lewis had arrived. I kept on working. She came outside again. Ruth knew that I hadn't seen or talked to Lewis in two months. Wanting to make him grow up a little and learn how to tell someone no, I kept working on the fence.

I heard the door open a third time. "Come on, Bobby," Ruth said gently, "Lewis has come to see us. Swallow your pride and come to lunch."

Entering the kitchen, I joined a mood of carrying on like nothing happened. We laughed and cut up for over an hour.

"How's your game?" I asked. Lewis said he wasn't pitching the ball well. Before walking him to his car I put four clubs down about five yards apart, dropped four of his balls, and said, "Look at a club and just swing and drop your ball on top of it. No thinking. Just trust your eyes." This was all he needed. We agreed that if he made the U.S. Open I would caddie for him.

Joking, Lewis asked me if I could handle his bag.

"Are you kidding me?" I laughed.

I gave him a hug, and off he went. Claude Harmon used to say, "In life, business, and golf, ego and ignorance make a lethal combination." That was the last time I saw Lewis Chitengwa.

The qualifying was on Tuesday and Jason was carrying the bag. The U.S. Open is a 36-hole deal; Lewis played well but missed by two. He already planned to leave on Wednesday--if not for Tulsa then for western Canada and an event in British Columbia, where he would play for four weeks. Jason called after the qualifying. "Lewis said to tell you he holed out two pitch shots, and your lesson helped." Lewis flew to Vancouver filled with fresh optimism.

***

On June 30, 2001, after saying good-by to a junior player who had come from Greenville for a lesson, we discovered that Jason Corley had just left a message. His voice sounded odd on the answering machine, and worse when I reached him. "I don't know how to tell you this, but . . . " Jason struggled to get the next part out. "Lewis passed away today."

Then he composed himself to convey what he knew. He had gotten a call from a hospital up in Canada. It was some kind of infection. But there had been no warning of anything wrong. Speechless, unable to make any kind of sense out of it, I heard Jason saying the doctors would be calling me.

Ruth, Rob, and Elizabeth totally broke down. Matthew was still away at Furman. I just locked up. Maybe it was a defense mechanism. I thought I needed to be strong for the kids. Rob was screaming and crying, losing it, so I tried to console him. You can only think about one thing at a time, even in a situation like this.

The first doctor gave us the diagnosis, a deadly form of meningitis called meningococcemia. Lewis had woken up that morning feeling terrible and called 911. The ER doctor told him he had the flu and sent him home, where he got progressively worse. By the time some friends went over to be with him, he was so weak he fell to the kitchen floor. Lewis told his friends he was hurting like he was on fire all over, but he couldn't feel his hands and feet; his body was fighting the ravages of this deadly infection by sending all of his blood to his vital organs. He died of cardiac arrest within fifteen minutes of arriving at the hospital.

The doctors who attended to him described Lewis as "calm, peaceful, and brave." They didn't know one thousandth of it, but they were compassionate.

The second doctor had been in the gallery at the Vancouver Open and followed Lewis the entire second round, where he had shot a 67 to put himself in second place. Seeing Lewis enter the hospital on a gurney, the doctor recognized him from the tournament. "Mr. Chitengwa," he had asked, "how are you?"

Lewis responded, "I'm fine, and I hope you are."

These were his last words. Hearing them brought tears to my eyes, finally.

The doctors asked about notifying the family. I told them I needed to be the one who made that call.

It was the middle of the night in Zimbabwe. When Lewis's father answered, I heard his mother already wailing in grief. A friend of Lewis's from Zimbabwe had seen the news on Golf Channel and the family got his call a few minutes before mine. Lewis, Sr. kept asking what happened. I explained the best I could, saying that it was an aggressive infection. The autopsy had not been completed, so I didn't know the cause of death definitively. We were all in shock. The Chitengwa family's pain, traveling over the telephone lines, erased the distance between Harare and middle Tennessee. I wished I could be there with them.

The next day, Sunday, Dick Harmon and John Drake both called. On Monday, July 2, the Nashville Tennessean ran a feature article about Lewis Chitengwa that filled the first page of the sports section, and we began the process of arranging for his body to be returned to Zimbabwe, and his family.

Josephine Chitengwa and Ruth McIver, Christmas 2001

{ 14 }

WITHOUT A COURSE

What saves a man is to take a step.
Then take another step.

–C.S. Lewis

July 4th was Daddy Will's birthday. Up until he died, in 1961, it had always meant a big party at the Gordon house. When we returned to Tennessee in June, 1999 I sent out word that we were reinstating the celebration. Over a hundred people came from Chicago, North Carolina, and all over. I invited our Zion Presbyterian pastor and his wife, and the contractor who built the little white house and his wife. Willie Earl Webster and his extended family attended. The rest were Gordon family members, including all six of Horace's living brothers and sisters. A big rented tent, a fish fry, kids running around having fun: I was back HOME!

The 1999 gathering was the first time many of the Gordons got to know me as an adult. Most of them hadn't seen me in forty years. The youngest of Horace's siblings, Buddy Gordon, had become a major in the U.S. Army. He had joined the Army after graduating from Tuskegee Institute. My mother had loaned Horace the money to pay for Buddy's tuition. Horace paid her back when he could, and Buddy paid back Horace. That weekend I told Buddy that Daddy Will's death when I was thirteen had been the saddest day of my life.

Buddy was a nickname--his real name was Lewis Gordon. His gaze disconnected, he stared off into space. "I never thought about it," he said, "but when Mr. Horace died it was the same with me." Mr. Horace was Horace Armstrong, my grandfather. Buddy continued, "He used to take me with him to Nashville when I was nine or ten years old . . . I remember what I wore to the funeral."

Buddy looked at me, focused. "You remind me of your grandfather," he said. Horace Armstrong died in 1942, six years before I was born. Born in 1855, he was an old man even to Daddy Will and Mama Grace. All of the Gordons called him Mr. Horace, and I heard more stories about him from them than my mother. These tales tended to reinforce one dominant theme: my grandfather hated racism with a passion.

"Was it really as bad as in the movies, like 'Mississippi Burning'?" I asked.

"Your grandfather had a Model T Ford," Buddy said, "the first one out our way in the early days. A black man who wasn't a Gordon used to work on it. One day after tuning up the car he asked Daddy (Daddy Will) if he could ride it up to Stephenson's Store, about a mile away, to get some candy. Daddy said it would be okay." Buddy said that when this man got to Stephenson's, the men who hung out there--my mother always called them "po' white trash"--demanded, "Where'd you steal that car, nigger? We know where you live and we'll get you tonight." Back then this was lynching talk.

That night, Buddy said, "two cars came driving down the lane near our house. Daddy Will had given everybody a gun who was strong enough to hold it--they had a surprise waiting on them if they climbed our fence. About fifteen minutes passed, then they left."

Buddy stopped, as if the story had concluded.

"Come on, Buddy," I said, "I know that's not the end of it."

He laughed. "Daddy went up to your house about 6:30 the next morning and told your grandfather," he said. "We heard the car crank up . . . And that's all I know. Daddy told us 'Mr. Horace will know how to handle it.'"

Several weeks later I went to visit George Martin Armstrong. A cousin in his 90's and the oldest remaining family member, he had all the oral history down. When I asked him if he knew about this incident, he chuckled.

"They told me your grandfather went up there with his walking cane," he began. "He circled the place several times, staring everybody in the eye. Nobody dared mess with your grandfather. He was six foot four and he could be intimidating when he was upset. Well, he was seriously upset this morning.

"After he made eye contact with the eight or ten lowlifes present, he *slammed* his cane down on Stephenson's counter with him standing there. They say it sounded like a gun going off-- ol' Stephenson like to have jumped out of his skin. Waving that cane in his face, your grandfather says, 'I don't know if you were in on it, but you know who was. All I'm going to say is don't make me have to come back up here. If I have to come back, nobody is going to like what I'll be bringing with me.'"

George Martin laughed at the old memory. "Nobody messed with the Gordons. Horace Armstrong was a friend to everyone, but nobody wanted to cross him . . . No one knew what he intended on bringing--but whatever it was, they didn't want to see it."

***

After skipping 2000, I had sent out the word that we would pick the July 4th party tradition back up in 2001. This one, I emphasized, was for Horace--we all owed Horace and we needed to give him his flowers when he was still alive. Since Horace never liked big crowds, I'd planned with his family to hold the numbers down, but even so around fifty Gordon relatives gathered between the two houses for the big celebration. They could tell Lewis's death only four days earlier had really shocked me. They knew our hearts were broken.

Seeing the compassion in the faces of the family I loved, I urged myself to reach down and grab something when the time came to speak. "Horace," I started, "I know you didn't think I was paying attention . . . but I saw how you took care of your mother and daddy. Horace, I know you didn't think I was paying attention, but I saw you wait till last to get a drink of water in the field. Horace, I know you didn't think I was paying attention . . ."

I had no sermon in mind, but something was spewing like an oil well gusher out of my wounded heart. I just kept going until I was finished. "Horace," I said finally, "You are a man's man and I love you. Everybody here loves you." Nobody said a word. Horace wiped the tears with his napkin. It was the first time I ever saw him cry.

***

We thought Horace didn't have much time left, but Douglas, Wallace, Anne, and Buddy Gordon all died prior to Horace's death in February 2010. Mary Frances died early in 2011.

As long as Horace Gordon was alive he was the man on this farm. I moved where we fed the cows hay in the winter to a spot where Horace, now in the late stages of Alzheimer's and bedridden, could see them from his bedroom. He hadn't spoken in several months when his daughter, Mary Elizabeth, reported, "Daddy said 'cows need hay.'" His farmer spirit was still watching. After he died I told Mary Elizabeth that it was our turn to make it work--the baton had been passed. Our relatives who came before are dead and gone, but their spirits are with us every day. Whenever I'm stumped on the farm, I stop and ask: what would Horace do? His life proves you don't have to be rich or famous to make a difference.

Rock-solid partners for close to fifty years, Horace and my mother could communicate without talking. Mother handled the business details of the farm and Horace worked the land. When I was small, I rode in Horace's lap while he drove the tractor; when I got older, I sat on a toolbox built into the tractor's fender. I always wanted to be with him. He exuded calm and humility. Though known as one of the best farmers in the county, Horace Gordon showed no trace of pride or an ego. He wore work clothes and grease outlined his fingernails.

My dad dressed impeccably. He wore suits, a tie, and a starched white shirt to work as an accountant. I never once saw dirt or grease under his fingernails. But my father and Horace Gordon were alike in many ways: quiet, gentle men with the highest ethical values who always put others ahead of themselves. One just wore work clothes and the other a suit.

My father always maintained a certain distance, not just from me but from all of us. Horace wasn't letting anyone get too close, either--they both had a lot they weren't talking about. But you could depend on them. I feel like God gave me two fathers.

My own race-blindness had to come, at least partly, from my father. As a child, I saw him hold the door for a black lady and address her as "ma'am" in the Columbia, TN, of the 1950's. This came naturally to him. He displayed respect and compassion for every soul who crossed his path. The repulsion I feel when confronted by racism is the result of everyone in my two families showing by example how much better the world could be, if only we could heal the gulf between our races.

Growing up, I spent more time around Horace than my father. This wasn't a decision I made, just the way it was. Horace could perform the most sophisticated and strenuous manual labor and make it look easy. When my friends and I worked on the farm as teens we were in top shape, but none of us could come close to keeping up with Horace cutting tobacco. First you drive a tobacco stick in the ground and put a steel spear at the top, and then you chop six-foot plants and "spear" them onto the stick--all in August when it's 100 degrees in the shade. From so many years of doing this, Horace's stroke and movements involved no wasted motion. He was utterly efficient. In this regard, Horace Gordon was an artist.

***

A citizen of Zimbabwe, Lewis Chitengwa had been living in the United States with a green card; he died while traveling in Canada with a visa. It took about a week to disentangle the knot of red tape involved in getting his body released. At first we considered making the trip to Zimbabwe, then we realized there needed to be a service for Lewis here since he had so many friends. We planned one for his church outside Nashville and another for our old church, Trinity Presbyterian, in Charlottesville. Wally Armstrong would speak at both services, which we would videotape to send to Lewis's family.

Mark Arnold organized the Tennessee service, held in Franklin at Christ Community Church. Because of the constant chatter of our houseguests, I told Ruth early that morning that I would see her at the church later and left for the quiet of Maury County Park. At 6 a.m., from a spot where I could see in every direction, I prayed, "Lord, you tell me what to say and I'll say it," and then just handed it over.

The church was thronged with people I didn't know: white, black, all grieving for Lewis. I could see the Lord in their faces. I felt His presence as He gave me the words to say, about how an eagle has a premonition when it's going to die. "It will fly to the top of a rocky crevice and stare directly into the sun," I said. "Those two doctors in Canada got to see an eagle die--a man looking into the SON." Addressing the camera that was filming the service for Lewis's family in Zimbabwe, I spelled it out: "S-O-N."

The next day I returned to work at First Tee. On the drive up there I heard my cell phone chime. Picking it up I saw a text message: "The joy is in the pain." I almost had to pull off the road. I never wear sunglasses, but that day I knew I needed them. I was wearing these wrap-around sunglasses like David Duval's. It was very hot and humid. With everyone sweating so profusely, my tears went unnoticed (or unacknowledged) amid the perspiration. I tried to contain my emotions, but every black kid I looked at--even just a fraction of a second--I saw Lewis.

Usually I gave a motivational wrap-up in the classroom after the session. That day, telling them I couldn't do it, I went around to a private space behind the classroom. John Drake came to be by my side. "I know you had a lot of yourself invested in Lewis," he said. "I'm so sorry."

I broke down and John embraced me with compassion. I collected myself by the time the wrap-up session ended. There was a boy about eight years old in John's group from PAL. His father was dead and he had taken to me. Without knowing anything about Lewis, he came looking for me that day. He hugged me around the waist and looked up, smiling. *The Lord has work for me to do,* I thought right then. *I have to keep going.*

***

Like the Nashville service, the memorial in Charlottesville the next week was packed. I had stood with Lewis when he was baptized in that church where he made so many friends. It seemed like the entire UVA athletic department attended: the athletic director, coaches, trainers, secretaries, and players from many teams showed up to pay their respects. Lewis's teammates sent messages from all over the world. Mike Moraghan, who organized the Charlottesville service, had also gone to Harare for the funeral; Mike said the outpouring of love there was beyond his ability to describe it.

UVA gives the Dixon Brooke Award to the golfer who best demonstrates leadership, cooperative spirit and unselfish service. Lewis had barely processed the news that he was receiving this honor when The Board of Visitors (Thomas Jefferson's term for board of trustees) invited him to a black-tie function.

There, in the boardroom in the Rotunda, The Board asked Lewis to speak on the spot.

At the memorial service, Mike Moraghan recalled Lewis's extemporaneous remarks.

So proud to be a University of Virginia student, Lewis had declared that just walking across campus made him feel blessed. He told the Board that he treasured the relationships with his fellow students and faculty members. Not once did he mention golf.

The talk was his heart speaking. Lewis never lost the awe that he had the opportunity. He knew that he was chosen in some supernatural way. When he concluded his remarks the Board of Visitors gave him a standing ovation, many with tears in their eyes. Mike Moraghan informed Lewis that French general Lafayette once spoke in that room. Winston Churchill, Margaret Thatcher, Ronald Reagan, John F. Kennedy; an endless list of statesmen had visited Mr. Jefferson's university. "But Lewis," Mike had told him, "none of them affected a crowd of people like you just did."

Back home we received tapes of the casket being removed from the airplane at night with Lewis's family and friends present. This surreal scene triggered memories of President Kennedy's body being returned to Washington after his assassination. When films of Lewis's funeral service and the burial first arrived, I couldn't bring myself to play them. One night I finally got out of bed in the middle of the night to watch alone.

There was an open casket during the service. Ruth found me on my hands and knees, still unable to believe my eyes.

Lewis would have been the role model of role models. On numerous occasions I saw how the children whose grade-school classes he spoke to swarmed around him--they didn't even want to return to recess, let alone class.

I had shut him out over a trip to Orlando.

Eventually we had to gather up Lewis's personal belongings to send to Zimbabwe. Some things were passed around to friends as personal reminders. After he graduated from UVA, I had helped Lewis shop for a car, a burgundy used Honda that he'd kept spotless. Now we planned to sell it and send the money to his parents. Ruth dropped me off at his apartment to drive the car home. I unlocked the driver's side door and got in.

There on the dashboard I saw that shiny white rock I had given him for Christmas.

Our hands have body oil--it's why we clean our grips. When I picked up that white stone and held it in my palm, I could see the body oil: Lewis had been rubbing it.

My note had said, "When times get tough, rub this stone knowing I love you." I slumped out of the car and fell onto the asphalt. "God," I pleaded, "if I hurt him, strike me dead. If pulling back caused him any pain, Lord, just take me right here."

***

Things were going so well with The First Tee and the Golf House that the two ladies who ran the Golf Academy pulled out a contract saying they had exclusive rights to instruction. The Legends Club champion approached me for a couple of lessons that he said had turned his game around. Then he declared loudly in the Grill Room, "If you want a real golf lesson, you need to go to the other end of the range." One of the lady pros overheard this and decided that I was taking money out of their pockets.

Yes, I was scrapping and hustling (so as to make 20% of my previous income), but I'd never promoted lessons to adults. Players were just finding me. Most adults I taught didn't have anything to do with Legends. My employers knew this. But thirty days after Lewis's death I was called in and notified I couldn't teach at the Golf House anymore. Grieving, angry, and suddenly unable to provide, I began to feel like I was dying inside.

A driving range opened in Bellevue, a 120-mile round trip from my home. I paid them a visit and asked if they could use me; given my decent following I was allowed to teach.

With range instruction fees set low and a third of what I took in going back to the owners, I couldn't make it long-term this way, but at least I didn't have to abandon my players.

That year I trained five novices for state competition-- without a golf course. The Tennessee State Amateur in Memphis drew players who had qualified from all over the state, in addition to college players, and the five I was training had never contended at that level. But I believed they could handle it. I convinced them that the time was now, and they were ready.

I had to coach differently at Bellevue. At a private club, you are in constant contact with your players. Now, working at a range in a twenty-five acre field, I had to paint the shot in my imagination, describe it to them, and ask them to hit it. "Imagination is more powerful than knowledge," I told them. "The subconscious can't tell the difference between what is real and what is vividly imagined." I asked each player course-management questions such as "What will you do if the pin is back right, with your natural fade?" and got each one to develop a "bread-and-butter" shot: when you have to keep it in play, what shot do you have?

At the time a hotshot teacher in Memphis was getting a lot of attention, but at the tournament my players whipped his guys soundly. Scott Haile and Eric Lee finished 5th and 6th. Charlie Gibson and Graham Worsham tied for 16th, better than they'd ever done before. Dan Crockett, a tournament novice, ended up a few shots behind them.

I had never had so many play so well in a state championship --with all the mental prep work on a driving range! No one probably noticed except my players; but this was a great accomplishment for them--and a much-needed boost for me.

***

We talked about spending Christmas and New Year's in Zimbabwe, but Ruth wondered how we were going to afford it. "If we don't go now, we never will," I said. "Forget the money. It all belongs to God, and He promised to see us through."

On our way to visit Lewis's family we all crammed into a direct flight from Atlanta to Johannesburg. There we had a five-hour wait. It was the middle of the night when we finally walked into the terminal in Harare.

We looked up to see Lewis's family on the next level, jumping up and down, waving. I hadn't realized how much our visit meant to them. Lewis's brothers and sisters had been anticipating our trip for months. When we met you would have thought we had known each other forever. Lewis's mother Josephine hugged Ruth, tears streaming down both their faces. Lewis, Sr. and I shook hands, looked each other in the eye, and embraced. A bond had already been forged, but this sealed it.

We were staying with Tom and Janet Hall, whose son Ryan was Lewis's best friend and played on the UVA golf team with him. Tom Hall had designed their lovely house. From one side you could see for miles: Zimbabwe has a riveting beauty that makes you just stare. Its landscape and vegetation--neither desert nor lush green but something in-between and otherworldly--did not resemble anything I had seen before. It felt like another planet.

The next day we drove out to the Wingate Park Golf Club, to see what we had been hearing about for so long. The Chitengwas had lived on the course property ever since the club closed the swimming pool, and the humble building that had served as the pool house became their home. Walking into their living room Ruth and I saw pictures of our family on every wall. That first night they had a party at the club in our honor. Asked to speak, I described how we treasured and cherished Lewis as one of our family. Filled with love and sadness, I could feel Lewis watching over us all.

I spent several days with Lewis, Sr. while he gave lessons. He taught mainly in his native Shona language, but as a fellow golf professional I knew what he was saying: we spoke the same language when it came to golf. The guy was simply a brilliant teacher.

Christmas morning the Chitengwa family gave us seats of honor, serving breakfast in the living room, as if we were royalty. They wanted us to feel special, and we were deeply touched by their kindness. Like Lewis, his siblings were polite and comfortable in social situations, in addition to being strong competitive golfers. Rob had picked out a gift for Farai, a year-and-a-half younger than Rob. Lewis's older brother Elias shared his good looks; he was trying to make it running a bar. Helga and Rhoda, the two sisters, were stunningly beautiful. On the wall hung the UVA diploma that Lewis worked so hard to attain, and tables in every corner were stacked with trophies. I felt Lewis's spirit. I could see the trademark smile that had endeared Lewis to strangers on the five continents, wherever golf took him.

Later we went to church. The Dutch Reformed congregation was primarily white. Segregated Zimbabwe reminded me of stories about the early 1900's in the United States. The Shona people just seemed to go with the flow; I could see poverty and people living on the fringes, but little or no violence. Lewis never understood the resentment blacks in the United States felt toward our country. He used to say, "If they want to see prejudice, let me take them to Zimbabwe." Lewis's father had achieved something really exceptional in conquering this racial division to become a respected golf professional. Still, his family had very little in material possessions. In the big picture, perhaps, none of that stuff matters, but I could see how in the United States we took so much for granted.

The day after Christmas all of us, including the Halls, made the long drive to the cemetery. The women in Lewis's family wore black dresses and hats. The Chitengwas had tried to find Lewis a plot closer by, but so many people were dying from AIDS that nothing was available, so Lewis had been put to rest in a public cemetery. Somehow this seemed fitting: when he played, he had carried the hopes and dreams of so many who never got a chance.

We parked and approached the grave. It was a beautiful day, and I couldn't believe the number of fresh graves we passed. Lewis, Sr. led us to his son's new black headstone.

For whatever reason seeing that headstone, shining in the sun, made it all real.

We stood in a circle, taking it in silently. I had brought a bag--twenty-five or thirty pounds--of pea gravel from the United States. I wanted to scatter these tiny stones around the grave to symbolize how many people in our country loved Lewis. When I asked Lewis, Sr. for permission, he gestured to go ahead. "Of course, please." After placing pebbles around the tombstone, I put my hand on its smooth hot black surface and closed my eyes. For some time we stood without speaking. Then Lewis, Sr. asked me to pray.

I had everyone hold hands. My words--about how we knew the body was beneath the ground, but Lewis's soul was in heaven and we would all one day be reunited--are a blur now. Lewis, Sr. filled a bucket with water. Then, very reverently, he sprinkled water with his hand over the grass that had been planted around the grave.

Just before we left, Matthew, Rob, and Elizabeth fell on that grass, touching the tombstone and weeping. We all needed to see Lewis's grave, and place our hands on the reality of that headstone.

Our two weeks passed in an eye-blink. In memory they linger as a sequence of images: a pride of lions glimpsed on a safari arranged by the Halls, statues carved by Shona artisans, Victoria Falls, beauty beyond description.

Lewis's family accompanied us to the airport when the time to leave arrived.

The Chitengwas had looked with such anticipation to Lewis's future. His death still made no sense to me. During times like this we have to just wait on the Lord to see us through. Our days might be filled with dark clouds, but above them we knew the sun is still shining. His hands were on all of us during this time.

What courage Lewis had shown in leaving so young, not knowing what lay ahead. I was grateful he didn't lose his nerve and turn around, glad he stayed on the course that brought him to us. Lewis changed us all forever.

I headed back to Tennessee a long way from healed. I doubted I would ever be the same, but maybe we aren't supposed to be the same again.

When we got back we learned that my Labrador retriever, Babe, had died just four hours before our return. I didn't know that the veterinarian had recommended putting her down sooner, but Ruth had broken into tears in the vet's office, saying, "I don't know if Bobby can handle it--you may have to put him down, too."

Babe hung on. She just couldn't last until we got home.

{ 15 }

ON THE BUBBLE

Courage is resistance to fear, mastery of fear,
not absence of fear.

–Mark Twain

Mark Arnold had referred most of my Bellevue players, and when one of his associates was considering buying a golf course, he brought me in. A Michigan developer had started construction in Spring Hill, near the Saturn GM plant, about fifteen miles from me. With $3 million sunk into the project, the original developer had gone bankrupt. The lender had foreclosed and was putting it up for auction.

Initially Mark's associate hired me as a consultant, to do a feasibility study and assess how much it was worth. Within about a month I handed him a forty-page document detailing my findings. The demographics looked promising; the vital area within fifteen minutes of the course was rapidly becoming densely populated. The course had been carved out and nine holes were almost completed. My study concluded that if he could buy it for $1 million or less it could work. When my employer was the only bidder who showed up, it became a regular buyer-seller real estate deal, and he got it for half the price I had targeted.

In 2002 he offered me the job as head professional. Opening as nine holes, the course would be eighteen holes in several years. My salary as head pro of the nine-hole course was supposed to increase by a third when we expanded to eighteen holes. This was a handshake deal. I slugged it out to open that course, an Arnold Palmer design that I felt had potential. But finishing a new course is just the beginning--you still have to market the facility effectively. I came up with the name King's Creek and designed the logo myself. Working out of a doublewide trailer, we didn't even have a paved parking lot.

At King's Creek I was earning less than half my Greenville Country Club salary. I had always been able to provide, allowing Ruth to shine as a housewife and homemaker, whatever those terms mean. When I couldn't make the handsome incomes I once did, Ruth went back to work, first at a hospital, then doing travel nursing.

In December 2003 Ruth was working on Long Island. She wouldn't be home until the day after Christmas, so I got up and made Christmas breakfast for everyone. After experimenting with a rich dessert for our (December 26) family Christmas, I went to bed and didn't feel like getting up. I wasn't in distress, exactly--just constantly thirsty and going to the bathroom incessantly, feeling this light pain in my chest. When Ruth called, Matthew described what was going on and handed the phone to me. She told me to go to the emergency room. "I know indigestion when I feel it," I responded, "and this is nothing more."

She asked to speak to Matthew again. He was now a senior in college and a big strong young man. "You have two choices," he informed me. "You can cooperate and *let* me take you to the hospital, or you can be stubborn and I'm going to bust you over the head with an iron skillet. Either way, you're going to the emergency room."

The emergency room on Christmas Day is the pits. They checked my heart and drew blood. I lay there for forty-five minutes before the doctor came back with a verdict: "Mr. McIver," he said, "your heart is fine. You have Type II Diabetes." Ruth had already surmised as much--to a nurse, excessive thirst and urination were sure signs.

When I see pictures from Zimbabwe now, I realize that I was in denial. My weight had climbed over 250 pounds. High blood pressure, sleep apnea, elevated triglycerides, and now diabetes: it all added up to a heart attack waiting to happen. Not if, but *when.* For the first time I actually wondered how much longer I could survive.

Only 55 years old, I was on the ropes and knew it. Muhammed Ali used to rest against the ropes, cover himself with his forearms, and let Joe Frazier or George Foreman wear themselves out body-punching him as hard as they could. He would take a beating for half the fight. But Muhammed Ali had a plan and it worked--unlike Ali, I had no plan.

Life had been anything but smooth since leaving Greenville. When I sought their counsel, R.C. Sproul and General Grinalds had both said, "Trust providence going forward." I don't know why I thought it would be easy.

Early Type II diabetes can often be controlled with a pill, but I was soon taking two big doses of insulin a day. Maury Regional Hospital offered a class called "Living with Diabetes." It lasted all day and went from grim and discouraging to grimmer and totally disheartening. Diabetes requires management of the minutiae and total commitment to lifestyle changes. I have the hardest time staying organized to begin with--if it weren't for Ruth helping me, I would never have had such success in the golf business.

When the final segment concluded, I lagged behind while everyone else left. "Y'all have this thing named wrong," I told the nurse who taught the course. She looked puzzled. "It should be *Dying* with Diabetes . . . It seems like you die, one toe at a time."

Managing a smile, she said, "If you can follow the plan, you can do okay with it."

I called Scott Verplank to talk about my diagnosis. With juvenile (Type I) diabetes, he was a success story. Scott kept everything strictly regimented: When and what he ate. When and how much insulin to take. Exercising to stay super-fit. He had grooved these into routines, totally habituated to the point where he could manage his condition--as serious as it is--effectively. In March of 2011 Scott finished second in the Houston Open at age forty-six. At the time he was dealing with a problem with his wrist; he has had two surgeries on his elbows and been out of action for a total of almost three years. And Scott has taken impeccable care of himself for decades.

When coaching I ban the words "can't" or "quit" (except for "can't quit"). Now I faced an uphill battle I really couldn't afford to lose. Despite the changes I made, my insulin requirements kept climbing. That seminar on diabetes was in February of 2004. I still couldn't understand why God had taken Lewis at such a young age. Part of the grieving process is anger, and I had been stuck there a long time: on some level I was mad at

God. Trust providence going forward? That hadn't worked out. Now, facing my own mortality, I wanted to know *Why me?*

***

Accustomed to getting my pick of assistants, at King's Creek I had to settle for whoever was available. In the past, big and exclusive clubs had trusted my judgment and experience enough to give me almost total control over their operations. This developer, however, wanted to make every little teeny decision, and he rarely had enough cash to follow the business plan. It took forever just to get the parking lot paved. And because the driving range hadn't yet opened, my coaching couldn't serve as the magnet it had been at my previous clubs. Nevertheless, I decided to persevere--I had nothing else.

Ruth found out about a surgeon who was using an innovative procedure that might help me. Recent research has confirmed that this procedure, called a duodenal switch, can eliminate Type II Diabetes in most people.

Dr. John Husted told us a patient needed to have five comorbid conditions to qualify: high blood pressure, sleep apnea, elevated lipids, Type II diabetes, and morbid obesity. My weight put me in the "obese" category. For my body mass index (BMI) to rank as *morbidly* obese, I needed to go from 250 to 264 pounds. Even stuffing myself, I could only reach 256 pounds. I was about to leave for our final visit, eight pounds short of qualifying, when I remembered that a gallon of water weighs eight pounds. On the way to the doctor's office I drank a gallon of water . . . and made the weight.

Drinking that much water could have led to "water intoxication," even death, I learned later. But without that surgery, I knew I was in trouble.

I had the duodenal switch procedure in February 2005. I went from taking two big shots of insulin a day to needing none just the day after surgery. Released in five days, I went home to a detailed post-op protocol: along with handfuls of supplements, I needed to eat eight times a day to get enough protein. Never a compliant patient, I ate when I wanted. When I went back to work my fellow employees were astounded at my weight loss, week after week.

***

King's Creek was ready to go to eighteen holes in June, 2005. That salary increase I was supposed to get? When the developer came into my office, he acted like it had been erased from both our memories. "I know things are moving slower than we anticipated," I told him. "I will be willing to forego it, but our agreement *was* a raise when we went to 18 holes." The following week he let me go and hired a pro for half what he was paying me.

Ruth and I made a trip to Oxford, Mississippi, to visit my college roommate, Bill Mosby, and his wife, Karen. Julian Allen from CMA had moved to Oxford too, and Julian's daughter Katherine was working with a developer from Texas on a Fazio-designed golf course under construction nearby. I met with the developer to talk about my qualifications and what I could do for him. He offered me a position as director of marketing during the start-up, after which I would become head professional. My salary, which started low, would go up commensurately. Oxford had a high cost of living, so Ruth would stay put while I found a condominium and went to work. Returning to where I'd gone to college was exciting, and Charlottesville had given me a taste for university towns.

A company from Scottsdale, Arizona--guys in their late twenties--was managing the development. One commented to me, "This isn't your first rodeo." Apparently it *was* theirs, however. From day one I knew we had big problems. After convincing the developer they would sell $50,000 memberships, they had already spent $13 million and only had twelve holes completed. This developer was really an oil and gas producer, worth a ton of money: I went from one developer who had trouble making payroll to another so wealthy I couldn't get his attention.

Like many university towns, Oxford has an illusion of prosperity. Donnie Kessinger, who had played baseball for Ole Miss and later the Chicago Cubs, was the biggest realtor in town. I went to see him, and ask if this deal made financial sense to him. Donnie had heard about the money being spent on the course. Knowing the demographics, he told me there were fewer than a hundred and fifty residents who made more that $100,000 a year.

I finally got the developer's ear and laid it out for him: the most he could get for a resident membership would be $15,000 and even then it might be slow. His best chance lay in attracting non-residents the way Farmington did, but that would take time. The management company didn't understand this market--or else they were incompetent; they seemed to think Oxford was like Scottsdale, or Palm Springs, California, where $100,000 thousand memberships aren't uncommon. The developer, a finance guy, soon understood.

I rolled up my sleeves and went to work selling memberships--*trying* to sell them would be more accurate. In October Julian's daughter Katherine asked, "What's going on with your weight?"

Absorbed with helping this guy get off the hook in Oxford, I wasn't taking care of the duodenal switch protocol. Our daughter Elizabeth was getting married on December 31, so I was traveling back and forth to Tennessee and didn't have time to pay attention.

At Elizabeth's wedding, relatives and friends questioned my sister in whispers after the service: "Does Bobby have cancer?" Matt King asked his mother who that man was, escorting Elizabeth down the aisle. This finally got my attention.

Back in Oxford the developer agreed that I had done everything possible. As he put it, "the calling was premature." They didn't even have plans for a clubhouse yet.

I weighed about 150 pounds and my skin was grey. Stumped by my condition, our family doctor in Columbia rubbed his head, saying, "You look like you've been in a concentration camp." He had me checked for lung cancer. It came up negative, as I anticipated--the surgery and my neglect were sapping me. I still couldn't escape the drumbeat in my ears: provide, provide, provide. Somehow I had to fulfill my role in the family.

Trying to draw on my natural salesmanship, I spent weeks studying to get a state license to sell health insurance. The company that had hired me provided a prospect list. These "prospects" were often struggling families facing eviction who didn't have a prayer of being accepted for coverage--or would be charged an arm and a leg if they did qualify. I sold a good policy on my first call. Beyond that bright spot, I never felt so out of my element.

***

One day John McNeely called. When I started joking around with him he cut me off. "Rusty," he said, "Dick died this morning."

Dick Harmon had contracted walking pneumonia. That morning he woke up in Palm Springs having trouble breathing. His family took him to the hospital, where he had a massive heart attack on the gurney. They worked valiantly to revive him, John said. He just didn't respond.

All this had happened within the last hour. John had called me immediately after hearing it from his brother, who worked out there--this bad news traveled fast. I told John I would see him in Houston for the funeral, then hung up the phone and cried. It felt like the call about Lewis. Dick Harmon had seen the news of Lewis's death on the Internet and immediately called me from Austria, where he was teaching. Dick was so kind. He always cared.

Before leaving I put together a photo album for Nancy, Dick's wife, thinking their children might enjoy having the pictures. My mind roamed the River Oaks of the past as I reflected how great those years had been. Now I was wasting away and didn't really care.

In Houston I stayed with Ruth's best friend Mary Lu Campbell and her husband Jim. They loaned me their big Chevrolet Suburban so I could drop the pictures off at Dick's house. There I learned that the family, former assistants, and some close friends were meeting an hour before the doors opened. Driving back to Mary Lu's to change clothes, I was going with the traffic when an elderly lady suddenly and without signaling made a left turn that put her Honda broadside in front of me. I slammed on the brakes but that big Suburban wouldn't stop. Mid-swerve, I caught the right rear of her car.

We pulled into a service station. Although I told her it wasn't necessary any longer, the insurance companies would deal with it, she insisted on calling the police. The Campbells' Suburban was leaking radiator fluid while her small Honda was hardly damaged. Go figure. You can let this upset you or you can go with the flow, I reminded myself. I just sat on the curb and prayed for Dick's family.

Finally the lady said, "let's go." She had just pulled away when I realized I'd written my insurance information on the other side of the map Mary Lu had drawn for me to get back to their house.

In the Bellaire section of Houston all the houses looked alike to me. I couldn't recall the name of the Campbells' street. After driving up and down identical streets with that Suburban leaking fluid, I had just found their driveway when a Houston police car pulled up. He was after me for leaving the scene of an accident. I told him how the other driver wanted to wait for the police and then she wanted to leave, how I gave her my map. My best friend had died. All I wanted to do was get dressed and go to the funeral home. He kept talking about leaving the scene of an accident. I sighed with frustration. "Do you really think I have a big enough imagination to think up such a lie?" At last he listened and understood.

The Suburban was out of service, likely totaled. Mary Lu said that Jim would be home in an hour to take me to the funeral home for the private gathering. While I showered and got dressed, I started anticipating how Dick, with his great sense of humor, was going to love this story. It made me laugh just thinking about it. Then reality slapped me back. My great friend had died. The Lord had His hand inside my chest, squeezing my heart, just like with Lewis.

Fourteen hundred people attended Dick Harmon's funeral. The family was receiving condolences, but the crowd was so big that I just stood under a big tree trading stories with Ervin Wilson, who worked in the bag room at River Oaks. Ervin told me that he had once admired a pair of Dick's expensive street shoes. "Dick just took them off and said, 'Here. They are yours.'" Dick had that kind of heart. Then Cameron Greenwood, one of my River Oaks juniors, spotted me, and before long I was visiting with young men I hadn't seen in almost thirty years.

The sky was grey but the rain held off. Bruce Davidson, who was replacing Dick as head pro at River Oaks, was hosting all the assistants and a few friends for lunch at the club. Mark McMurrey--the late bloomer I'd coached in Houston at the same time as Scott Verplank--had given me a ride to the funeral. When it came time to leave for the club, Mark found me outside. Just as I opened the car door, a BOOM of nearby thunder recalled that storm in 1977. Without that storm I might never have met Dick Harmon, much less worked for him.

Not in the mood for small talk, I sat with Ervin and Mark at the luncheon. Mark drove me back to Mary Lu's afterwards. It was raining pretty hard now. Mark talked about being with Dick in Scotland the previous summer when a group of friends went on a golf trip. One day, with a van too small to accommodate everyone, Mark and Dick had walked the two miles to the hotel. Mark told me how glad he was, now, that he'd gotten to tell Dick how much he meant to him.

It was pouring by the time Mark pulled up to the curb. "Wait a minute, Rusty." Mark came around the car and wrapped his arms around me. "Rusty," he said, "I have some unfinished business with you, too . . . You gave me the most attention. You got me into Wake Forest. You gave me so much--I can never thank you enough."

I started crying once again. "No," I said, "you just did."

The Lord promises that He will provide. He says He will see us through. Mark McMurrey let me feel something we tend to forget: what it is like to be in His hands.

***

I came back home and worked on the farm, driving the tractor. Mowing grass--you never get through. I had plenty to do, just no paying job. Playing golf was the last thing on my mind. When I finally got around to writing Nancy Harmon, I said that loud clap of thunder after the funeral reminded me of meeting Dick because of that other thunderstorm, 30 years earlier. I described how tight we all were back at River Oaks. If it came down to it, I believe we would have been willing to die for each other.

Back in the late 90's, when I was still at Farmington, a sportswriter friend named Kevin Record had traveled to Houston for a UVA-Rice basketball game. Covering golf in addition to UVA, he wrote with a lot of heart and soul. When these guys are on the road they have free time, so I arranged for him to meet Dick Harmon and visit River Oaks while he was in Texas. Dick rolled out the red carpet. Kevin told me he spent all afternoon talking to him and watching him hit balls. Dick supplied enough material for ten columns.

But Kevin Record wasn't just after Harmon stories--he was after McIver stuff, too. If Dick had to describe Bobby McIver in one word, what would it be? "Dick never hesitated," Kevin told me later. "'Loyalty' is what he said--'Bobby is the kind of guy you want in a foxhole with you.'" I wrote to Nancy that if there was one quality I would hope Dick would choose for me, this would be it. After all, if you were Dick's friend, he would do anything for you.

That thunderstorm in 1977 changed the course of my entire family's lives--I just never had time to think about it before. When we are busy, all we do is run around in circles and think. Without a job I felt events slow down. Now I had time to contemplate and listen to that inner voice. My health was bad and it seemed like it would never get better, but this period alone on the farm was when things began to start making sense. I could see all the breaks I had gotten, the doors that opened, and some that closed.

So much came together as I wrote to Nancy Harmon. Later, when we finally spoke, all she said was "That letter . . . " Both of us knew.

***

In August 2001 Miguel Coles--Matthew's classmate at Woodberry Forest--and his family had invited me to their home in Caracas, Venezuela. Miguel had rounded up a dozen or so players for a weeklong Double Eagle golf school during my stay.

In Venezuela I saw exceptional wealth alongside staggering poverty. I was dealing with elite, Ivy League-educated world travelers who spoke three languages. Using the slogan "It's Not as Hard as You Have Been Made to Believe" and an outline that moved from one shot into another, I started with three-foot putts and emphasized keeping the short game simple.

One morning Felipe Montemayor, the premier architect in Venezuela, said, "Bobby, our philosophy is the same in architecture: less is more."

I stopped and looked at him. "That is exactly right," I said. "Excellence in coaching golf is when you have nothing left to take away . . . Some of these professor-type pros get it backwards."

In 2001 Miguel Coles also first suggested that I write about how I coached; by 2006 I had another book 80% completed. That brief exchange with Felipe Montemayor led to the title: *Playing Great Golf: Less Is More.*

***

Mike Keliher was teaching at Harpeth Hills Golf Club in Nashville, but I hadn't seen him since returning home. Finally in July of 2006 I made plans to meet up with him where he was coaching. When I got to the course, I spotted Mike sitting in a golf cart some twenty yards away from his student. Most pros teach from the right side or the rear, but I can see everything I want to see from the left and slightly behind. Mike was observing from this position, too, but he didn't get it from me--I didn't start looking at swings this way until after he left me.

As I hung back about thirty yards, I could tell he didn't recognize me. The Bobby he knew was a 200-pound redhead. I now weighed 145 pounds and had a full head of gray hair. It took a few glances, but once Mike realized who I was he jumped out of his cart and gave me a big hug. Then I watched him give three or four lessons.

Mike Keliher had left the Country Club of Jackson when he realized being a club pro wasn't his deal. But that didn't negate his passion for the game, or his extraordinary ability to instruct and encourage others. He taught like a "golf whisperer," keeping his distance and using short phrases and even hand signals. His students, clearly comfortable with his unique style, were all good players.

When the coaching ended Mike and I sat on a cart with our feet propped up, talking golf and reliving stories. With his beartrap mind Mike remembered tales I had long forgotten. The subject of Mr. Harmon got us laughing, and took us back to Texas.

Mike recalled his trip to River Oaks to get ready for that U.S. Amateur qualifier in 1978, almost 30 years earlier. He reminded me how he hit the towering six iron over a pine tree that fronted the green. We watched his ball roll within six feet of the hole. "Then you threw down a second ball, Bobby, and yelled, 'Hell, anybody can get LUCKY--Hit that damn shot again and show me you are GOOD!'" This, he said, had jolted him into hitting the next one four feet away.

Mike still had two more days in Houston. I locked his clubs in my car trunk and wouldn't let him touch them. Mike had a tendency to practice too much, so I took this option away from him. We went to an Astros game and had fun. The main thing was anchoring in his subconscious mind not just the idea but the *belief* that he was ready. Mike *was* ready. He needed to see I believed it. Mike Keliher left Houston on autopilot. A week later he called. "I shot four under," he said. "I was medalist."

"Am I supposed to be surprised?" I'd responded.

Sometimes the smart ones struggle: they are thinking too much. Mike called again from Plainfield Country Club in New Jersey after learning that he was matched against Bobby Clampett, the best college player in the country. As a pro, Clampett later got to thinking too much himself, but he was rock-solid back then. "What room is he staying in?" I joked. "Why don't you call and offer to help him pack? Mike, you can win this match. It's 18 holes--get him down early and keep putting it on him. Call me as soon as you close him out."

Every detail of that long-ago match seemed to come back to Mike. "I got him two down on the front, I had him three down through twelve. But he birdied four out of the last six holes--he beat me one up."

I had heard Mike was shooting some scores in the low 60's. This guy I'd taught as a junior and a college player was approaching age fifty, but when I suggested that he give the Champions Tour a try, Mike dodged the indirect compliment. Once I told him about my book, however, he immediately asked to see what I had written. I said I had covered everything but the full swing. Mike agreed that it is the non-swing areas that determine a champion. He would appreciate the sections on sports psychology, course management, and effective practice-- not so much doing things right as doing the right things--and didn't need an explanation.

We went to a famous restaurant in Nashville, Loveless's Cafe, which specialized in fried chicken and biscuits. Noticing I wasn't eating much, Mike grew concerned. I'd already told him about my surgery. "Don't worry," I said, "my stomach will stretch. I'll get it back." I suggested that we do some teaching together, maybe a corporate outing-type thing--we would make a charismatic duo. Mike liked the idea. He had learned of Lewis's death from the news, and I told him about Double Eagle Golf Group. "Hey," I said, "it's a good name and I have logos and stationery already on hand."

Mike was headed to the U.S. Amateur in Minnesota, with a good player from California he had coached for five or six years. Anticipating he might want to read my book, I had a copy in my car--over 200 pages without the section on the full swing. As we went our separate ways, Mike said, "*Eat*. Get your weight back." It was coming, I assured him, I just needed time.

That night Mike called. Already well into the book, he said, "This is a lock. This book will get published--I know somebody who can help us." I knew it wasn't false flattery. Mike called me two or three more times to talk about passages he'd read.

For some reason Mike had just purchased a large home. After two divorces, he was single and a four-bedroom house seemed incongruous. The U.S. Amateur was held in August. After his player lost early, Mike came back to that big new house.

***

A friend of mine had a cabin on the Buffalo River. I went there just after Labor Day. Planning to stay until the swing section was completed, I ended up spending eight weeks alone in that cabin. It was an almost magical experience--when you get that still and quiet, your mind responds. Even focused intently on that section, however, I was having trouble.

It took me a good while to figure out that I was still looking for "The Swing," when it didn't exist. I coach the *player*. No two swings--much less temperaments--are alike. I read a lot about how everyone else taught. Frustrated, I looked back over the other sections. I had been pleased with them, but something wasn't right. I couldn't put my finger on it.

With no phone service at the Buffalo River cabin, Mike Keliher couldn't reach me there. When I drove to where I could make a call he didn't answer, and when I left messages he didn't return my calls.

Finally, late in October, I went to his house. I hadn't been around Mike in a long time, but I knew him. After his excitement and enthusiasm in the summer, he now seemed really low. He was showing signs of depression. After that visit I kept getting his answering machine.

I hadn't seen or talked to Mike's mother since serving as best man in his first marriage. As Thanksgiving approached, an inner voice told me to call.

Toni Keliher was surprised and excited to hear from me. "Toni," I said, "I'm calling out of concern. I know something about clinical depression--I've been treated for it--and I'm pretty sure that Mike is in a major depression. I'm urging you to have a family intervention and get him help if he needs it."

I soon heard from Diana, Mike's sister. She wanted the name of a psychiatrist. I told her that Dr. Glenn Yank, former head of the department of psychiatry at Vanderbilt, was compassionate and brilliant. At this point I felt it was my place to bow out unless the Kelihers thought I was needed.

Thanksgiving, Christmas, New Year's: the holidays came and went with no news about Mike. I saw it as a good sign.

{ 16 }

INTO THE SILENCE

*For as this appalling ocean surrounds the verdant land, so in
the soul of man there lies an insular Tahiti, full of peace and joy, but
encompassed by all the horrors of a half lived life.*

–Herman Melville, Moby-Dick

If you're going through hell, keep going.

–Winston Churchill

Somehow the Ivy League scholar Cornel West had made his
way into my consciousness. That winter of 2006-07 I acquired
The Cornel West Reader and quickly concluded he is a genius.
Now a professor at Princeton and Union Theological Seminary,
Dr. West has taught at Harvard and Yale. But what persuaded
me that he spoke *my* language too was his account of his childhood experiences in a black church in Sacramento.

I bought the book for a section about the influence of popular
African-American music on our culture. Rhythm and blues has
always been my music--give me the Temptations, the Four

Tops, James Brown, Marvin Gaye, and Tammi Terrell. I couldn't care less about the Beatles.

Reading Cornel West made me try to understand Marvin Gaye's song "What's Going On." The studio version that everyone knows is the product of takes and retakes, including Marvin singing back up to his own lead vocal. These carefully composed studio recordings can lack the improvisation and heart of a live performance. Among the videos I found on You Tube, a slow "What's Going On" features Gaye on the piano fronting a small four-piece band. Another, taped in Canada, combines a very upbeat tempo with a big orchestra and back-up singers for a very different, tent-revival feel. I realized that just as a golfer will never play two rounds the same, these creative artists never play a song the same way twice.

I had long been a fan of R & B genius Donny Hathaway. Browsing around a music store I discovered his 1972 live album, which included a smooth, jazzy cover of "What's Going On." Hathaway and his band had recorded it in Los Angeles in 1971, shortly after Marvin Gaye's single was released. This soon became my favorite version. Listening to it through my headphones, I went deeper and deeper into the song every time it played.

At this time Miguel Coles and my writing coach, Megan Macomber, were trying to help me finish that final part of *Less is More*, the swing section I had struggled to complete. After many exchanges by phone and email, Miguel finally said, "Hey, you keep looking for the secret--just give us your ideas."

On a Sunday morning I got out of bed and went to the computer keyboard. It all came together: that music filling my soul, the way those artists improvised, how strongly I wanted to convey that golf at the highest level comes from the heart. Seeing that I was totally focused, Ruth quietly went to church, leaving me behind undisturbed. It felt like the words were coming from outside myself. Totally in the flow, I finally got to the root of the problem--not just with the swing section but, I now realized, the entire book: I had been writing what I *knew* about golf, not the way I coached. I had been writing another textbook.

One more book in the trashcan. Once again, I was starting over.

***

That Sunday afternoon, Megan called. This was unusual. She was a hands-off coach who believed in the natural learning process, too. "How did you write this?" she asked. She knew I had been reading Cornel West. Her intuition told her I had been in some contemplative place and writing from my heart "in spirit." She wanted to make sure I recognized it, like me with Mike Keliher on the number 10 hole at River Oaks. I had previously felt self-conscious and tentative in writing this book, but now I discovered I could free it up, when nothing was at stake--when I wasn't "writing a book."

In several weeks I would be heading to Orlando for Arnold Palmer's Bay Hill Classic, where Scott Verplank and I usually met up.

In June I would turn 59. After attempting to qualify for the U.S. Senior Open in 1999, when I was fifty and still had my A game, I had given up competitive golf. Sure, I played maybe three or four times a year--"jolly golf," Mr. Harmon called it-- but this wasn't me. I had to have the adrenaline flowing. I had to have something at stake . . . something that I felt for the first time in years as it woke inside. I decided to give the U.S. Senior Open another try.

Filling out the entry form, I opted for the Connecticut qualifier, instead of the Nashville site. I couldn't show up near a Nashville-area golf course without people wanting to joke around and hear some stories. With more good players up north they have more spots, and I always play better on a hard course with stiff competition. And I'd heard the emotion in Mike Keliher's voice when he was reminiscing. That U.S. Amateur championship I'd helped him prepare for had been played in the northeast. Maybe asking Mike to help me get ready for this event would lift us both. After I mailed off my entry, I called to tell him my new plans, and ended up leaving another message on his answering machine.

I departed for Scott's tournament in Orlando in a deep and contemplative place, inspired by reading Wayne Dyer's *Wisdom of the Ages*. For whatever it's worth, there is no new wisdom: just when you think you've come up with something brilliant, you find a scholar who had the same ideas six hundred years ago.

Sometimes we fixate on particular ideas or philosophies, to our detriment. Greek logic prevails in our education systems-- the American mind wants to understand, measure, and label everything. Dyer's book helped me become aware of this tendency. This ingrained empiricism might help bakers or geometry students, but I see it as a serious interference to great golf. The inner chatter of the conscious mind mires most American golfers well below their potential.

I just wanted to get inside the ropes on Monday, Tuesday, and Wednesday with Scott Verplank and his caddie, Scott Tway--"Scott Squared." Early in the week Josh Points, a teammate of Matthew's from Woodberry Forest, spotted me and I waved for him to come inside the ropes. As he walked with us, Josh told me he was teaching for Jim McLean at his Miami golf academy. Jim and I were the same age and our pictures ran side-by-side when *GOLF Magazine* named us Top 100 teachers. Through Josh, I felt connected to my earlier life.

In Orlando I focused on observing Scott Verplank's game. Whatever the coach could learn from his player might help me prepare for the U.S. Senior Open qualifier in early June. A visual learner, I was absorbing the images. By spending time with Verplank on the practice range and during dinner, I hoped to find out what was going on inside his head.

There is nothing easy about great golf. Ideally, it begins with observing excellence and ends with playing from the heart, but in between you must put in thousands of hours of training. I don't think true mastery is possible. What we aspire to is efficiency and effectiveness under pressure, the qualities Scott Verplank displays so consistently.

I spent this whole week in an almost blissful state. Even without competing, my mind was absorbed in a pleasurable experience--the most basic definition of flow.

Lewis Chitengwa once said that during the 1993 South African Amateur, "It was like I was riding a wave. It felt like something was going on. I felt I was destined to win." That feeling of destiny is the ultimate victory in the inner game.

Writers and musicians find their livelihood in the flow, a peak spiritual experience that some define as "divinity within," a creative circuit that somehow connects the artist with the Creator. I've enjoyed the friendship of some creative writers with immense talent, and some classically trained musicians. We don't have any problem identifying them as artists.

Bobby Jones said that golf, played skillfully, could be compared to ballet. Golfers, however, are considered athletes, and people do not generally consider athletes to be creative artists: they are jocks. But all the great ones, players and coaches alike, were and are artists.

***

On my last night in Orlando I got a call on my cell phone from Mike. "Hey, this is Keliher," he said. "I wanted you to know I'm doing fine."

"Great," I replied. "I'm in Orlando with Verplank."

"I'm doing fine," Mike repeated. "Call me when you get home--I will return your call." He paused. "Just don't call my mother again. I'm fine."

"OK," I said. "I'm glad you are better. I was concerned. I only called her because I love you."

I heard him say, "I love you, too." Mike had pulled himself out of depression without medication in the past--he did it while working for me--so I assumed this was the case now.

***

I love traveling alone in an automobile, free to think about whatever bubbles up as the mile markers pass by. During the twelve-hour drive back to Columbia I began considering what it would take for me to get ready to compete again. During the eight years since my last tournament I'd undergone major surgery and lost a hundred pounds. I would have to understand my different, weaker body and train accordingly, coming up with a process or regimen to make the best use of my time.

Mostly I had to *believe* it was possible. Shifting my focus inward, I consciously recalled events where I had turned on the after-burner, like at the Austin Country Club. The inner game had been the backbone of my coaching. Now I had to get it done myself. While working on my physical or outer game, I would rehearse my inner-game skills every time out. If I felt myself losing my focus, I decided I would walk off the tee.

I believe in synergy, the phenomenon of people's communal intelligence exceeding the sum of the individuals'. Mike Keliher was brilliant and I had plenty of experience . . . Together we could surely accomplish something special. I was looking forward to connecting with him.

Back home I had to get my equipment squared away. The standard length of a putter is 36 inches. I had this putter I'd never used that was 48 inches and heavy in the head. The easiest putt is a tap-in. In theory I could make *every* swing a tap-in: adjusting my hands up and down that long grip--holding it at 48 versus 34 inches, say--would make the putter head travel different lengths as my hands swung the same "tap-in" length. It might take a little time, but the laws of physics told me it should work. When I called to run this idea past Mike Keliher, I kept getting his answering machine. But Mike marched to a different drummer. I figured we would get back in touch at some point.

Once I was back on the farm, practicing, it really hit me: I weighed 150 pounds now, and my swing felt like someone else's. Like my flowing and natural high school swing, it used centrifugal force to generate power. In golf, there are swingers and hitters. The difference has to do with how the right arm straightens. A swinger just lets centrifugal force snap the club through. A hitter uses centrifugal force, too, but powers the right arm through the ball like a piston in a gasoline engine. But whether you're a hitter or a swinger, you feel like you are snapping the club-head off the shaft at the moment the shaft and both arms straighten just in front of the ball.

I had to reprogram my brain. At 150 pounds I found myself having to hit two clubs more than I was used to; it was really hard pulling the trigger on a six iron when I was used to playing an eight. I needed to come up with ways to get as much distance as I could.

I had told Scott Verplank about my Senior Open intentions over dinner the first night in Florida. "Bobby," he said, "everything has changed out here--this technology is letting people blast the ball 350 yards and even more. Plus, you can hardly hit these drivers off line. The balls are a part of it, too--they're taking the skill out of playing golf." Scott was hitting his driver towering heights and at least twenty yards further without straining. I asked him to call Taylormade and get me a driver just like his, only with a stiff shaft.

Graymere Country Club had a short and easy course, and growing up I became accustomed to shooting 65 with regularity. As a result, my comfort zone and self-expectation was under par and in the 60's. When I competed on a longer and harder course, my subconscious didn't know the difference. The mind can be your servant or your master--you get to choose. Using my experience coaching the inner game would give me the best chance of getting in the flow and staying there for 18 holes. Once I could trust my outer game, I knew I could let go and play unconsciously.

First, you must stake your claim. I resolved to give all of my body, mind, heart, and soul to this quest. I kept telling myself three things. *Anything is possible*--that was the foundation. I don't believe in luck, but I do believe in miracles. Finally, I would be ready. I would train with all I had in me: I couldn't control the outcome, but I could control the process on my end.

***

Jimmy Ward called on a Wednesday morning in early April. He said, "I hate to have to tell you this . . . They found Mike's body in his house last night."

Jimmy had been by Mike Keliher's side at Belle Meade and again at the University of Tennessee. His son was coming on strong with Mike as his coach. I asked Jimmy what he knew. "It was suicide," he told me.

I found my way into our family room. I was alone. Ruth was at work. She had been holding us up financially for some time. I remember just putting my face in my hands. Like with Lewis, the tears would not come. Here's a guy who cried for two days in 8th grade when his dog was hit by a car. But now, as an adult, I'm locked up.

Checking my cell phone, I discovered a voice mail message left at 2:30 a.m. by Mike's family. By the time I called Mike's mother it was around noon. "Toni, I just heard," I said. "Would you like me to come be with you?"

She hesitated. "Yes, I would like anyone who loved Mike to be near me." The day was overcast, threatening to rain, when I knocked on the door. Toni answered it and we embraced. Nothing needed to be said. As people came in and out, Toni introduced me to them as "Mike's golf coach." The world was somehow upside down: these young men taught me how to coach.

Mike's sister Diana came over and put her hand on my back. "We appreciate your being here," she said. "You were almost like a second father to Mike . . . Would you be willing to participate in the memorial service?" The service was set for that Saturday, which happened to be Easter Saturday. A Catholic priest who didn't know the family, much less Mike, would preside. I would deliver Mike Keliher's eulogy.

***

Bob Wolcott was working in Tunica, Mississippi, just south of Memphis. He planned to come in on Friday. When I told him Diana Keliher had asked me to bring the primary message at the service, Bob replied, "Don't forget, this is a celebration of a great life." Before the service I planned to find a room to be by myself. "I'm going straight to that room and get on my knees," I told him. "Will you be there with me? I need you, Big Man."

"You can count on me," Bob said. "I'll be there with you."

I got home Friday afternoon and got quiet. Among the people attending Mike's service, one or more would probably suffer from a mood disorder. Mike Keliher was beloved--his death could nudge vulnerable friends or relatives into depression, which makes you feel so hopeless. A suicide leaves people hurting and asking why. I didn't have an answer, but somehow I had to bring a message of hope. I sat at my computer for three hours. Finally, deciding I needed sleep, I gave it to the Lord. In the middle of the night I woke up, and forty-five minutes later an outline for my remarks lay on the desk, under my Bible.

Saturday rolled around beautiful and sunny. I'd wanted to grab a golf club; one of those fiberglass devices with a golf grip was handy at the back door. On the farm we used it to separate cattle, so its lack of a club-head didn't matter. I was going to use it in Mike's service somehow, I just didn't know how. Ruth drove us to the funeral home. We arrived an hour early but people were already pouring in. Spotting Bob Wolcott, I gave him a nod and then walked through the crowd with my eyes on the floor. This is a tournament tactic: if you don't make eye contact, you can transit without speaking. Bob followed.

Finding a tiny room with two chairs, we talked about 'Mike-isms,' all the unique expressions and traits that made Mike Keliher's imprint on your life indelible. About half an hour before the service we shut the door and got on our knees. Bob put his hand on my shoulder. For about twenty minutes we prayed that this would turn into a celebration of a good life, and that the words would minister to those in attendance.

After the last "Amen" we opened the door to find the place packed. People were standing in the rear. As a hush greeted the appearance of the priest, I noticed that Mike's golf bag had been placed in front of the pulpit. The priest made a few comments. Scott Keliher's young daughters sang like a tiny, perfect choir. Then I slowly made my way up. Taking several deep breaths, I scanned the crowd. So many faces I knew, wrinkled now and framed with gray hair. Mike's high school and college teammates were all present, folks I hadn't seen in thirty years.

I started by saying that Mike Keliher had something more-- much more--than a case of the blues. Everyone close to him tried to persuade him to get help, but for some reason Mike refused our attempts. Nobody had any reason to feel guilty. We did all we could, and that's all anyone can do. Depression was the common cold of mental health and help was available-- medication could be very effective. I was talking about this, I said, because the family hoped it could possibly help someone else. I saw Mike's sister Diana nodding approval.

Then I spoke about my history with Mike, starting when I spotted him on the golf course at Shelby Park wearing his white Hogan cap. Mike's curiosity had made him my best student ever. I had better players, like Scott Verplank, but my best *student* was Mike Keliher, hands down. His keen intellect, along with exceptional sensitivity and an ability to communicate, had also made Mike "the best instructor nobody ever heard of" in the country, and one of the five best teachers I knew. Working out of the spotlight, he turned out some great players.

Bob Wolcott had reminded me about his first trip to Belle Meade, and how Mike, Matt King, and the crew had gathered to greet him. After Bob hit three or four balls Mike had said, "Wolcott is so PURE, Bobby, what in the world are you going to teach him?" Mike was right: if I tampered with that swing it should have been a crime. Mike loved to use the word "PURE," and he knew pure when he saw it.

So did I. Mike's action was totally pure, too. For him I changed it to KELI-PURE.

Mike had game and he was definitely a competitor, but he always celebrated a teammate's success. *Always* . . . Mike's University of Tennessee teammates--Jeff Jones, Jeff Walker, Jimmy Ward, and Stuart Smith--were all nodding emphatically. Mike was such a good leader that few realized until afterwards that he was the chief.

Mike Keliher had this loud and spontaneous laugh that was just Mike. When Claude Harmon did that golf school back in Jackson, Mike soaked up everything he could learn--including the humor. I could still hear his laughter from that day the previous summer, when we'd sat on that cart at Harpeth Hills, and Mike recalled Mr. Harmon holing out his second bunker shot in a clinic, throwing his arms up, and declaring, "That's it. That's how you do it."

Mike had been married twice. His two ex-wives sat together and held hands during the service. Another mystery way beyond my ability to understand.

Mike's death, I said, was "a mystery best left to the mind of God." Recalling the movie *Chariots of Fire*, I quoted Olympic track athlete Eric Lidell: "I know I am called to serve in China, but when I run I feel His pleasure." I said, "Mike ran a good race . . . even now I can somehow feel God's pleasure."

Then I heard myself declaring my intention to qualify for the U.S. Senior Open in June. "I plan to play with Mike's clubs," I said. "I want his spirit with me . . . We all know it's not the arrow. It's the Indian." I had entered the tournament in an attempt to draw Mike out. The first day or two after his death I was ready to withdraw. But now--staking my claim in front of four or five hundred people--I could taste the bit in my mouth.

I was holding that fiberglass shaft with a golf grip. "You all know that a 'sound' golf swing has . . . well, a *sound?*" The experienced players nodded. You could blindfold me and I could tell my players by the sound. When we were together at Harpeth Hills, I'd asked Mike to "hit a few and let me hear that music again."

Mike Keliher had beautiful timing and rhythm, but what I remembered most was his balanced finish. I walked down from the podium holding that fiberglass shaft. "Let me give you something to remember," I said. Then I swung in slow motion, finishing with my knees touching--Mike's signature. Everyone who knew him as a golfer *knew*.

I held that trademark finish a moment. Then I went over and gave the white headless shaft to Mike's mother along with my notes, in a white three-ring binder, before taking my seat.

***

On Monday, two days after Mike's memorial service, it was time to start coaching myself. When I got Mike's clubs, there was no turning back. I wasn't just playing for myself, but for everyone named Keliher and more. That little sterling silver medal was mine until someone proved otherwise, but I had work to do.

First I had to determine my set make-up. You can only carry fourteen clubs in the bag, so determining what combination works best for you is essential. This involves factoring in how well you are swinging along with the course you are playing. During the service for Mike I had said "It's not the arrow that matters, it's the Indian." But like arrows, *clubs have to fit*. If just one club doesn't fit you, a poor swing with compensations will result.

Ben Hogan said the driver was the most important club; Harvey Penick said the putter; Raymond Floyd, the sand wedge. I agree with all of them--these three clubs tie for first priority.

The high-tech driver Scott Verplank had Taylormade send me was perfect. The loft was just right. Too little loft will make a player unconsciously hang back, as if his body were trying to help the ball get launched on an ideal angle; too much, and the mind and body will try to adjust and hold the trajectory down. Proper shaft length is also essential. My arms are proportionally short for my 6'1" height, so I already knew my club-shafts needed to be one inch longer and one degree upright from standard. The shaft that worked best for me at that time was a stiff that was about a 6.5, using techno lingo. A shaft that is too stiff makes you unconsciously swing harder. The shaft flexes and releases several times during the swing, and you want to get all the help you can from the shaft "springing" during impact. Contrary to common belief, a player will hit a more flexible shaft farther because there's more shaft kick; the catch is that you give up something with regards to accuracy.

The lie angles of the irons are critical. A toe that is down too much (flat) will send the ball right of target with a good swing; if the toe is up too much (upright), the ball will go left. To determine what suits you, put tape on the bottom of the club. Hit a shot off a smooth hard surface and read the impact evidence. The mark should be centered. Too flat and you'll see the mark out towards the toe of the club-head; too upright, the mark will be in towards the heel.

Grip size matters. My grips are standard size but I use a few layers of extra tape under my left hand. This is a preference; the larger grip helps me take the left side out of play. I just know it works. Claude Harmon used to have twelve wraps under his left hand, saying, "I can talk to a fade but a hook won't listen." If you can take one side out, you effectively make the fairway twice as wide. Knowing your ball is going to fly straight or fade to the right slightly, you can aim down the left edge of the fairway, then have the entire fairway width to work with. Hogan understood this. Nicklaus gets it. Case closed.

Scott Verplank had told me the new technology made curving the ball harder. On the tour, no matter what kind of swing they made, the ball was almost assured of going relatively straight. Nevertheless, I still held Mr. Harmon's belief that the hardest shot to hit was a straight one. He believed golf was a game of curves, and his preference was a fade. My eye was also used to seeing a fade, so this would be my game plan once again.

The wedges are crucial. Sets today have more wedges; I had a 60-degree wedge, a 52-degree gap-wedge, a 48-degree pitching wedge, and a 56-degree lofted sand wedge with ample bounce or flange on the bottom of the club. This means the trailing end of the sole was about 5 degrees below the leading edge, making the club slide under the ball without digging--unless you are buried, you want shallow divots out of a bunker. Mike Keliher's set included a 64-degree wedge. It is intrinsically harder to control a shot with high trajectory, but I resolved to keep an open mind.

The PGA Tour had begun keeping all sorts of stats. I ignored most of them, but controlling your distances does matter. I had told Lewis that the distance wedge game was the single most important factor in the number of birdies made. Great putting has more to do with where you are putting from than your stroke--I am better from eight feet than Ben Crenshaw from 30. Pros on the Tour make half their putts from 6 feet, but it falls off dramatically farther away, even for tour players. We control distance better with our full swing because it's more familiar from all the repetitions. When I was heavier and stronger, I hit a 60-degree wedge 75 yards without straining. The other wedges would extend that at approximately 15-yard intervals.

I had started to work on "finding" my 150-pound swing the previous fall. Ruth would come home from work to see me, illuminated by the headlights of my car, hitting balls into my practice fairway on the farm. Sometimes, hitting in the chilly

November air with a slight rain, I built a roaring bonfire to keep warm.

Relying on my senses, I kept trying to discover my new move. I wanted a flat left wrist and a lagging club-head that snapped and squared through impact. Suddenly I realized I was feeling my old high school swing, which relied on rhythm, timing, and centrifugal force to deliver the clubface squarely--pointing at my intended target through impact. The ball doesn't care what swing you use--Newton's laws work every time!

The grip is the #1 fundamental. Always has been and always will be. I used what is called a "neutral" grip, which allows the forearms and hands to rotate equal distance both ways, opening and closing. You want to stand "proudly," as Mr. Harmon would say, "showing some neck," with proper leg flex and a straight back. The swing works most efficiently if the arms simply hang under the shoulders. The other essential position, in my view, is the balanced finish that Mike Keliher demonstrated so well. If you can arrive at the proper destination, chances are good you took the right route: what preceded it was most likely sound too.

A pendulum, even one with a hinging of the wrists, will take the same measure of time to complete an arc. Whether a four-foot putt or a full swing, any golf swing should take the same time from the start to the finish. With enough repetitions, I would ultimately be able to execute unconsciously. Sam Snead used to say the perfect rhythm for his swing was a 3/4 waltz time. Not conversant with music theory, I don't know what it means other than the rhythm and timing are the same. Practicing with a CD player in my back pocket and headphones on to shut down the conscious-mind chatter, I discovered by accident that Donny Hathaway's live version of "What's Going On" provided the right timing for me. With the CD player set on Repeat, I rarely hit a shot without this song playing softly in my ears, burrowing into my heart and soul. Hathaway's rhythm section kept me in time when I walked and played 18 holes.

Jack Larkin and his wife Lee Anne live in Atlanta with their three children. Jack was invited to join the Peachtree Golf Club--the premier club in Atlanta and Bobby Jones's home club. To maintain his great rhythm and timing with much less practice, Jack uses a metronome with headphones to serve the same purpose as Sam Snead's internal waltzes and my "What's Going On." Jack works on his pitch shots and short game one afternoon a week, practicing his putting with the metronome before hitting a few drivers. He understands that if his timing with the scoring shots is right, it will be the same with the long shots.

Jack Larkin's swing has always had a flowing, unhurried power. This might seem surprising, but you can generate more club-head speed and power with an unhurried natural swing. I never worried too much about my players being "on-plane." Kids couldn't care less about theory, and more importantly *the human body will give it to you if the set-up and takeaway are right.* Once that downswing starts, you let the club-head "snap" through the ball and coast into the balanced finish. A golf swing will repeat if some damn fool doesn't coach the inner artist out of you.

In *The Pro*, Butch Harmon's 2006 book about his father, Butch brings up Jack Larkin as an example of how "talented kids" can be "ruined by bad teaching." After "someone told [Jack] he needed to get longer in order to have a chance on tour," Butch writes that Jack tried to increase his club-head speed; Butch implies that this caused Jack to lose his accuracy, and his game never recovered.

Jack Larkin gave his dream of playing the PGA Tour a couple of years before pursuing a career in the wine business. When I spoke to him recently, Jack told me he'd never met Butch and had no idea what he was talking about. He never experienced any slump or needed to change his swing. Jack Larkin has twice won the Georgia State Golf Association Public Links Amateur Championship, which tells me that he didn't lose his game. Jack has continued to excel in match play because he's retained the utter calm he displayed when he won the 1979 U.S. Junior to become my first national champion. I admire and respect all the Harmons and Butch is a friend, but I suspect he couldn't resist what sounded like a good story.

My players have praised the way I got them prepared to compete mentally, physically, and spiritually. Coaching came naturally to me, but now for the first time I had embarked upon such a mission with *my* game as the focus. I like the motto "dance with the girl that brung ya." I believe in keeping it natural, going with what works, and . . . well, keep on going with it.

If you are thinking about your pre-shot routine it isn't a routine. It has to be natural, simple, and suited to your individual personality. I used to time my players' routines with a stopwatch. When they were swinging on autopilot, unconsciously, their pre-shot routines always ran around thirteen seconds. Playing basketball I'd learned that having a routine at the free-throw line gives you your best chance of making the shot. The same applies in golf. The swing truly begins when you initiate the routine. If it is unconscious and automatic, the rhythm of the routine meshes with the swing. It all flows.

Having a reference point from which to self-coach means you don't have to rely on some guru. Keep your approach to the swing simple and natural, and you can never go damagingly wrong. Certain specialty and trouble shots require an imagination . . . but everyone has one! Einstein was right: imagination is more important *and powerful* than knowledge. A mental picture (shot visualization) held until the finish will serve you far better than breaking the swing into pieces with swing keys.

Good basketball coaches say the game starts at the opponent's basket and unfolds backwards from there; their team can shoot poorly and still win by playing great defense. *The game of golf starts at the hole and works backwards to the tee.* A great player can hit just eight greens and still shoot 69--that rock-solid short game is the true measure of mental toughness.

I had to believe that I could make every putt and short shot where I could see the hole. I worked on making everything from six feet and in. Once you can do this, all those long putts, chips, pitch, and bunker shots feel that much easier. Believing you can make the six-footer coming back frees you up to be more aggressive.

Tom Watson's game provides a great example of this. Watson was 59 when he played in the 2009 British Open; missing a short pitch shot and five-foot putt sent him into a four-hole playoff with Stewart Cink. He lost. Every golfer in the world was pulling for him to win at his age. In his prime Watson might have holed the pitch, claimed the Claret Jug, and made history, but when he started missing the comeback putts his confidence diminished. That's what I saw in the 2009 Open playoff: Watson no longer believed he had that comeback putt in the bag.

***

Can you see it?

Do you have it?

Do you need it?

Sound course management can be summed up right there. When you examine and picture the shot, your subconscious mind will usually impel your body toward the best option. Then go into #2 and #3 and play your shot. But keep this in mind: Bobby Jones said it took him years to understand that just because he had a shot didn't mean he needed to play it. Sam Snead summed up his course management philosophy with the declaration that he always played the easiest shot. Keep both your swing and shot selection simple.

Make as many decisions ahead of time as possible. Your course plan should be pretty much set. Know which limb in a distant tree will be your aiming point. Determine the club you plan to play and the shape of the shot. Even when weather conditions such as wind and rain force a change, a plan should still have you thinking *less*, executing your pre-determined decisions, and just reacting to the target on each and every shot.

I looked over Mike Keliher's clubs. He had a set of beryllium copper Ping Eye II irons; I'd once owned a set and liked them. Mike had big hands, so a change of grips was in order, but the length and shaft flex fit my specs. I needed to adjust the lie angles and make them 2 degrees more upright. His Titleist driver was too heavy and stiff, but the Taylormade driver Verplank had sent me was perfect. Likewise, Mike's three wood wouldn't work, but I had that hot one Bob Wolcott had gotten for me from a tour van at the Kemper. I always like a three wood I can hit longer, and a driver I can hit higher, shorter, and straighter--these clubs accomplished this. Mike had favored the four-wedge system for distance control. I kept pondering that 64-degree wedge loaded with lead tape. Whatever his thinking had been with that club, it remained inscrutable.

Once I spent some time with my long putter, I really did convince myself that every putt was a tap-in. The subconscious can be tricked, but it only uses perceptions--sensory information--and imagination. My hands would swing inside an arc defined by the creases of my two pants legs, the same length every time. Holding the shaft at 32 inches let me roll it about four feet, whereas holding it close to the end at 48 inches would let me "tap" a 60-footer. I wrapped blue plastic tape around the square, enlarged grip, which had no taper, then placed strips of black plastic tape around the grip at two-inch intervals. I used a conventional reverse overlap grip; I've never had any reason to go with the claw or other yip-prevention split handgrips.

Greg Powers, who played well in two U.S. Opens, used to practice putting on his club's hardwood ballroom floor. By the time he got there, Oakmont's greens felt slow to him. Davis Love's father used to have him hit drivers 150 yards to help groove the sequence of his swing. My practice fairway on the farm curved left to right from one direction and, of course, right to left from the opposite end. I mowed it 15 yards wide, then placed white stakes in the ground flanking it 45 yards apart. Teeing up Scott Verplank's driver, I swung at half speed, dropping my shots in the fairway. I visualized each shot, went through my routine, and let it go just like on the course--holding a picture of the shot and thinking about nothing.

Seeing white out-of-bounds stakes can instill fear. But telling yourself to stay away from that water hazard or those OB stakes usually results in exactly what you *don't* want. With your mind drawn to them, where does the ball go? Directly at what you are looking at. Hitting to a fifteen-yard fairway with OB stakes 15 yards on either side would reset my perceptions: up in Connecticut, with a 40-yard wide fairway, it would feel like I was hitting into the Gulf of Mexico. I might not even see a white stake up there. But if I did, it would look so far out of play it would be a non-factor. *Our brains adjust to extreme situations if we practice that way.* Greg Powers' strategy made the Oakmont greens seem slow to him, while mine would make the Darien fairways appear wider than they were.

After settling on that putter I found myself acclimating quickly. I stuck a tee in the ground and putted at it from four directions, first from 30 feet to give me a sense for that distance, then from 8 feet. Soon I was moving my hands up and down the grip without thinking. This proved exceptionally effective from 50 or 60 feet; even long putts seemed like tap-ins. I decided to use *paces* rather than feet with my putting: "ten paces" seems shorter than "thirty feet." I'd take four paces from the hole to my ball to convince myself I had a tap-in. This also helped me calibrate where to hold the putter and thereby control the length of the arc.

I have never known a player who couldn't putt better at night. When you can see, you look at the line too much, or even worse notice spike marks. Putting by moonlight allows you to see the shadows and contours, but you're not tempted to over-read a putt or look for spike marks to avoid. I would recommend this kind of practice to anyone.

I had decided to practice my short game and play only with Titleist Pro VI balls. They performed the best for me; my shag bag was filled with about forty brand new balls. This had been my players' practice for thirty years. *Don't practice your short game with a range ball.* They are inconsistent and respond nothing like what you will be playing. Bob Wolcott gave me six dozen Titleist Pro VI balls, all imprinted with his name.

***

Every time I played or practiced, I had the CD player in my back pocket, the headphones on, and the same disk on Repeat, Repeat, Repeat, hearing it and not hearing it at the same time. While his band jammed behind him, Donny Hathaway introduced his players: "On the bass . . . the baddest bass player in the United States . . . from Salemburg, North Carolina . . . Willie Weeks! Willie Weeks, y'all!" Like the music, these words grooved themselves in my mind.

Bob Wolcott hosted a fundraiser for his hometown of Dickson, TN, outside Nashville. Vince Gill and his band would play, and Bob raised thousands of dollars through the years. That spring Bob invited me backstage with my son, Rob, who was sixteen. As Vince introduced me to his band, a thin African-American man, maybe fifty years old, flashed a nice smile. When Vince said his name, I stepped back. "On the bass," I said, "the baddest bass player in the United States . . . from Salemburg, North Carolina . . . Willie Weeks! Willie Weeks, y'all!" I had never met him and had no idea he was Vince's bass player.

Willie's eyebrows went up and he smiled. "You have been listening to some good music," he said. Willie Weeks was just 18 when he played with Donny Hathaway back in 1972. It was now 2006, so I was taking him back 34 years, but his reaction conveyed that this was a special memory. He told me working with Donny Hathaway during that stretch was magical. This music had a powerful effect on the people he saw from the stage:

"Their heads would sway back and forth, looking like wind blowing across a wheat field." Hathaway's band toured both coasts and even played Carnegie Hall. Hathaway was a musical genius, Willie said, but he suffered from schizophrenia. Donny Hathaway jumped to his death from a New York City hotel room in 1979.

Vince Gill said Willie Weeks was one of the best bass players on the planet, and he has since played with Eric Clapton. When I told Willie that I was using that music to groove my swing, he got it. These musicians get things others miss.

***

I spent 75 percent of my practice time with the putter, sand wedge, and driver. As I moved further away from the hole-- making twenty in a row from six feet and working toward fifty-- I kept telling my gullible subconscious, "This is just another tap-in." They were finding the hole; my long putting was especially strong. Holding that 48-inch putter on the end and swinging between the creases in my pants simplified things for me. But would it hold up under pressure?

I fed my subconscious positive expectations: "This is Verplank's driver and he never misses a fairway." "Look, here's another tap-in." On putts, when I pictured the ball entering the hole from the direction the ball was rolling, my body's alignment adjusted without any thought.

Picturing what part of the hole the ball will enter is crucial. The inner artist, (spirit, soul, or heart--labels don't matter) feeds on pictures imagined in what we call *visualization*. If you are *trying* to visualize, you aren't visualizing--you are thinking about visualizing. Don't let this inner game stuff intimidate you. Before I am through, I hope it will be clear.

I decided to practice/play at Stoney Brook, the little daily-fee course where my prep school team at CMA used to shoot 65 all the time. I told the course manager that I planned on carrying my own clubs and playing 18 first thing in the morning, then practicing. He offered to waive all fees. Now that I was playing with what felt like my high school swing, walking back on that course gave me deja vu: it seemed like it was 1966 again. Playing five days a week, just swinging with no expectations, I was training myself to get in the flow every single day out. I wanted to play with my eyes in Connecticut--*observe without labeling the shot as good or bad*--and let the pictures into my subconscious. I decided to name this non-judgmental awareness the *Eagle*. I would get a yardage, picture a shot, and play away, holding my finish and watching the shot intently until the ball stopped rolling.

Between shots I focused on my breathing--the best way to stay in the now and play one shot at a time. This breathing pattern became unconscious with training (see pp. 352-53 for instructions). It was hard hitting a six iron when my eye was used to playing an eight, but the driver was on autopilot. I was intentionally not keeping score. At 59 years old, weighing 150 pounds, I was playing a new game. A lot of physical changes occur in our fifties--none positive. Competing with the newly eligible fifty-year-olds, I would need to get into the flow and stay there for 18 holes to have a chance. With my experience in the inner game, I believed it was possible. The subconscious doesn't know age as a number: you are as old as you perceive yourself to be.

Before long some of my old classmates spotted me at Stoney Brook, and everyone who knew me wanted to talk. "What are

you doing?" "We haven't seen you out here!" "Why are you playing by yourself?" Too much chitchat wouldn't help at all. With
less than two months before the tournament, I needed to put in
the reps in the inner game, too. Time to find another place.

I went to see the pro at Saddle Creek Golf Club in
Lewisburg, the heart of Tennessee Walking Horse country,
about 25 miles away. Once I told him what I was doing and how
he could help me, he agreed to everything, including keeping it
quiet. For the remaining five weeks I worked at Saddle Creek,
practicing for about three hours with numerous *breaks*. Ever
since someone told me that when you're using your mind it's
helpful to break every twenty minutes, I have always advocated
short, focused practice sessions spent working on the inner and
outer game simultaneously.

Saddle Creek had a perfect little area to work on distance
control with the wedge. Nobody ever used the space but me. I
could hit my bag of Titleist Pro VI's uphill or downhill, putting
towels down at various yardages to gauge shots. I had always
been a good wedge player controlling distances, but after an
eight-year gap I needed to groove it and establish some confidence. Wondering what Mike Keliher had seen in that 64-
degree wedge--he must have had some kind of plan--I kept it in
the bag for now. Did I want to have longer clubs? I was hitting it
shorter. Brad Faxon once threw a 60-degree wedge in a lake. He
said he was so tempted to use it that it cost him more shots than
it saved him . . . so he gave it a new home.

Saddle Creek provided a decent test without being too hard
or easy. I was just freeing it up: picturing the shot, aiming,
swinging, and letting the ball go wherever it wanted to. That's

how it feels when you are in the flow. If nothing else, I had time to *pretend* I was in the flow.

Willie Weeks and Vince Gill know all about getting in the flow and giving it to the inner artist. The music itself helps them attain this creative place, like "What's Going On" coming through my headphones. The inner artist resides in the subconscious. Great ones don't have to *think* about playing music; it just flows out of that silent place where the spirit resides. Spirit, soul, heart . . . take your pick. Timothy Gallwey in *The Inner Game of Tennis* labels this Self II. But the inner artist isn't another "self," it is the spirit in the subconscious. There is only one self playing. This is why, like music performed with artistry, great golf also transcends technique.

Every year Foot-Joy gave me ten pairs of shoes, size 10C and never anything but the best. I had collected twenty hardly-been-worn pairs of shoes in a closet in the spare bedroom. Those Saddle Creek fairways were firm; after playing 18 holes five days a week, my feet were killing me. Hoping to find a pair that didn't hurt, I kept switching and finally found a pair of black and gray saddle oxfords that worked; at last my feet were comfortable. There was a brown and white pair in the same style. These two pairs of shoes had belonged to Lewis Chitengwa.

Verplank's driver, Keliher's irons, Wolcott's Titleist balls, and now Lewis's shoes . . . Every one of them was accompanying me on this quest. Oh man, I wanted to make it.

***

Several years earlier, googling "NLP-Golf," I had discovered the website of Wade Pearse, a mental-game coach in Vancouver, British Columbia. In the field of education NLP stands for natural learning process. This NLP stood for "neurolinguistic pro-gramming." As I read a well-written article by Pearse I was starting to think there might be something to it, but he kept talking about the need for certain "concepts" in order to play well. I fired him an email: "Someone may play pretty good and get to a ten or twelve handicap playing with 'concepts.' But if the player wants to be a champion, the only way to play great is with 'sensory perceptions' . . . and no conscious mind interfer-ence." Three or four days later I got a response. When he first read my message, Pearse said, he thought I was a smartass. "Bobby, I am a very sound sleeper," he wrote. "Last night I woke up at 3 o'clock and I knew you were right."

We developed a friendship over the phone and by email. I found Wade intelligent, energetic, and engaged. In April of 2007 I asked him if he could offer any advice for my Senior Open preparations.

"Think back to your best competitive golf experience," he said. This stumped me at first, but Wade was patient; he said it might be in there with a color. All of a sudden winning that qualifier at Austin Country Club came up on my mind's screen. I described Mr. Penick helping me and told Wade I'd shot eight under for thirty-six holes.

"Can you remember a vivid color?" he asked.

That was thirty years ago! But then it came to me. "Yeah, I was staring at a beautiful blue sky all day . . . I didn't want to talk to my playing partners and I was praying for more birdies." Wade kept coaxing me to remember the emotions I was feeling then, pulling the good stuff out of my subconscious.

Finally he suggested something completely new to me. "When you're into your pre-shot routine," he said, "imagine a sky-blue cylinder encircling your ball where you will take your stance. Don't change your routine, but imagine that cylinder going to heaven. Let it go as high as you can imagine it." Now came his kicker. "Bobby, when you step into the Circle of Excellence you will have the same mindset as you had in Austin." This was outside the box, but Wade was a nice guy and a little research had revealed that his NLP wasn't that radical. I was willing to give this Circle of Excellence a try.

And so help me, it worked. I felt like a racehorse getting ready to run again. Whatever your best competitive experience, be patient, let your mind recall it . . . then use it.

As a coach I know that players rarely change a swing for keeps. They tend to slip back to their natural inclination. Bob Wolcott's stance used to get too narrow; I would know it before I saw him. Like a steel bar, people may bend, but that steel will bend back. "He'll be back doing the same thing in three weeks," Claude Harmon would say to me when the player he'd just helped was out of earshot. After thinking about this at home, I grabbed my five iron, three balls, and some tees. Outside, I moved my left thumb and squared my stance the way Harvey Penick had suggested in that one-ball lesson. Just like in Austin, I started hitting it really well.

I decided to practice full swings--not just putting--in the dark. The first time, I did it just to see what it was like. Wearing Lewis's black shoes and a pair of black pants, in barely enough moonlight to see the ball, was as close to training blind as I could get. A full moon washes out most of the challenge, but when you can't see your feet and legs it's something different altogether. I was working on rhythm and balance but wanted to elevate my awareness by listening for where the ball would land.

After four or five balls to get used to it, I was soon swinging by feel and going to a balanced finish, just trusting that the clubhead would make contact with the ball. That first night I hit about seventy-five balls. The next morning I found those balls in the tightest pattern I had achieved all year.

I have described some things that helped me. What works for me may not work for you. Following my intuition, I didn't have a manual. That soul music I was listening to helped me shut down or tune out the conscious mind. The silence and solitude of being exiled to the farm by my lack of a job allowed me to focus with an intensity I had never known, while stretching myself beyond where I had been before. I had never wanted anything so intensely.

When Scott Tway and Scott Verplank won at Lake Tahoe, they'd made a decision to have fun--they weren't going to *try* to have fun, they were *going to* have fun.

The most basic definition of flow is being absorbed in a pleasurable experience. I was having fun, totally into it. If you have to think about being in the flow, you will just be thinking about the flow--it has to be unconscious to *be* the flow. I was getting there every day, unconscious. I wanted to run up to Connecticut . . . but I had to hold on and let the day come.

Lewis Chitengwa with the South African Amateur trophy, 1993

17

GIVING IT TO THE MAGICIAN

*In basketball--as in life--true joy comes from being
fully present in each and every moment, not when
things just go your way.*

–Phil Jackson

The journey is more fun than the inn.

–Robert Frost

In the process of training for the Senior Open I detached myself from everyone but my wife and family. I saw other players at Saddle Creek but didn't stop and talk with them unless I felt like it. With that focus came a higher level of awareness and consciousness than I had ever known before. I heard every bird singing, smelled the sharp smell of fresh-cut grass, even felt Mike and Lewis with me at times. I felt the spirit inside with every one of my five senses, and a few others the scientists haven't named yet. It might be in an older and weaker package, but my spirit was in there--I just had to coax it out.

Coaxing and coaching. Sometimes the processes match as closely as the words. I was learning more about the inner game with each day. Because the key lies in the repetitions I needed to give myself as many quality repetitions as I could, consistently holding my finish and feeding my mind good pictures. If you are only working on the physical game you are doing the job half-way, so I rehearsed the inner and outer games simultaneously. The natural learning process was doing the job: I just had to *keep showing up.*

Daddy Will used to tell me, "It doesn't take any longer to do something right than halfway." When we went to the movies, we sat in the balcony with all the other "colored" folks. I would buy us ice cream cones for a nickel each at a little diner close to the theater. They wouldn't let him buy anything. But he also used to say, "Nobody can bother you unless you let them."

Daddy Will was old and walked with a cane. I learned how to wait and not be in such a hurry when I was with him. I can still hear him. "If you aren't going to do it right, don't do it--wait until you are ready to do the job right." "We need to take care of these tools . . . They will take care of us." Have you ever seen someone sharpen a garden hoe? Daddy Will did, with a file.

These clubs were going to take care of me if I took care of them. This meant getting the dirt out of the grooves and scrubbing the grips with soapy water and a stiff wire brush. Clubs feel better when the grips are tacky and not slick. I had to keep these clubs right.

Claude Harmon said, "The big picture is in the details." I told my guys "Success is the sum of small efforts, repeated day in and day out," (I've recently learned that those words originated with Robert Collier) along with faith in the things that you do.

After Scott Verplank went to Oklahoma State he adopted the saying "Everything is a learning experience." I've always wondered if Mike Holder hammered this into them. Another valuable attitude: "What did we learn today that will help us going forward?" Played bad? Don't be upset . . . What did you learn? At fifty-nine years old I was taking it one day at a time, learning whatever could help me.

Using my experience in Austin, I visualized winning the Senior Open qualifier. Once Wade Pearse helped me retrieve that memory, the feelings and details returned. I started keeping a gratitude journal, writing down everything I was grateful for each day and using the words grateful and thankful at every opportunity. Like a hummingbird flapping its wings, the conscious mind flutters through thousands of thoughts daily; to quiet my mind I returned to the practice of meditating twice a day. Of all my preparation strategies, the meditation may have had the greatest impact on my ability to get into the flow every day and stay there.

Many people believe getting into the flow--or the zone, as some call it--just happens randomly several times a year. Learn how to detach the ego and quiet the conscious mind, and you can get there regularly. I had a more ambitious goal, however. My intention was to *stay* there for all eighteen holes in Darien.

I had to prepare for obstacles that can disrupt the flow. Making a triple bogie, getting a bad break, dealing with an official, getting angry, getting six or seven over, or letting a bad pairing grate on you--I wanted to be ready to handle any or all of these. Probably eight times a round your ball will come to rest in a place you're not expecting. Once you accept this, when it happens it'll just be part of the game: you can stay in the flow and play the shot.

***

I hadn't seen Dale and Sherry Kahlden in twenty-eight years, since we were at River Oaks together. The Kahldens lived in Norwalk--not far from where the Senior Open qualifier was being played--and Dale was the pro at Shorehaven Golf Club. After arranging to stay with them, I decided I'd rather have Shorehaven's best caddie than a bag toter at the other club, but Dale wasn't there when I called his shop. As soon as I said why I was calling, the young man who answered said, "I'm Dale's son John, and I'm the best caddie out here. I'll caddie for you." That made one less thing to think about.

I made reservations to fly into New Haven on a Wednesday. The qualifier was the following Monday, giving me four days to relax and get used to the change in climate and playing conditions. With an early morning flight out of Nashville, I planned to spend Tuesday night at Mrs. Keliher's house. Mike's sister Diana invited me for dinner, with Scott Keliher and his family, and we talked about Mike, sharing some humorous stories. "I don't believe in luck, but I do believe in miracles," I told them when they asked about the upcoming tournament. "It may take a miracle, but I'm going to give it all I have." The next morning Toni woke me up for the short trip to the Nashville airport. Mike had told me it was a tradition for his mom to take him to catch a plane. When Mike won that U.S. Amateur qualifier, as medalist he had received a sterling silver medal with the USGA emblem on it. As we arrived at the airport I said, "Toni, if I win that medal, it's yours."

Those "What's Going On" lyrics repeated endlessly in my head. I still couldn't understand why Lewis and Mike died so young. But instead of grieving I thought about how they lived, and how close we were. Once the plane was airborne I tilted my seat back and focused on my breathing, imagining the oxygen going in and out of my heart. If you have any desire to get into the flow on a regular basis your heart must be filled with love, gratitude, and compassion--you cannot be carrying around anger, bitterness, or any other emotion that will interfere. On that day I couldn't have hauled any more love. I was grateful for all the players God had sent my way, thankful to have such a wonderful family . . . so many people had helped me get to this point. I felt nothing but good will now. "I'm playing for every soul who has ever been kind to me, dead or alive," I pledged to myself.

***

In New Haven I rented a car and made my way to East Norwalk, about forty miles. Dale and Sherry Kahlden, both tournament players, knew not to upset their routines and just let me chill out. I met John, their nineteen-year-old son and my caddie, and we spent some time at Shorehaven getting acquainted. I hit a few balls but mainly played wedge shots out of the tall, thick grass around the greens--typical for courses in the northeast-- using Mike Keliher's 64-degree wedge. The greens were quick, as I anticipated. The bunkers also tend to have steeper slopes, but ever since Claude Harmon taught me the finer points, the sand game has been one of my strengths. The main thing with Mr. Harmon was getting up and letting trajectory help stop the ball. Pleased with how I was rolling it, I didn't worry about the bunkers.

The very exclusive club hosting the qualifier was allowing practice rounds after 1:00 pm on Thursday. John wasn't available so I ended up riding a cart with some nice guys. The course conditions were excellent. It was a good northeastern layout--a lot of elevation changes, many of the greens well above the fairways--with a few places where you needed to lay up and a couple of quirky holes. It wasn't Winged Foot, but I liked the golf course; the more challenging holes were right there to see.

It was still chilly up there and the bent-grass fairways were soft. Aiming for the center of the greens or past it on every hole, I wanted to have enough club playing into the greens. I was hitting my driver very solid and straight, but still being two clubs shorter after all this training meant paying attention to yardage to the back edge as well as the ideal position for every tee shot. John Kahlden had said he knew the course well. With sixty players for two spots, I had no idea what score it would take, but it didn't matter--I had prepared to put one foot in front of the other, play one shot at a time, and let the Magician invent some shots.

On Friday I hit a few balls and played six holes late in the day, meditated, listened to music, and talked to John. His parents called him Johnny. He told me he had recently made it to the semi-finals of the Metropolitan Golf Association match play. He had laid out a year after graduating from high school, but his heart's desire was to play college golf. Our conversation turned to the qualifier. Because there were only two spots available, I told him, "Let's free it up and have fun! The worst we can do is third." This puzzled John, until I explained that third and sixtieth get the same result: they get to play a great course, enjoy it, and go home.

On Saturday I drove the forty miles back to New Haven to see Megan Macomber, a college English teacher and a gifted writer. We had become friends several years earlier and she had been to Columbia for a visit. I had heard a lot about the Yale golf course designed by Charles Blair MacDonald, so after lunch at a good Italian restaurant, we headed across town to check it out. That Yale golf course exceeded my expectations, with deep, shaggy bunkers much like those at Winged Foot. The course in Darien would be much easier. It was fun playing that monster; I just cruised around, dropping another ball and playing some shots. I was hitting it solid and all I wanted to do was relax, have fun, and enjoy being with Megan.

My plan for Sunday was to walk to downtown East Norwalk, a neat small town on Long Island Sound. A couple of miles from Dale and Sherry's house I happened upon a Missionary Baptist church about to start worship. When you see Missionary in front of Baptist, you know it's a black church and it will be a lively worship. Attending Canaan AME had made me comfortable with their traditions and brought a real appreciation for how they do it. This Connecticut church was packed, but a lady signaled for me to sit with her. In the black church guests are asked to stand and identify themselves. I rose and said, "I'm Bobby McIver from Tennessee. I'm here to qualify for the U.S. Senior Open tomorrow, and I'll need all of my game to make it. I'm very grateful and thankful to be able to worship with you today."

It was a spirit-filled worship. The pastor prayed the Lord would be with me. As I exited the church he grabbed me, told me he was from Tuscaloosa, AL, and wished me well. After that I walked around just counting my blessings. I went down to the waterfront and sat for a while on a bench. The cool breeze off Long Island Sound felt good. With my CD player I listened to the music that had helped me get into the flow during my training.

My tee time was around 10 the next morning. I was paired with a big Japanese-American gentleman I had seen at the practice round. Knowing he would hit it by me, I asked John Kahlden to hustle and get to my ball ahead of me--I wanted to know how far I had to the back edge and to the pin. I would pull the clubs, but if John favored another club he should speak up. If there was any wind he needed to let me know. I wanted John to read every putt--I would ask if I was in doubt.

We planned to get there two hours before our tee time. My warm-up would consist of twenty minutes at the short game area, twenty minutes on the putting green, twenty minutes on the range, then twenty more minutes at the putting green, holing three-footers and getting a feel for the pace. This allowed time to go to the locker room and get to the tee fifteen minutes ahead of the tee-time. The mind likes routine and process, and with plenty of time there is no need for rushing the warm-up. I wanted to be in the flow from the time I left Dale and Sherry's home through the entire round. I went over this with John, explained the rationale, and asked him to keep up with the time.

Monday morning Sherry prepared a big breakfast for us. Then I went to my room to stretch out and listen to some music. Finally I sat upright in a chair and did the three-part deep breathing, as a meditation, for twenty minutes. Here's how:

Count to four as you inhale, filling your lungs to capacity. *(In-2-3-4)*

Hold your breath for a three count. *(Hold-2-3)*

Exhale very slowly, for a six count. *(Out-2-3-4-5-6)*

All breathing is through the nostrils. Squeeze all the air out using diaphragm muscles. With your eyes closed, put your awareness on the abdominal muscles. The rhythm of this breathing will become automatic.

If you need a name, call this mindfulness meditation: it stills and quiets the mind. It also gives you more energy, increases your awareness, and gives you a higher level of consciousness. Practice this breathing while walking on the course; focus your awareness on your heart area. Breathing is one of the least understood essentials for staying in the flow. The conscious mind inevitably comes into play regarding yardage and club selection, but deep breathing helps keep the ego and conscious mind out of the way between shots.

All my training had the simplest goal: to *breathe properly and stay totally in the present* for the 18-hole tournament. I wanted the Eagle (nonjudgmental sensory perception) to see each shot and relay the images directly to the Magician. Holding a picture of the shot effectively displaces the ego, silencing intrusive conscious-mind chatter. Maintaining the Eagle's intense gaze would give my body the chance to make adjustments unconsciously, without the Professor judging, or interfering with conscious thoughts. I wanted the Professor to go to lunch or take a hike. The Magician doesn't need his help--the power is in the unconscious.

What I was striving for through meditation is called the beginner's mind in Zen. At eleven or twelve my players did all this stuff naturally. I just wanted to play with the freedom of a twelve-year-old. Adults have to unlearn these mental game problems, the concepts and swing thoughts that clutter your mind when you get older. The body is doing, the mind is know-ing, and the spirit is being: to BE a good player, *let your spirit have it. Pretend you are twelve.*

I had trained this way with my mental game for over two months. It was now automatic and required no thinking or try-ing. This period of walking and carrying my bag had actually made me feel like a kid again.

***

It was time to tee off. Walking over to my playing partner, I stuck out my hand and introduced myself. "They have two spots," I said. "They belong to us--let's get it done!" The polite Japanese-American man seemed a little taken aback, but I had broken the ice and turned him into a teammate. I wanted him to know that I truly felt goodwill towards him and wished him well. This set the tone for the round.

We started on the number 10 hole. A par four that played up a steep hill, it allowed both of us to make easy pars. Number 11 was a short par 4. After driving it pure I had a nine iron into the pin, which was tucked on the back right. The ball flew right and landed in a bunker. I could barely see it. When I stepped in, my feet sank down to my shoelaces: the bunker had recently been filled with sand and seemed to have no bottom. After studying it, I decided to hit Mike Keliher's 64-degree wedge and swing as hard as I could. The ball popped up. Failing to clear the lip, it buried again, staying on the slope. A bunker is supposed to have a firm base and about an inch of loose sand on top--a shot that hits on the slope should roll back to the bottom.

I was facing my first test. After running so many tourna-ments, in my judgment that bunker should have been "ground under repair"; I should have been allowed a free drop. I hit it in there, though, so I couldn't let it jar me out of the flow. Setting up to play my third shot, one foot in and one out, I asked John, "Will it go forward?" He said it would. Once again I swung as hard as I could. The ball popped out, carrying three feet.

All of this took some time. It was my putt. With a thirty-footer coming off a slope, I hit it six feet by and missed. Since I had only played the course once, starting on the tenth hole had the course out of order in my mind. Already three over, I found myself confronting number 12, the hardest par 3 on the course. During the practice round they'd placed the tee at about 210 yards, but now it was on another tee playing 235 yards. I asked John to bring the bag on the tee. Based upon that practice round I was carrying four wedges: I didn't have a club for the shot, all carry over a lake. The 7 wood I'd put in the bag instead of a 3 iron would carry 200 yards--max. I had to use my imagination, the only club left I could rely on. Choking down on my 3 wood, I aimed over the water to the left and finessed an incredible cut shot into the middle of the green. It was pure subconscious magic.

Coming off the number 12 green, our third hole, we were met by a very young rules official. "You are behind," he said abruptly. "I'm timing you."

In the past I would have told him that he didn't know his job. I just smiled. "You got it, pal," I said. "We'll catch up." My playing partner was rattled. Seeing him rushing, I went over and said, "Hey, everything is cool . . . I'm the reason we're behind. I don't play slow. I'm just going to play at my normal pace--the clock is on me, not you."

I got in a groove: three over, just playing one shot at a time and looking for some birdies. I kept doing my breathing. On number 15 my ball came up short on my second shot. In that heavy greenside rough, with the pin on the front and a steep bunker to carry, I took that 64-degree wedge again and swung as hard as I could.

The ball must have popped forty feet in the air. It dropped almost straight down, took a bounce, and rolled within six inches. I walked off the green with a par that felt like a birdie--even three over, I could hardly feel my feet touching the ground.

That triple bogey and the rookie rules official combined couldn't rattle me out of the flow. By the time we came around to number 1, our tenth hole, we had closed the gap as I anticipated. Number 1 had two greens. We'd played the straightaway one during the practice round, but today we were playing across a big ravine to the second green. After a good drive down the right center, my ball was on a downslope. With 200 yards, I needed to hit the seven wood, swing with the slope, and catch it solid. But the slope had me off-balance and my ball failed to carry the ravine. I took my drop, hit a five iron on the green, and two-putted for a double bogie.

With eight holes to play it was time to make a move. My putting was good, I just wasn't hitting it close enough to the hole: nothing was falling. I stayed dialed in with that driver Scott sent me, driving it solid and in the fairway. On the fifth, a tough par 4, I missed the green to the right. I had to hit it about 90 feet up a steep slope, off hardpan, to the hole on an upper tier. Letting my intuition invent a shot, I took the 7 wood and played a low scooter. The ball came to rest about three feet away and I made the putt. My playing partner couldn't believe it.

I was playing every shot with pictures, my attention in the present moment without thinking about it--so deep in the flow that I had to ask John what hole we were playing. Feeling like I was floating, I made a par five on number 8.

The next thing I knew we were back at the clubhouse on our last hole. It seemed impossible. With as much energy as when we started, I could have just kept playing.

Number 9 was a good par three with a big terrace that extended above the pin, which was front right on the lower level. Picturing my ball catching the edge of the upper level and releasing to the hole, I hit it solidly--the shot I'd visualized--but it stayed on the upper level, about three feet above the lower one. It was a difficult pin position. I had visualized the ball trickling to the hole and flopping in the high side.

It was a new green, however. The ground felt firmer under my feet, the surface broke about ten feet from the hole, and the green was lightning fast. After hitting a good putt that caught the edge, I made a five-footer coming back for par. The round was over.

***

John Kahlden had been keeping my playing partner's card along with mine. I hadn't really thought about my score all day. We sat down at the scorer's table and went over that card four or five times. I knew I hadn't made it but still wanted to turn in a correct card. After I signed it, John took it to the scoreboard for me. Wanting to just be alone for a moment, I spotted a stone wall about forty yards away in the shade. I walked up the gentle slope and sat down, looked around, and took in the magnificent setting.

Several trips around this particular course might have helped me. At 150 pounds my old power wasn't there--there were no six birdies like at Augusta on this day--but I felt fine about the round.

Artists say flow means "the God within," and I played a round of golf that was inspired or in spirit for sure. How did I know? I felt an unmistakable joy and inner bliss. Musicians describe it as feeling like someone else is playing the music through them--this is how it felt for me. The Magician that really is my true self on the golf course played some great shots. I felt peace. On that day, I knew this was the best I could play.

Bobby Jones said there are two types of golf: social--or as Claude Harmon described it, "jolly"--golf, and tournament golf, which caused Jones to be nauseated before every round. I was rarely satisfied with my tournament play. Many times I used to get in my own way. My ego was judging--my main opponent had been myself. There was a time when I would have been throwing my bag in the trunk and spinning my tires in frustration over the score I returned at the Senior Open qualifier in Connecticut.

Not today. Today the ego was totally detached--I accomplished what I had intently trained myself to do. When Lewis Chitengwa went off to sit on that other stone wall in Charlottesville, I had told him, "That scoreboard is just a bunch of numbers." On this day, on this stone wall in Connecticut under the lush green trees, I felt love and compassion for myself, grateful to have played. My score didn't matter: that scoreboard really *is* just a bunch of numbers.

An inner voice was becoming audible. Would this be my last competitive round? Tournament golf had given me plenty of thrills--I had many memorable moments playing with that scorecard on my hip. Satisfied with everything, I sensed this might be a good place to end it.

When he saw me sitting on the stone wall, my Japanese-American friend walked over, thinking I was dejected. A nice, gracious, and gentle man, he was also extremely well mannered. I'd learned he lived in Manhattan. "Bobby," he said, "you played with a lot of courage and heart . . . You just kept playing. You taught me a lot--I will never forget you or this day." I thanked him. I'd had a lot of fun, I said, and was happy to be paired with him. I stood up, shook his hand, and gave him a light hug.

Seeing John Kahlden approaching, I took one last look around. "Johnny," I said, "it looks like we have third place locked up. Let's go home." We loaded up and John drove us home.

In a very real sense, that was the best round of golf I ever played in my life.

Bobby McIver and Mike Keliher, 1979

18

THE DIRECTION YOU ARE GOING

How old would you be if you didn't know how old you was?

−Satchel Paige

My return flight wasn't until Wednesday morning. Knowing I would be preoccupied by the qualifier, I'd wanted to save an extra, unburdened day with Dale and Sherry Kahlden. After another trip to New Haven to see Megan, I got back to their house about an hour before sundown. Sherry was putting some mulch in the flowerbed when I drove up. "Johnny's out there playing," she said. "Go catch up with him and play a few holes."

At Shorehaven they loaded my bags on a cart. Finding John on a par four, I watched as he set up, went through a smooth routine, and smashed a towering tee shot that flew straight down the middle, carrying at least 300 yards. I stepped back, thinking: Lord, what do you have me looking at? I played away, but my attention was on John. He kept blasting his driver, and then hitting shots flush and right at the hole. When I threw several balls in a bunker, he hit every one within four feet. His putting was solid. I had coached some great juniors, but none of them had this kind of controlled power at this age.

We played five holes before darkness set in. The next day, before I left for the airport, I made a point of thanking Sherry for sending me out to play with John. "I think this trip was about him, not me winning a tournament," I told her. "I'm going to see what I can do."

***

Toni Keliher understands golf and these qualifiers. When she picked me up, I told her I'd played with all the heart and soul I had in me. At her house I transferred my luggage to my car, gave her a hug, and headed out. After running on adrenaline for so long, I was beginning to realize how tired I was. At Diana's house I returned Mike's clubs. They were glad to get them back and I was kind of sad to let them go. They were a great set of irons.

After a decompression period I got around to trying to help John Kahlden. Mike Holder was now Oklahoma State University's athletic director. He had coached the OSU golf team to eight NCAA Championships; the team won its ninth title with Mike McGraw as coach. Like UCLA when Wooden was coaching, the OSU program attracts the top players year after year. Buddy Alexander had moved from LSU to the University of Florida, where he too has won national championships. I sent both Holder and Alexander the same message: John Kahlden had had some success in Met Golf Association events. While I had observed the work ethic--practicing and weight training in addition to caddying two rounds a day--I had only seen him play five holes and never seen a score posted. But having witnessed PGA Tour-quality shots coming off his clubface, I felt he could play for any team in the country. In fact, I would stake my professional reputation on it.

Within a half-hour Mike Holder emailed, asking me to call him. After catching up, since we hadn't seen each other in many years, he said, "Bobby, if you think this young man is a fit for our program, we like his chances. But Mike McGraw is our coach now, so you will be hearing from him." I told him I understood.

"I took one other player based upon someone's intuition," Mike Holder added after a brief pause. "Tommy Moore called me on the turn at an AJGA event in New Orleans. Tommy said we needed this player. His name was Scott Verplank, and he did a pretty good job for us."

Hanging up, I found myself almost moved to tears. I had no idea Mike Holder would respect my opinion to such an extent. I was always hard on myself--like most people, I never seemed to see my positive qualities as clearly as others did--and struggling with my health and no job had brought my self-esteem pretty low.

Mike McGraw soon called. "I have talked to Mike Holder and Scott Verplank, who both said you wouldn't have endorsed a young man like this unless you believed in him." He continued, "We had two players turn pro, so we can use another player or two. We're willing to give John a chance, but since we never saw him play or recruited him, he needs to call us." As he gave me his cell phone number I had to chuckle, recalling that wrist-buckling NCAA rule book in the office of the UVA compliance officer, thirteen years and several worlds ago. OSU's policy, Coach McGraw continued, was the same for walk-ons and scholarship players. "If we determine that they likely won't be able to get into the lineup for competition, we'll suggest they transfer and we'll help them find a good fit."

Dale answered my call to the Shorehaven golf shop. "By chance would John and Sherry be there?" I asked. They were-- Sherry doing his bookkeeping and John just in from caddying. "Good," I said, "Get everyone on a phone. Make sure Johnny has a pencil and a piece of paper." Dale got everyone in place. "Hey, Johnny," I said, "write down this number--Mike McGraw, the golf coach at Oklahoma State, is expecting your call. They have a spot for you. Looks like you are going to be a Cowboy."

When I told Mike Keliher's sister Diana about these developments, she asked me up to her house. Without even knowing John Kahlden, Mike's family were all touched and thrilled for him. They gave me Mike's OSU head covers, shoe bags, and a travel bag to forward to John. My parting words to the Keliher family were, "I don't begin to know what God is doing in all of this, but He is definitely in it--it was all God and all grace." Diana agreed.

John Kahlden made an impression at Oklahoma State, maintaining a 4.0 grade point average and working tirelessly in the training room. When it became apparent to Coach McGraw that the team was so loaded with talent that John might never get in the lineup, John transferred to St. John's and then Southern Mississippi. At Southern Mississippi he played for Jerry Weeks; a friend from the Country Club of Jackson, Weeks had been the pro at the Hattiesburg Country Club and helped with the Harmon schools. As a member of Coach Weeks's team John played some good college golf, achieving his long-held dream. John Kahlden turned pro in January 2012, worked at Lost Tree Golf Club in south Florida, and is now pursuing a playing career.

The Heart of the Game

***

After the U.S. Senior Open I began losing weight again. By the time my older son Matthew got married, in August, I weighed less than 140 pounds. Family and friends came from all over to Greenville, SC, for the wedding. My sister Mary Dale and her husband Jim traveled from San Francisco. An anesthesiologist with a medical degree from the University of Kentucky, Jim Scheller had spent four years in the middle of his career getting a degree in Chinese medicine. Western medicine is dominated by Greek logic. The Chinese look at health differently: many of their most effective practices--which have been around thousands of years longer than ours--cannot be understood with our logic. That Sunday, after I requested his opinion, Jim suggested that I find a local doctor competent in Chinese medicine.

A Google search turned up the clinic of Dr. Stephanie Mouton. An anesthesiologist at Vanderbilt Hospital with a medical degree from Tulane, she had also studied Chinese medicine like my brother-in-law. In the place to write a message I described my surgery and what had been going on with my weight, and asked when I could see her. She wrote back that afternoon, words I would never forget: "You are fortunate to have survived. I want to see you tomorrow."

Chinese medicine focuses on energy flows in the body, among other things. After a thorough examination Dr. Mouton began treating me with acupuncture. She did not like the duodenal switch surgery for anyone. Seeing me once a week for several months, she took blood, saliva, and hair samples, and put me on so many nutritional supplements I can't remember them all. My color, energy levels, and weight started coming back. This Chinese medicine--as practiced by Stephanie Mouton with her abilities and compassion--was a Godsend.

John Wooden said that love was the most effective motivator he had available to him--second, he added, was the bench. It seemed like God had benched me. I couldn't understand why. I was just grateful for Dr. Mouton, and to finally be feeling better.

***

The University of Tennessee Department of Agriculture offered seminars for small farmers. The UT experts proclaimed that demand for organic vegetables had become almost unlimited: people want food that hasn't been treated with chemical fertilizers, pesticides, and herbicides. I'd already had an early hint of this from the sophisticated Venezuelans at that golf school in 2001. They had shocked me when they said they had homes in the United States but couldn't stay more than two weeks because the chemicals in our food affected how they felt after even this short period.

Once Ruth and I invested in an irrigation system and other equipment, we had no problem growing a wide variety of beautiful vegetables. I got six young men with leadership potential to help out, three twelve-year-olds and three older teenagers, most from our church. At critical junctures I would ask them, "What do we need to do?" Letting them make the right decision helped to build their confidence. Starting at 6 a.m., we worked hard and had fun too. Nothing is better for your body than strenuous activity that causes you to perspire, and working with these young men was a joy.

The Franklin Farmer's Market was the largest venue in the area, with several thousand customers. Every Saturday the twelve-year-olds helped me load the tents, tables, and produce on a trailer at 5:30 a.m. They improved each week, but we were not selling what those University of Tennessee Department of Agriculture experts had led us to expect. Market manager Deb Grant kept moving us to spots with more foot traffic. We did better, but the vegetable business wasn't coming close to showing a profit. Finally she put us next to the area where the musicians played.

Each week a group of veteran bluegrass players in their 70's and 80's performed from 8 until 10 a.m. Then, from 11 until 1 p.m. when the market closed, Deb would bring in aspiring musicians from the pool of Nashville talent. Under a large tent I usually noted fifteen or twenty people either silently enjoying the performance or treating it as background music. Occasionally there was light applause.

On a sunny day around the middle of August I noticed a pretty young lady pulling an electric piano behind her as she zipped across the pavilion. Glancing past her, I saw another young lady with a fiddle case. A good crowd was gathering and unfamiliar electricity charged the air. When these two started performing at 11:00 I couldn't stop looking over my shoulder-- one song after another, they kept bringing it with energy and enthusiasm. I can't play music or sing, but I can see heart: these girls had it. They radiated joy.

They identified themselves as High Road and said they were selling CD's. It seemed like a magnet was pulling the crowd their way. A florist whose booth was tucked out of sight of the music area sent them two beautiful bouquets of flowers. Fifty to sixty people crowded under the tent that typically sheltered only a couple dozen disengaged shoppers.

Going over to buy a CD, I wound up buying two while Sarah Davison played a ragtime piece on the piano. With her blond hair and lovely face she looked like a petite prom queen, but she was no rookie as a musician. Her singing voice was crystal clear. Anna Grace Kimbrough, a beautiful tall brunette, played the fiddle with incredible speed and precision. Her voice made a velvety counterpoint to Sarah's and they harmonized like angels. Anybody could hear how good they were. What impressed me was their contagious smiles and something extra in their eyes. You could *see* they were having fun.

At 1:00 p.m. the market closed. All the vendors, who had been there since 7 a.m., broke down, loaded their trucks, and exited like a bunch of gypsies. The boys and I had a system; we could have our trailer loaded in fifteen minutes. I was carrying a table to my trailer when Sarah Davison walked up to me through a crowd of people and smiled. "I want to thank you for coming to hear us."

Stunned momentarily, I finally said, "You are thanking *me*? The pleasure was mine--trust me, it was a pleasure listening to you."

I put up my table, then walked back over to where Sarah was also breaking down. Calling her over, I looked her in the eye. "I'm not sure you girls know how good you are," I said. "I'm really a golf professional--this vegetable farming is just something to do--and I coached a lot of gifted golfers who became champions. They knew they were good, but it took me to tell them they were better than good. Sarah, you and Anna Grace are better than good! Something tells me I'm supposed to help you. Give me your card and I'll see what I can do." She retrieved her card and I gave her mine.

After exchanging emails several times, Sarah asked me to meet her and Anna Grace for breakfast. I found out that both were classically trained graduates of Belmont University's School of Music. They were just getting started professionally. Sarah had finished third in a world ragtime piano championship, and Anna Grace told me that as a singer Sarah had perfect pitch with a two-octave range. I relayed some of the advice I give my best golfers. We talked for two hours. A few weeks later we picked the conversation back up for two more hours at the same place. This time we decided I would become High Road's coach.

I was more than thrilled, and they were eager to be coached. I didn't know music, but I knew Sarah and Anna Grace had the magic to go to the top. The principles for the pursuit of excellence are the same regardless of the game. As with gifted golfers, I needed to build up their self-esteem and create an attitude of positive self-expectancy. I joked that it had cost me thousands in vegetable-farming losses to become their coach--and it was worth every penny.

I served the girls for about a year and a half. Working with them expanded and stretched me. It made me a better coach, and I couldn't have had more fun. Every Wednesday morning, when we met, I paid attention to their eyes and coached intuitively. As I guided them through the principles of human potential, I kept telling them ANYTHING IS POSSIBLE. I asked them for their dreams, then said DREAM BIGGER. Like me at their age, they had a hard time dreaming and seeing a bigger picture. This is the norm . . . and why a good coach needs to *coax*.

My lack of connections in the music industry eventually caught up. Trying to get High Road some engagements, I called maybe fifty influential friends, but these people couldn't associate me with anything other than golf. The idea of me coaching two musicians didn't compute on the other end (and I'm a persuasive salesman). My game is coaching, not being an agent for High Road; they needed someone with experience in the music business at this stage. With an agency representing them now, they have already appeared on TV twice.

Sarah and Anna Grace started playing the piano and violin at age four, before they could process verbal instruction. Sarah first learned by putting her fingers on top of her father's. After telling them "twenty hours a week for fifty weeks times ten years equals ten thousand hours," I once asked them how much time they had put in playing their instruments. They looked at each other. Both said, "Thirty thousand easily." The good stuff may be in you, but you have to have the passion to do the work. Excellence doesn't come cheap.

***

In October of 2009 I traveled to San Antonio to spend a week with Scott Verplank as he played in the Texas Open. I knew only a few of those playing, which showed my age, but those who knew me would come over to chat, like old acquaintances Davis Love and David Toms. Scott was hanging out with Justin Leonard in the practice rounds, so I got to meet him for the first time. Scott, inspired so much by Ben Crenshaw, had himself fueled similar dreams for players like Justin who followed behind him in Dallas.

Scott was playing his normal steady and predictable game. He is always among the leaders on the PGA Tour in percentage of fairways hit, along with great putting and short-game stats. Even now that he's getting older, barring injury he can still win any time--never make the mistake of writing off Scott Verplank.

I'd last seen Mark McMurrey at Dick Harmon's funeral. One of my best players in Houston, Mark had started as a 15-year-old beginner in 1977, the year I arrived at River Oaks. By working very diligently on his game, doing everything I asked, just three years later Mark earned a spot on the Wake Forest team-- long an incubator of great golf, beginning with Arnold Palmer and continuing through Lanny Wadkins and Curtis Strange-- demonstrating that a player can get a later start and still excel. Mark now lived in Fredericksburg, not far from San Antonio. When I called, Mark suggested we play golf on Friday so I could meet his fourteen-year-old son, Harry. I decided to stay for the entire tournament and bring my clubs.

I knew Harry McMurrey was an exceptional athlete-- quarterback on the football team and point guard in basketball- -but Mark said his son was ready to focus on golf, and Harry could play. It was obvious from observing how easily they got along that they had a close relationship, and Harry's upstanding character was all the proof anyone should need that Mark was a good father. Harry had a strong desire to play well, but he was relying upon his dad for "swing tips." Without knowing it, Mark was filling his mind with concepts and words about how to play. I convinced Mark to back off and let Harry figure it out for himself.

After I suggested taking Harry to the tournament to see Scott Verplank and other champions play, Scott arranged for badges and spent time with Harry after Saturday's round. I could see what this was doing for Harry, his imagination igniting before our eyes. For Mark this underscored the importance of a young player just absorbing it all. It's like the final round of the Masters: at the end Jim Nance doesn't have to talk--the unfolding drama speaks for itself. I had given Mark *The Inner Game of Tennis* years ago. Now he realized that Gallwey's natural learning process applied to his son, too: let Harry witness excellence, and feel the rush.

Scott Verplank's tournament allowed me to reconnect with Mark McMurrey and meet his son Harry. This eventually led to a coaching relationship with Harry. I typically communicated with Mark about Harry's progress, and Harry and I would talk on the phone about once a month. In April 2010, I flew down for a four-day visit. I watched Harry play during the day, then did human-potential and inner-game coaching for an hour or so each night. Harry had already shown that he was a natural, so I emphasized trusting his ability and keeping things simple. I explained how the conscious and subconscious parts of the mind work, encouraged him to observe with non-judgmental awareness, and taught him methods of quieting his mind and just playing with pictures. He learned why it was best not to play with swing keys. After Mark saw the wisdom of getting out of the way and letting me work with his son alone, I watched Harry's confidence grow. He reminded me of those time-lapse sequences of a flower blooming as he realized that his body, mind, and spirit would give him everything he needed if he just understood and trusted some universal truths.

I only did physical (or outer-game) coaching once. I didn't change Harry's technique, just showed him how to make pitch shots using different clubs that permitted a shorter swing. He caught on to this in twenty minutes. On Sunday, my last day with him, Harry played a really good final nine at the Lady Bird Johnson Golf Course in Fredricksburg. I'd watched him play the River Hill Country Club course, in the Texas hill country, but he played Lady Bird's course most of the time. It was a pretty good test of golf; the wind always seemed to blow fairly hard there. Finally, I prepared a notebook for Harry to keep, with readings for him to ponder. We got our work done and I flew back home on Monday.

On Tuesday, Mark McMurrey called. "Harry has something to tell you," he said. I could sense some excitement on their end as the father put the son on the line.

"I made seven birdies, one bogie, and had a 66 today," Harry announced. "My previous low score was a 73." Players develop what is called a comfort zone, making it very hard for a player with an all-time best of 73 to shoot a 66. In four days of coaching, I was able to show this smart young man how to tap into his ability. Then Harry's own eyes gave him a glimpse of his true potential.

***

In *Rethinking the Future*, Sociologist Alvin Toffler writes that in the 21st century illiteracy will not involve those who cannot read or write, but rather those who cannot learn, unlearn, and relearn. Eleven- and twelve-year-old children see great golf being played and mimic intuitively. Older players who once played well and want to regain that form can fulfill their own special potential--if they can *unlearn* whatever conscious-mind interferences they've picked up. The key is understanding and using the inner game.

When a coaching opportunity of the latter type presented itself to me recently, I didn't have to think about my goal. Just as I'd prepared myself for the Senior Open, my intention was to get this student playing like a twelve-year-old again.

In February 2010 I was getting a bite to eat in Nashville when I saw a guy waving for me to join him. I hadn't seen George Creagh in decades. We had participated in that Jack Perry group together, studying the Earl Nightingale course, and it was George who insisted I read *The Inner Game of Tennis* when it first came out.

That February morning George told me he had a goal: winning the U.S. Senior Amateur at the age of sixty-nine. I almost jumped out of my seat--I loved George's heart for dreaming so big at this age. Then he asked if I would coach him, which excited me more than he could know. George Creagh was a great player, with one of the most natural swings I have ever seen. His tempo was silky smooth, and better yet it would repeat. Add our shared knowledge of the inner game and belief in human potential . . . *Let's go!*

When I asked George if he had any injuries I needed to know about, he said his left shoulder was on the verge of needing to be replaced. "If you trust me," I said, "I have a genius trainer I want you to see."

Mark Noble specialized in treating orthopedic injuries without surgery. After working with the Duke men's basketball fitness program for twenty-five years, he was now teaching at the University of Alabama in Huntsville. Like I expected, he disagreed with the orthopedic surgeons. Mark told George he definitely didn't need surgery, instead giving him a program of exercises to strengthen the muscles that supported the shoulder.

With George (or any player) you have to get the body in shape to do the job. Given a program prescribed by a world-class trainer, George was going to focus on working out--starting in the spring when the weather would cooperate--and getting that old childlike mental game back.

Like many players, George didn't know how far he'd gotten away from what he was doing when he played great. But with George, the unlearning would come easier.

I had barely finished saying that I wanted him playing and practicing totally in pictures when he interjected: "Be the observer and not the judge." When I told him "Just picture the ball rolling in, no swing thoughts or focusing on the stroke--the body will give you what the mind is picturing," George got it. He remembered those Nightingale and inner-game precepts.

I mainly worked on his confidence. George Creagh had won several Tennessee State Amateurs and many other tournaments, but even with a great champion like him you have to build up the self-esteem. For whatever reason, most players' self-perception falls short of how good they are.

Once we got started I only watched George three times, coaching him mostly by phone and email. He was so experienced--and I knew his game so well--that this worked. While George was intently observing the ball his body would unconsciously make the swing changes. This is the inner coach at work: let the Eagle do his job in silence. I believed George would progress more rapidly without me being there. I wasn't teaching him to play, just awakening the 'peaceful warrior' within.

I had one coaching idea that definitely fell outside the box. To execute it, I attempted to enlist Bob Wolcott's son, who was fourteen at the time. I wanted George to observe the ease that

Benjamin Wolcott displayed pulling the trigger with an empty mind. George understood my reasoning, but the Wolcotts live thirty miles away and we couldn't coordinate everyone's schedule. I still like the theory: to play like a kid again, find a good one, watch him play, and mimic--the natural learning process upside down.

Practicing with a purpose, George concentrated on letting go mentally and physically. We designed shorter, highly focused practices with two-thirds of his time devoted to the short game. The times I saw him, he was hitting it very well. As we got closer to the qualifier I encouraged him to visualize playing the course, Wyndyke Country Club in Memphis; having won the Tennessee State Amateur on that course, George had lots of good memories connected to it. He played a practice round the week before so he could get there the day before and rest.

There were fifty players for two spots. George failed to qualify by several shots. He called me afterwards, almost apologetic, going so far as to say something about letting me down. I straightened that out quickly: I was proud of his effort and that he had enough "kid" in him to dream and believe anything is possible again. We both gave it all we had. It's golf--you can't control what anyone else does. What more could we have done?

Hey, the fun is in the chase. Happiness comes in the direction you are moving. If you are moving toward a goal that you are passionate about, the journey gives meaning and fulfillment. You are that much closer to realizing your dream. Once you commit to a dream, the question isn't if but *when* you will see it realized. George gave it a run and showed us both his heart. Before we hung up I said, "if you choose to maintain the dream at age seventy, count me in."

George Creagh trained the next year. At the 2011 Qualifier in Lexington, Kentucky he played well but came up short. He hasn't thrown in the towel--he's still playing. George's inner child still wants to have fun, and he's not in any danger of forgetting how.

***

My parting words to all my players before any competition or performance are "Let 'em see your heart." If they do this, I can't ask for anything more. When they come home I will love them regardless . . . And regardless, it's time to get ready for the next one.

Ruth and I recently went to hear High Road perform at a local restaurant. We got there about forty-five minutes before show time so we could visit with Sarah and Anna Grace, and the owner gave us a table right in front of the stage area. Then I noticed a young girl entering the restaurant carrying a guitar case, accompanied by her mother. After they got organized, Anna Grace went to the stage and introduced this young lady--I didn't catch her name--adding, "she's opening for us." She looked about eleven or twelve and this seemed like her first performance before a crowd: as she played her acoustic guitar I could see she was nervous. Anna Grace got up and accompanied her on piano, something that clearly wasn't planned. This kind gesture did not surprise me, since Anna Grace is such an encourager herself.

After the young girl finished, she and her mother took seats on barstools, right in my line of sight. As I expected, she didn't take her eyes off Sarah, Anna Grace, and Vicki Vaughan, a stand-up bass player and vocalist who had joined High Road. It had been some time since I last saw them perform. Anna Grace's mother Susie Kimbrough--a choir leader and talented musician herself, and once homecoming queen at Mississippi State--had traveled from Mississippi. I walked over to Susie, to share my opinion that Vicki had added another layer and they were playing better than ever.

When they took a break it gave me an opportunity to speak to the young lady with the guitar. I met the mom first; Kelly Russell told me her daughter Kimberly was eleven and this was indeed her first public appearance. When I finally got her attention I introduced myself to Kimberly, asked her to come near me so she could hear, and reached out to hold her hands. "Kimberly, you know you are good?" I paused and she modestly nodded. "Then let me be the first to tell you that you are *better* than good." She beamed. "You've got it, girl--I know what I'm talking about."

It took a lot of courage to get on that bandstand ahead of High Road, and I wanted to make sure she got some encouragement. Later her mother said, "You are an answer to prayer." Kelly told me that Kimberly mainly played the electric guitar. After taking lessons for only six months she was scheduled to perform The Star Spangled Banner in a school assembly several weeks off. "The Jimi Hendrix version?" I asked, and her mother said yes.

That this eleven-year-old could play something that complex after six months of lessons was astonishing. But I was not totally surprised--she had a beginner's mind. Her ego hadn't shown up yet to tell her she couldn't do it. At this age they are pure potential: Kimberly hadn't "learned" that playing the guitar at this level is supposed to be too hard.

"Kimberly proves one of the main points of my book," I told Kelly. "Human potential is unlimited if life hasn't made you old inside." I had already described the process of "coaching" (or coaxing) High Road. Now, explaining that eleven- and twelve-year-olds were actually the ones I understood the best, I tipped my head toward Kimberly. The girl was really *watching* High Road.

"Her imagination will take off," I told her mother, "and she will start dreaming. I've seen it happen this way more times than I can count."

The Sheriff of Armsdale Farm, ca. 1954

19

THE 19th HOLE: GOING THE DISTANCE

We are not rich by what we possess,
but what we can do without.

−Immanuel Kant

The ache for home lives in all of us, the safe place
where we can go as we are and not be questioned.

−Maya Angelou

Joseph Campbell called the pursuit of excellence "the hero's journey." This book includes many of the heroes in my life--the family, friends, and special people who helped and have been there for me. Some, like Daddy Will, hoisted me on their shoulders and gave me a chance to pursue my dreams. My hero of heroes is the lady I first saw on that dance floor way back in 1976. Ruth picked me up and carried me when my health put me on the bench. Quit? Give up? Not a chance.

Don't confuse celebrity and stardom with being a hero--a true hero possesses nobility and personal traits and virtues to emulate. Regardless of their game, everyone has heroes. If you can't think of any right away, go deeper . . . and tell them! However they show it, they will be thrilled when you recognize their contributions.

My players have won too many state opens and amateurs for me to keep up with. They won every major amateur championship, some numerous times. They have qualified and played in major pro championships . . . and I was never there to see a single victory. Going the distance is something we talked about in advance, when we made the decision to never lay down and quit.

This game isn't about being perfect. In fact, I coach my players that in golf the quality of your bad shots is more important than the quality of your good ones. Golf and life are about having the heart to finish the race and keep fighting when things aren't going your way. The greatest motivator a coach has at his disposal is love--not shame, or the fear of punishment for failure. A close second is trust, on both sides. These qualities make for coaching contributions that will long outlast the physical presence of the coach.

When I took part in Jack Perry's course in 1974, I was a rookie just getting into the business. I didn't even know if I could coach. Asked to dream as big as I could, I came up with six goals. Let's check them out and see what happened:

1. Help my players earn college scholarships.

Eighteen players earned major college scholarships.

2. Develop a national champion.

Jack Larkin won the 1979 U.S. Junior Amateur.

Scott Verplank won the 1984 U.S. Amateur and the 1985 N.C.A.A. individual title.

3. Have two players named first-team NCAA All Americans the same year.

Scott Verplank and Bob Wolcott were both first-team All Americans in 1984.

4. Become a head professional at a metropolitan country club by my early thirties.

I was named head golf professional at the Country Club of Jackson at age 31.

5. Be respected by my peers as a good coach.

1991 Teacher of the Year for the Middle Atlantic PGA.

GOLF Magazine Top 100 Teacher, 1995 through 2001.

6. Write a book on my philosophy of coaching.

You are reading it.

I have embedded my mental, physical, and spiritual game philosophies in my stories. But there is no new wisdom. I got the good stuff from Penick, Harmon, Wooden, Nightingale, and many others--I am just passing it on.

I like to say I did my best coaching when I wasn't there. If you do your job, players will learn to coach themselves. Scott Verplank hasn't needed a lesson from me or anyone else in decades and his lifetime prize money exceeds $30 million. We must have done something right. At some point you should coach yourself out of a job--if not, you're doing it wrong.

The UCLA Brain Research Institute has determined that the creative potential of the human brain is, for all practical purposes, infinite. Success, according to Earl Nightingale, is the progressive realization of a worthy goal. You are already successful when you set the goal and begin the journey. Anything the mind can dream up and believe in can be achieved. The one thing that contributes most to success is a positive attitude.

These universal truths have worked for successful people forever. In addition to paying attention, the people I've worked with who eventually succeeded have adhered to the following six precepts:

Declare your goals and stake your claim.

Dream bigger and believe anything is possible.

Maintain a positive attitude and respect everyone.

Nurture self-esteem and positive self-expectancy.

Focus on the process and reach the goal inch by inch.

Pledge to never give up: we can't spell "quit."

Now that I've fulfilled my goals and seen those development of human potential principles proved true, it raises an obvious question. Do I wish I had dreamed bigger?

No. I'm very content. I married a great lady and we have three wonderful children. We now have four grandchildren. For eight miraculous years Lewis Chitengwa was essentially our fourth child. It has been tough at times, but my dreams definitely came true. I wouldn't change a thing or trade for any other players--my guys were the best and I told them so very often. The beautiful and talented musicians of High Road have brought joy and helped me understand that the fundamentals of excellence apply to any game.

After achieving most of our dreams we can fail to come up with new ones, especially as we get older. You should always anticipate when a goal is about to be reached and come up with a replacement well in advance in order to avoid letdown periods in between. I have been guilty of seeing my dreams come true and not having any new ones ready as replacements. As we age the possibilities diminish. We have to stay in touch with our inner child and artist to be happy in later years. I have been taking guitar lessons. In my sixties, I may not be playing Jimi Hendrix like Kimberly, but maybe I can learn a few chords and play like her.

***

When we returned to Tennessee in 1999 we had to spend the first night in a hotel while we waited for the movers to deliver the furniture. With my biological clock still set on Eastern Standard Time, I found myself awake at 5 a.m. Not wanting to disturb Ruth, I dressed and went to a 24-hour place to eat breakfast. Then, still having time to kill, I decided to drive out to Cecil's Store just below our farm, where the locals would congregate for coffee. As soon as I walked in the door Jack Cecil, the owner, asked, "Where in the world have you been, boy?" It was like I had been away for two weeks instead of thirty years. I provided a brief summary of where my career had taken us. Mr. Cecil laughed. "You are just like a rabbit," he said. "It jumps up and runs in a circle, but it always comes back to its hole."

He was right: we had made our way back home. I was pretty attached to my life as a high profile club pro, but the past thirteen years of raising my cattle and farming organic produce have taught me to embrace the land my ancestors worked for two centuries. How much is this farm worth if it isn't for sale? I sometimes wonder. Nothing . . . or a billion dollars?

My childhood friends used to call Armsdale Farm The Magic Kingdom, because we had fun out here (Disney got our name later). Scott Verplank won the first tournament he played with Scott Tway as his caddie. Asked what allowed them to click like that, Tway told me, "Our goal was to simply have fun." Bingo! Old folks just have to unlearn and relearn how to think like our younger role models. "Unless you become like little children,"

Jesus said, "you shall never enter the kingdom of heaven." Jesus isn't instructing us to be childish, but childlike. I firmly believe He is talking about detaching the ego, the false self that creates constant inner noise. You need periods of silence to hear the voice of intuition and inspiration. It is impossible to be in spirit unless the ego is detached, which takes years of training. But when we adults manage to detach the ego we can find the magic again and have fun. You are only as old as you think.

I believe God wants us to have fun regardless of our age or circumstances. The first question in the Westminster Catechism is "What is the chief end of man?" The answer: "To glorify God and enjoy Him forever." I feel certain we are pleasing God when we are content and having fun. As kids we didn't need much to have fun on this farm. Subtraction leads to contentment as an adult; the fewer things we require to be happy, the happier we will be. To play your best golf, you need to let go of all swing thoughts and just PLAY. Armsdale Farm has proven an ideal place to do just that.

It's also where I've come to lick my wounds and get ready to play again. A decade of pain and suffering--losing Lewis, Mike, and my health--put me on the bench and finally got my attention. Long periods alone in contemplation coaxed me past the "why me" stage to the realization that He has a bigger master plan. In the process of getting older I was letting myself forget my true purpose in life. Training for the U.S. Senior Open and coaching Sarah and Anna Grace resurrected--and expanded-- my belief that anything is possible if the body, mind, and spirit work together naturally and in harmony. I feel like a child again.

"Blessed are the poor in spirit for they shall see God," Jesus said. This sounds like the opposite of the Kingdom of Heaven. But C.S. Lewis urges us, "Pay attention to your pain because God is drawing near." As I have gotten older and experienced more sudden heartache and pain, I have discovered this to be true. I saw the spirit of God at Mike and Lewis's memorial services. As I spoke to those in attendance, I could see and feel the compassion and understanding emanating from the congregations. Somehow when I'm the most despondent and down, I can miraculously sense His grace and goodness.

The kingdom of heaven is a spiritual place in your heart. It knows no geographic location, nor is it restrained by any limiting boundaries. In this kingdom filled with love and understanding we experience great joy, contentment, and feelings of bliss. When you get there you will taste a bit of heaven. This isn't just something one finds after death--it can be discovered in the here and now. It's not a place but a state of mind, a higher level of consciousness. The Kingdom of Heaven can be experienced anywhere. I found it when Harvey Penick gave me the simple tip that led to me winning that qualifier in Austin, when Mike West and I made fifteen birdies to capture the Middle Atlantic Pro-Assistant, and when I teamed with Mike Whiteside to shoot ten under against those boys at Augusta National.

This higher and blissful state is not reserved for athletics. I reached it when I first met Ruth, and then on our wedding day. The days my three children were born let me enter the Kingdom. And I felt it while I channeled the inspiration that allowed me to write this book. Everyone has experienced it at one time or another. The challenge is to stay there for an extended period. It takes experience not to let the routine challenges of life knock you out of this most desirable spiritual state. The Kingdom of Heaven and really being in the flow are the same, from my perspective. Flow is a state of grace. At its essence is a heart filled with unconditional love.

Daddy Will had an expression, "Let me see, let me see, said the blind man." I was once blind but now I see: since I have slowed down and gotten older I notice more. For me, God is in happy smiles and the twinkle of an eye. As a coach, I can see heart the same way. Every human life is a miracle to me because we are said to be created in God's image. When I look at a beautiful scene in nature I am witnessing evidence of the Creator. "There are two ways to live," Albert Einstein said. "One is not to believe in miracles at all. The other is to believe everything is a miracle." Your premise or starting point matters: when you believe in miracles, you can see them more clearly. Let me see, let me see . . .

I still do some golf coaching when someone asks. Where I planted turf grass on the farm, I now have a three-hundred-yard fairway that allows us to hit from both ends. My gifts lie in motivating and mentoring young people to achieve their dreams, and summoning the inner child inside any adult who wants to finally live up to their true potential. What do you want to be when you grow up? Whatever it is, go for it.

Robert Frost said, "The journey is more fun than the inn." Joseph Campbell talks about the hero's journey. Where do these journeys end? I believe Herman Melville's word picture of the soul as "an insular Tahiti, full of peace and joy" in *Moby Dick* gives us a clue. Maya Angelou touches upon it when she says, "The ache for home lives in us all, the safe place where we can go as we are and not be questioned."

Can we experience this on earth? Yes, it's possible, with years spent learning selflessness, but it never lasts. It's hard because there is so much heartache and pain. But that's no reason to quit or give up on going the distance. I believe the journey isn't complete until we are in His arms and kneeling at His feet. Then we will be in that real and genuine peaceful Tahiti. We will have finished the race, fought the good fight, and made it to the inn that is more blissful than the journey. We will be home.

No matter what your game in life may be, play it with all your heart and soul. The principles for excellence are the same for every undertaking. They are not complicated, but there are no shortcuts. It takes hard work. When your true self emerges, you will learn your gift, calling, and purpose, and meet your spirit. And when you reach this point it isn't work anymore--it's fun. Anything you earnestly desire is possible, so DREAM BIGGER.

Every human being is marvelously unique, wonderfully made on purpose for a purpose. Your body, mind, and spirit are infinitely more powerful and capable than you can possibly know. Not sure whether you believe in miracles? Go look in the mirror!

"And now abide faith, hope, love, these three, but the greatest of these is love." That's what it's all about. Take some gold dust with you and sprinkle it around. You will find the magic inside and outside. Keep the flame burning, so you will be a shining light for others. Remember that all your talent and passion are gifts from above, so be grateful. Keep smiling, keep playing, and always let 'em see your heart.

Bobby and his sister Mary Dale, circa 1949

AFTERWORD

*The intuitive mind is a sacred gift and the rational
mind is a servant. We have created a society that
honors the servant and has forgotten the gift.*

-Albert Einstein

In May of 2011 a large package made its way by mail from
middle Tennessee to New Haven, Connecticut. The battered
manila envelope yielded a thick stack of pages contained by roy-
al blue covers. I had been waiting for this: Bobby McIver's book.

At 287 pages long, every line single-spaced, the manuscript
would convert to nearly 600 double-spaced pages of raw prose.
Not just unrevised--it had never even been read. Bobby had restrained himself from so much as glancing at anything he had
written. He was able to do this, he said, partly because he knew
it would receive the immediate attention of an editor: this
manuscript was my baby now. Stricken by guilt and terror (how
can you fail at a task you haven't started?), my mind went into
scrambling mode while my body made a drink.

Bobby had been "working on" this book ever since I'd known
him. Seven years earlier, he had seen my name in *Seabiscuit* and
sent me an email. It could not have been a worse time: in the
spring of 2004 I was evicted by a former-student-turned-
landlord; my career was collapsing in a morass of surgery, com-
plications, and diagnostic mysteries. But Bobby McIver's email

was different from others I had gotten: he said he was writing on behalf of a friend, who could use some help with a novel. As soon as I called that 931 area code and heard Bobby's gentle, Mississippi-inflected Tennessee drawl, I knew this was no scam. The friend existed, the novel existed; *Arrows*, by Buck Young, was published in 2007.

Now that Bobby McIver's own book existed, as evidenced by the weight in my hands, I had no idea what "editing" it would entail, starting with cyber logistics I couldn't imagine and proceeding through the sentence-level revision--which I could, but didn't want to. I needed to read the whole thing to get a feel for it before any editing took place, so I took the book out on the porch to get started. To pacify the inner voice already accusing me of avoiding my job, I brought a pencil along with the aforementioned drink.

I figured I would be using the pencil mostly to make big X's in the margins of Bobby's text. This assumption was based on years of squinting at the prolific but haphazard emails he obviously sent without reading them first. The X is my standard code for "take this out" or "there's a problem here" or "I should give this more attention but I have a drink in my other hand." The opposite of the X is the check, my own "Good Housekeeping Seal of Approval." As every teacher knows, you can make crude marks like these with one hand while holding a big manuscript like Bobby's open with the other elbow--leaving that hand free for your drink.

I soon realized that the marks my pencil was leaving were not negative X's, as I'd anticipated, but positive checkmarks. I had approached reading this manuscript as a chore to be completed, giving myself a week to get through it. When I reached the last page less than 48 hours after I started, I wished I'd paced myself--so there would still be more book to read.

I called Bobby immediately, excited to give him my opinion of his book. His manuscript needed a lot of editing, I told him, but it was worth it. When he asked me how long the editing process would take, I replied, "a few months."

Recalling this wildly deflated estimate now makes me wince--and laugh at my self-delusion. I had a professional (enough) conception of how my editorial vision would engage the gears of Bobby's prose; I just operated on the premise that I would perform at some sort of editorial Mach II. Some of it was hucksterism. Now that Bobby McIver had become "my author," I felt I had to keep him in the game. He was suffering from a case of post-writing depression, that void you fall into after completing a big project, before you can gather the research, concentration, or just oomph necessary to plunge into the next one. Neither of the two book-length manuscripts Bobby had finished previously required that he engage his heart as a writer. He had never felt the intense, consuming euphoria of living in your book--followed by the emptiness when it leaves your hands. Time wore heavy on Bobby that summer.

I didn't help much. It took weeks, and the effort and expertise of Bobby's son-in-law Mark Cooper, just for me to get an electronic copy of the manuscript that I could work with on my (Mac) computer. Mark finally solved that problem; I received the entire manuscript in one file (with the file name, "A Strong Foundation") on July 4, 2011. Then two months passed, during which I converted Bobby's single-spaced text file to double-spaced before revising the first twenty pages. After spending an hour per page on the revision in August I convinced myself that at this rate I would never complete the process, I'd already let Bobby down, and our friendship was irrevocably trashed.

The seasons changed. Like a two-year-old racehorse lollygagging at the gate, too distracted to focus for ten seconds before the bell, I finally realized the starting gate had opened. Once I got my legs under me, I ran myself silly trying to catch up to an imaginary field. By the end of September I was spending at least sixty hours a week on the book.

***

I want to make one thing utterly clear: Bobby McIver wrote this book. It was not ghostwritten. When I read his original manuscript I perceived two things clearly: it needed the time and effort of a dedicated editor, and it already contained the material from which to fashion a gem. This book had the potential to change lives. Bobby had honored me by asking for my help. Inspired by its message of love, perseverance, and hope, I committed myself to the project without a second thought.

Bobby's book accompanied me on a Thanksgiving trip to visit my family in Michigan. I bought a new, lighter laptop computer for the purpose of traveling with it. Despite struggling with a new word processing program, I spent hours at my sister's kitchen counter in Ann Arbor, tailoring sentences while she was at work; editing in a windswept motel in northern Michigan; and squinting at the screen on the train both ways. Later I would look back on all that work as merely the "first revision," but at the time I felt the excitement of transformation. Everyone noticed how much happier I seemed than in years.

***

Bobby says that he has never read the book he wrote. As soon as he got to "The End," he sent it to me. In the process of revising it I have read it so many times that I can recite many whole paragraphs from memory. What would motivate a person to devote months of her life to editing what my mother, a brilliant painter, called "someone else's book?"

After finishing the first revision around New Year's, 2012, I was in the process of constructing an outline of Bobby's entire manuscript (almost 500 pages of it at that point--my first time through, I'd managed to cut about 100 pages). Without the outline the book was and would remain a vast, unknowable ocean. The outline would render it navigable--for me, and, I hoped, eventually for readers. That outline would enable me to spot redundancies, correct errors in chronology, and give the book an organic framework. After I described all this, my mom was uncharacteristically silent for a moment. Then she asked, "But what about your own work?"

"This is my own work, Mom," I said. I tried to explain how pouring my time into "someone else's book" could feel as fulfilling as writing my own stories. Even fact-checking (which, take it from me, is never finished) and proof reading, which must be repeated meticulously with each revision, proved fun and beneficial. More complex and writerly efforts--like imagining a better context for an anecdote, excising, and re-situating it--could engage me so deeply I often found myself in a trance-like state. This is exactly what Bobby refers to as "flow," the epitome of being-in-the-moment sought by artists and golfers alike. "It's definitely creative work," I told my mother.

She could relate to my trance-like flow description; that was speaking her language. Since that conversation she asks, "How is the book coming?"

***

It took me three more revisions, honing the focus each time, to bring the page count under 400 (two-thirds of the original). In addition to the people who appear in it, we looked for some readers who could provide "outside" perspectives. Hoping to get a totally unfiltered response, I would then speak with each one-- Bobby's friends could convey any criticism to me without worrying about hurting his feelings. This process revealed more than I expected. Bobby has an extraordinary assemblage of friends, whose loyalty is matched only by their kindness. He has drawn into his life people of great curiosity and thoughtfulness--people like him--and their insights proved invaluable in proceeding toward a final version.

***

My favorite character in F. Scott Fitzgerald's *The Great Gatsby* is Jordan Baker, the female golf champion rumored to have cheated during a tournament. I have never been able to prove my theory about Ms. Baker to the satisfaction of my grad school advisor, but I became convinced that few sports reveal a player's character to the degree that golf does. I think that is why I became such an avid fan, long before Bobby McIver entered my life; I believe anyone who shares this enthusiasm will know what I mean.

About fifteen years ago I got the chance to attempt a real golf swing at a driving range, instructed by a talented teenage player. Already a fan of the game, I was excited to learn what it felt like to execute those motions myself. A group of us went, so there was safety in numbers. I was confident in my general athletic ability; in addition to running, I had been weight training for several years. I even did some inner coaching as we trooped up from the parking lot. No one cares how far you can hit it, Megan--it's just for fun.

Then we reached the range. It seemed like as far as I could see they were lined up: all men, all within a couple of decades of fifty, all dispatching those range balls with such decisive thwacks they should've gone into orbit. (Some did go plenty far--way beyond the farthest yardage markers I could see.) It was a Pickett's Charge of poker faces. No one laughed or even talked. For this level of conviviality I might as well have gone to the shooting range, where earplugs and safety glasses make every man an island.

My teenage friend had a graceful swing with lots of power, and a friendly, modest personality. He wasn't there to show off or make anyone look bad. He really tried to help me, most likely passing on advice he'd been given about posture, balance, the basics. I just couldn't shut up the voice in my head telling me "You suck." Bobby's Professor, Gallwey's Self I, Freud's Super-Ego . . . no matter what you call it, it's not the way to have fun.

Bobby McIver says that ideally a player starts learning to play golf before the period of "adolescent self-consciousness," when such acute insecurity normally appears. Some of us have trouble out-growing it, struggling to consolidate the positive sense of self necessary to displace these doubts. George Creagh told me that because he lacked the positive reinforcement he needed to feel secure in his ability, he resorted to the element that always generated the praise he craved--his great swing. As a result, he believes, he neglected crucial aspects of his game.

George wishes he'd had a mentor like Bobby McIver. But George was (and is) a member of Belle Meade Country Club, where Bobby served as an assistant pro for six years. In his thirties then, maybe George just wasn't young enough--yet--to allow his inner child free rein. As Bobby describes, George Creagh accomplished this fully in his late 60's, starting that February morning when he finally got Bobby McIver as his mentor, and coach and player formed a dynamic team of equals seeking the heart of the game.

***

"The question is not whether we are going to face trials, pain, and suffering, but what we are going to do with them when they show up. Life is a learning experience--we face adversity and learn from it. Without pain there is no joy, or life." I quoted this passage--from part of *The Heart of The Game: A Coach's Journey* that I cut--in the introduction. I include it again here as an example of words that have copied and pasted themselves into my memory, and the difficult choices those 287 single-spaced pages forced their editor to make.

That Bobby McIver trusted me to make such choices is probably the highest professional honor I've ever been accorded. That our friendship has not only survived the type of collaboration that notoriously rips marriages and partnerships apart, but expanded and planted stakes, is testimony to the same spiritual core that Bobby cites as elemental to great coaching--and coaches, in the pages of this book.

This book would not exist without Miguel Coles. Since providing Bobby with the original idea ("write how you coach") in 2001, Miguel has kept both Bobby and me on task and on target. I couldn't count the pivotal moments when Miguel has rescued me from editorial confusion with one of his invaluable reality checks. He professes not to be "the literary type," but in my experience this is exactly the type who can help the most, especially when they bring the intelligence, acumen, and insight Miguel Coles does.

Bobby and I would both like to offer our eternal thanks to Laura Valentine, proprietor of Penuel Ridge, where he wrote the first draft of this book. He arrived at her retreat inspired but burdened with too much advice, most of it from me. A true artist herself, Laura listened to him and her heart. When she told Bobby, "God doesn't need your outline!" it was the magic stroke that freed him to channel the spirit and write.

Throughout this project I have bombarded my personal coach, the indefatigable and all-knowing Dr. Carra Hood of Stockton University, and Assistant Coaches Terry Hanson and Kathleen Butler with questions on every subject from how to navigate Amazon's publishing site to when, exactly, it would be polite to call one of Bobby's former students in Texas. Between them, Hood, Hanson, and Butler solved problems I risked blowing up into catastrophes.

The first readers of *The Heart of The Game: A Coach's Journey* were anything but outsiders: Ruth McIver and Mary Huston McLendon, Bobby's wife and his cousin. Ruth brought her own Eagle eyes to book drafts suffering from my compulsion to re-re-re-revise while proof reading. (I'm doing it right now.) Mary Huston first posed the Hard Questions, forcing me to follow the advice I always give my students: "Kill your darlings." Bobby's first draft included a story involving an Adirondack chair. This scene was so well written I refused to let go, until Mary Huston's wisdom--and the good of the book--prevailed.

Bobby's sister Mary Dale Scheller provided a unique perspective on their Armsdale Farm childhood. Mary Dale also gave me incisive editing suggestions of the technical sort; the semi-colon count has been reduced by at least half due to her attention, and those that remain had to justify themselves strenuously ;).

My sister Sheila Macomber, who designed our fabulous cover, saved the book at the last minute. I've never felt anything quite as luxurious as the knowledge that my project was in the hands of someone who truly combines "professional" and "artist."

Our younger sister, Brigit, put me up in Michigan during a period when I could barely be extracted from my laptop. Brigit diverted me with episodes of *Psych*, fabulous mixed drinks, and most of all, talk--about everything, and nothing. It felt like home, in the best way.

Robin Fowler has been unfailingly helpful, and gone beyond the call of duty in offering Bobby and me her encouragement and support. I am grateful also for the clear-eyed insight of Jonathan Coles and Lyn Mattoon. Their unsparing assessments bruised at first, but they pushed me toward a vision of what this book could become.

"The only 'secret' about golf I know is all the lovely people involved in it," Bobby has written. My phone interviews with Bobby's students, friends, and family supplied the highlights of many a day. Andrew Trotter, Will Dale, and Kathy Kahan added dimensions to my understanding of Bobby's personal history. Musician Kim McFadden gave me his expert feedback on the sections of the book that concern Bobby's use of music to facilitate his training, and the parallels between golfers and musicians.

David Smith, an Episcopal priest who took his first golf lessons with Bobby McIver, described for me Bobby's focus on "playing through your own nature" as opposed to being forced into a mold. It is this individualized method that gives *The Heart of The Game: A Coach's Journey* its instructional focus.

Mike Gunn has known Bobby McIver since 1954. Bobby turned six that June. Mike's father was an outstanding basketball coach at Columbia Military Academy, with Bill Wade (who plays a crucial role in these pages) as his assistant. Mike Gunn remembers "a little red-headed kid with a wild imagination," growing into a man who has remained steadfastly loyal to his childhood friends. The Armsdale Farm of Mike's recollection was indeed a "magic kingdom," where the Gordons told stories of bygone times to entertain their young audience. Bobby himself was already practicing the art of telling (Mike's term: "enhancing") stories. Most important, the boys had fun.

I had the privilege of meeting Mark Arnold during a 2005 Thanksgiving visit, and I was excited to talk to him again after he finished reading this book. Mark is the consultant Bobby and Ruth sought out in regards to installing a learning center on the farm. Mark and his associate, Price Carney, became a support network for Lewis Chitengwa when Lewis turned pro and relocated to Nashville. Like Miguel Coles, Mark insists that he is "not literary." Don't believe it. In sharing his thoughts about this book, he reinforced what he had established seven years earlier: no critic I know of can trump the insight Mark Arnold brings to a piece of writing.

Bobby has spoken often about the importance of Phil Steele's contributions to his thinking. An Ole Miss classmate of Bobby's and self-taught biblical scholar, Phil received one of the last revisions of *The Heart of The Game*. Discussing the book with him was an almost mystical experience. Phil Steele's expression of this book's spiritual message reconnected me to Bobby's mission so powerfully I felt as if I'd stuck my finger in God's light socket.

Those looking to get "a pure golf lesson," Phil said, will meet a teacher with a lesson plan subtler than that and much more profound. In Phil's words, Bobby's essential lesson is: "'God has gifted you in this way. I want you to relax about it.'" After our conversation I found myself hoping I will get to read Phil Steele's own book. Soon. (Thanks also to Phil for the Einstein quote that opens this Afterword.)

Jean Pryor Beech generously offered reactions to Bobby's book despite my inadvertently calling at a very bad time. Jean was the embodiment of grace and kindness. Some day I hope to hear all she has to say about Bobby, his book, or anything else.

I regret that certain people central to this story won't have the opportunity to read it. Lewis Chitengwa and Mike Keliher leap to mind; but there are others. Peter Low told Bobby over dinner at the Farmington Country Club that he felt like Bob Travis was his friend "'--and I haven't met him.'" I feel like Bob Travis is my friend, too. I'll never meet him on this earth, or Buck Dearman, or Mike Whiteside. They come to life so vividly in Bobby's words, however, that I feel as if we've known each other for years.

Only love drives writing like this. John Coltrane, the legendary tenor sax player, named his inspired composition *A Love Supreme*. Like the notes he played, which are still emanating ever outward into the cosmos, touching ears we cannot imagine, this love will never die. It transcends the limits of life and death because it lives forever and ever without end.

Index

Readers can find Bobby McIver's coaching experiences, philosophy, and training recommendations gathered here and organized under his name. Page numbers in italics indicate photographs. This index is handmade. I apologize for any errors--they are mine alone. MM

Abell, David, 271
Alexander, Buddy, 169, 170, 202-203, 362
Allen, David, 152
Allen, Doug, 152
Allen, Julian, 300
Allen, Katherine, 300, 301
Ali, Muhammed, 133, 297
American Junior Golf Association (AJGA), 154, 200, 363
Angelou, Maya, 381, 388
Annandale Golf Club, 152, 162, 186-187, 195, 247
Armsdale Farm, 266, *380*, 385-386, 399, 401
Armstrong ancestors 207, 265-266
Armstrong, George Martin, 281-282
Armstrong, Horace, 280-282
Armstrong, James, 265-266
Armstrong, Neil, 207
Armstrong, Wally, 206-208, 236, 270, 285
Arnold, Mark, 271, 273, 285, 295, 401
attitude, *see* McIver, Bobby, Larger Lessons
Augusta National Golf Club, 51-55, *58*, 122, 135, 217-218, 358, 387
Aultman, Dick, 36
Austin Country Club, 40, 46, 141-143, 319, 341

Baker-Finch, Ian, 218-219
Ballesteros, Seve, 57, 170, 171, 181-182
Banfield, Andy, 271
Bannister, Roger, 62
basketball
    Benefits for young golfers, 33:
    Indiana summer leagues of the 1930's, 46-47

Index

basketball *(cont.)*
> *see also* Wooden, John; McIver, Bobby--Coaching Experiences,
> YMCA basketball; and Columbia Military Academy basketball team

Battle Ground Academy, 69, 88, 117, 140

Belle Meade Country Club, *see* McIver, Bobby, Coaching Experiences

Biggers, Fred, 255, 261-262

Blue, Vida, 140

Brackens, Jim, 191, 196-197, 199

Bradford, Lissa, 30

Bradshaw, Robbie, 256

Brewer, Will, 187, 267

breathing, *see* McIver, Bobby, Coaching Experiences and Self-Coaching

British Open Golf Tournament, 9, 101, 155, 170, 218, 332

Brooks, David, 10

Brooks, Mark 156, 215

Brotto, Andrea, 213, 237

Brown, Billy Ray, 156

Brown, James, 314

Bryant, Paul ("Bear"), 95, 145

Burch, John, 5, *18*, 30, 70, 87-88, 268

Burke, Jack, 137

Busching, Hal, 186

Bush, George H.W., 200

Bush, Marvin, 200

Bybee, Mrs. Elizabeth, 138, 172

Campbell, Jim, 121, 303-304

Campbell, Joseph, 381, 388

Campbell, Mary Lu Jordan, 121, 126-127, 303-304

Carillion, Bruce, *18*

Carney, Price, 271

Carr, David, 251

Cassidy, Jim, 262

Cecil, Jack, 385

Champions Golf Club, 140

Chariots of Fire, 325

Charter Resource Group, 271

Chinese medicine, 365-366

Chitengwa, Elias, 291-292

Chitengwa, Farai, 291

Chitengwa, Helga, 292

Chitengwa, Josephine, *278*, 290

Chitengwa, Lewis Sr., 234, 277, 290, 291, 292-293

Chitengwa, Lewis, *198*, 207-212, *243*, 265, 266, 270, 276-277, 282, 284-288, 298, 303, 305, 311, 328, 340, 342, 345, 349, 358, 384, 386, 387, 401, 402

    South African Amateur, *198*, 200, 209, 317, *344*

    UVA Golf Team, 207, 210-211, 213, *244*, 252, 257, 287

    ACC Freshman of the Year, 233

    using visualization, 235

    "Guru" in Orlando, 210, 234-235, 269-270

    seasonal allergies, 237-239

    PGA Tour qualifiers, 268, 271

    Playing Nike and Canadian Tours, 271, 275

    Dixon Brooke Award, 286-287

    Spiritual Law of Expectations, 236

Chitengwa, Rhoda, 292

Churchill, Sir Winston, 23, 229, 287, 313

Clampett, Bobby, 97, 98, 101-102, 141, 202, 310

Clarke, Doug, 96-102

Clayton, Jimmy, 154

coaching, *see* McIver, Bobby, Coaching Experiences and Self-Coaching

Coles, Miguel, 13, 213, 307-308, 314, 398-399

Collier, Robert, 346

Columbia Military Academy (CMA), 22-23, 401

    golf team, 23, 25

    basketball team, 22-23, 63-65, 150

Columbia (Tennessee) Race Riots of 1946, 260

Comer, Kandi, 200, 220

Cooke, Simon, 213, 237

Cooke, Tim, 213

Cooper, Elizabeth McIver, 60, 174, 223, 232, 240-242, *243*, 249, 253, 258-259, 276, 293, 302

Corley, Jason, 271, 274, 275-276

The Cornel West Reader, 313, 314, 315

The Country Club of Jackson, *see* McIver, Bobby, Coaching Experiences

Cowger, David, 159, 164

Cox, Cabell, 227

Cox, Frank, 225, 227

Creagh, George, 8-12, 63, 78

    on the advantages of a mentor, 9

    Jack Perry course, 55-56

    on The Inner Game of Tennis, 10-12

    U.S.S. Amateur (2010-11), 374-377

    self-perception 397-398

Crenshaw, Ben, 40, 43, 57, 154, 157, 328, 370

Crockett, Dan, 290

Index

Crosby, Nathaniel, 156, 168
Crowder, Rett, *128*, *132*, 152-153, 165-167
    PGA National Junior Camp, 153
    anchoring, 165
    youngest qualifier, U.S. Amateur (1987), 183-184
Cupit, Maxie, 86
The Curtis Cup, 200

Danton, Mark, 159, 164
Davidson, Bruce, 305
Davidson College, 107
Davison, Sarah, 367-370
Dearman, Buck, 160-161, 164, 402
DeChardin, Pierre Teilhard, 111
Denny, Walter, 152
Doty, Art, 262
Drake, John, 272-273, 277, 286
Duval, David, 285
Dyer, Wayne, 316

Eagle label, *see* McIver, Bobby, Self-Coaching
Eagleburger, Lawrence, 200
Ego, *see* Bobby McIver, Larger Lessons
Einstein, Albert, 177, 213, 231, 265, 332, 388, 391, 402
Elam, Jerry, 86
Elkington, Steve, 156
Els, Ernie, 9
Emerson, Ralph Waldo, 247
Entrekin, Hugh, 30
Epps, Charlie, 143
Eriksson, Anders, 67
E-Z-GO, 51-52

The Farmington Country Club, *see* McIver, Bobby, Coaching Career
Fazio, Tom, 271, 300
Fellowship of Christian Athletes (FCA), 207
Finger, Joe, 122
The First Tee, 267, 272-273, 285-286, 288
Five Lessons: The Modern Fundamentals of Golf, *see* Hogan, Ben
Fleischman, Jeff, 214
Fleming, Sam, 51
Flick, Jim, 36
flow, *see* McIver, Bobby, Larger Lessons
Floyd, Raymond, 77, 179-181, 326

Ford, Tennessee Ernie, 103, 125, 127
Foreman, George, 297
The Four Tops, 313-314
Frazier, Joe, 297
Frist, Bob, 114
Frost, David, 84
Frost, Robert, 345, 388
Funk, Dick, 14, 192
Furman University, 252, 259, 276

Gallwey, Timothy, *see* The Inner Game of Tennis
Garcia, Sergio, 217
getting ready, *see* McIver, Bobby, Larger Lessons
Gibbons, Willie, 25, 26, 27-28
    Echo Lake Country Club, 27
    the "Claude Harmon line," 27, 191
    on over-coaching, 73
    leaving Bobby McIver's position vacant, 108-109
Gibson, Charlie, 290
Gill, Vince, 336-337
Gladwell, Malcolm, 10, 67
goals, *see* McIver, Bobby, Larger Lessons
golf
    as art, 314-315, 318
    competitive vs. "jolly" (social), 30, 315, 358
    club-fitting, 153, 210, 256
    clubs
        most important, 45, 326
        impact of new technology, 327
            Taylormade driver, 326
        determining set make-up, 326
            controlling distances with wedges, 328
            Mike Keliher's 64-degree wedge, 328, 334, 339, 349, 354, 356
            Three wood / driver, 333
        Using long putter creatively, 334
    grip as most important fundamental, 73, 329
    grip size, 327
    stance,
        CH: stand "proudly," 329
        Importance of set-up, 31-32, 330
    flat left wrist, 36, 45, 81, 84, 329
    "The Swing" 311
        "there are no perfect swings," 203

golf *(cont.)*

    "The Swing" *(cont.)*

        "trash your swing keys," 12

    swingers vs. hitters, 319-320

    swinging on-plane, 30

    tournament strategies

        make decisions ahead of time, 83, 254 (GCC) 333

        "Never let 'em see you sweat," 80, 155

        pre-tournament routine, 85, 352-354

    course management, 333

        the Three Questions, 140, 194, 200, 333

    "There is nothing easy about great golf" 317

        National Golf Foundation 2005 study, 42

        "Some days you have it, and some days you don't," 143

The Golf Academy, 267-268, 288

The Golf Channel, 42, 277

Golf Digest, 36, 139, 157-158

Golf House, 267-268, 288, 289

Golf Magazine Top 100 Teachers, 219-220, 256-257, 383

The Golfing Machine, *see* Kelley, Homer

Gordon, Anne, 283

Gordon, Douglas, 283

Gordon, Grace, 50, 233, 280

Gordon, Horace, 26, 50, 51, 104, 116, 117, 222, 260-261, 266-267, 279, 282, 283-284

Gordon, Lewis (Buddy), 238-240, 279-280

Gordon, Lillian, 51, 104, 116-117, 222-223, *264*

Gordon, Mary Elizabeth, 266-267, 283

Gordon, Mary Frances, 283

Gordon, Wallace, 283

Gordon, Will, *17*, 20, 21, 26, 50, 51, 118, 279, 280-281, 346, 381, 388

Gordon, William, 260

Graham, Lou, 8, 53, 78, 102

Grant, Deb, 367

Grantham, Steve, 154, 164

Graymere Country Club, 20, 23, 25, 26, 320

Greasy Bayou Hunt Club, 160

Green, Waxo, 69

Greenville Country Club, *see* McIver, Bobby, Coaching Experiences

Greenwood, Cameron, 137

Greenwood, Jimmy, 125

Greenwood, Todd, 137

Grinalds, John, 253, 262, 266, 297

grip, *see* golf
Grout, Jack, 228

Haddock, Jesse, 140
Haile, Scott, 248
Hall, Janet, 291
Hall, John, 239
Hall, Ryan, 235-236, 291
Hall, Tom, 291
Hall, Wayne, 194
Hampton, Ernie, 63-64
Hanover College, 107
Harmon, Alice, 112-113
Harmon, Billy, 134
Harmon, Butch, 134, 182, 330-331
Harmon, Claude, 7, 41, 42, 45, 59, 63, 73, 97, 106, 111, 122, 125, 133, 153, 158, 164, 183, 189, 272, 283, 285
    the Claude Harmon "network," 27, 122; Al Mengert, "local notes" 170
    the "fallacy," 37-38
    manners and devotion to wife Alice, 112-113
    playing career, 134-135
        course records at Winged Foot East and West, Quaker Ridge, Seminole, 135
        "If you are playing great, enjoy it," 143, 243
    as a teacher, 135-136
        "the master communicator," 191
        "encourager" personality, 136 (234; 377)
            Bobby McIver's job coach, 149-150
            telling stories with Bob Travis, 164
            McIvers' last Houston visit, 186
        locating "gall stones" / "hangnail" of problem, 135
        getting a player's attention, 192
        on players' tendency to backslide, 342
        sand game specialist, 306; the "Lily Pad" shot, 139-140
        "Use an eyedropper," 213
    on recruiting golf staff, 199-200, 220
    "bread and butter shot," 194, 290
    Claude Harmon Golf Schools, 157-159, 174
    on the importance of reputation, 220
    on the ego, 275
    "The big picture is in the details," 169, 346
    coming up with nickname "Rusty," 137
Harmon, Craig, 134, 217

Index

Harmon, Dick, 5, 7, 15, *128*, 138, 150, 154,157-158, 159, 196, 237, 322, 332
    'Loyalty' statement, 306-307
    hired at River Oaks Country Club, 122
    "thunderstorm" meeting, 123-124
    interviewing Bobby McIver at River Oaks, 125-126
    Mary Lu Jordan's letter, 126-127
    assembling a golf staff, 133
        showing by example how to treat staff, 128
    Southern Texas Section Pro-Am, 143-144
    Jack Larkin visit, 146-148
    visiting the Country Club of Jackson
    Pro-Member tournament, Harmon reunion at CCJ, 159
    sense of humor, 159, 265
    Farmington Country Club applicants, 195-196
    response to Bobby McIver's manuscript, 203
    calling Bobby McIver a "grinder," 174, 191
    Houston memorial, 303-306
Harmon, Nancy, 303, 306-307
Harpeth Hills Golf Club, 308
Harvard University, 241, 313
Hatcher, Maddon, III, 101
Hathaway, Donny, 314, 329-330, 336-337
Hays, Mrs. Leah, 21-22
Hazzard, Walt, 48
Hebert, Jay, 140
High Road, 367-370, 377, 378, 379, 384
Hillenbrand, Laura, 3
Hiwan Golf Club, 95-96
Hodges, Jimmy, 118-119
Hogan, Ben, 9, 36-38, 42, 69, 77, *128*, 134-135, 156, 209, 326, 327
Holder, Mike, 166
    recruiting Bob Wolcott for Oklahoma State University golf team, 140
    Tommy Moore's recommendation of Scott Verplank, 154-155
    with Scott Verplank at the Masters, 153, 167-168
    positive influence, 156
    1985 CCJ Intercollegiate Championship, 168-169
    Homer Kelley and Golfing Machine, 185, 202
    Response to Bobby McIver's "translation" of Golfing Machine, 202-203
    handling John Kahlden referral while AD at OSU, 362-363
Holt, Jimmy, 26
Horton, Dick, 40, 267
Houston Open, 298
Hudson, Randy, 39

Husted, Dr. John, 299

Indian Creek Country Club, 122
The Inner Game of Tennis,
    recommended by George Creagh, 63
    Timothy Gallwey's attempt to examine the difficulty of match point, 63
    natural learning process, 63
    getting ready and "quieting down," 64-65
    ideas from Earl Nightingale 65-66
    breathing technique 65
    Self I and Self II, 65-66
    the book's "oversight," 7-9; "blind spot," 66
    peak performance, 66; *see also* McIver, Bobby, Larger Lessons, The Flow

Jackson, Bob, 30, 70, 71
Jackson, Phil, 345
James, William, 91
Johnson, Curtis, 222-223
Johnson, Marty, 104-105
Johnson, Rense, 104-105
Jones, Bobby, 310, 318, 333
Jones, Ernest, 35, 42
Jones, Jeff, 324
Jones, Robert Trent, 28, 122, 248
Jordan, George, 121-124, 126-127
Julie, Jeremy, 233, 238
Junior Orange Bowl International Golf Championship, 207

Kahlden, Dale, *128*, 343, 349, 361
Kahlden, John, 349, 350, 352, 357, 359, 361-364
Kahlden, Sherry, 348, 349, 361
Kant, Immanuel, 381
Keene, Robert, *18*
Keliher, Diana, 72, 312, 322-324, 348, 362, 364
Keliher, Mike, *18*, *128*, *245*, 312, 316, 319, 321, 322-326, *360*, 402
    at Shelby Park, 69
    joining Belle Meade group, 70
    U.S. Junior Boys Amateur, (1975), 86
    Tennessee State Junior, (1976), 87
    natural "encourager," 87
    Battle Ground Academy golf team, 87-89
    scholarship to University of Arizona, 91
    transfer to University of Tennessee, 140

Index

Keliher, Mike *(cont.)*

    visiting River Oaks before U.S. Amateur qualifier, 140-141, 309, 315

    serving on Country Club of Jackson golf staff, 158-159

    coaching at Harpeth Hills, 308

    vs. Bobby Clampett in U.S. Amateur Final, 310

    traveling to 2007 U.S. Amateur as coach, 270-271

    as training partner, 275, 276-279

    memorial service

        "Mike-isms" and laugh, 324

        "PURE," 324

        swing and signature finish, *245,* 325-326, 329

    clubs, 334; *see also* golf, clubs, Mike Keliher's 64-degree wedge

Keliher, Scott, 323, 348

Keliher, Toni, 89, 312, 321, 348, 362

Kelley, Homer, 102, 185, 187, 202, 203

Kessinger, Don, 301

Kimbrough, Anna Grace, "encourager," 368-370, 377

Kimbrough, Kim, 104, 108

Kimbrough, Mrs. Mary, 25-26, 104

Kimbrough, Susie, 378-379

King, Clay, *128*

King, Connie, 29, 157

King, Jim, 31

King, Matt, 1, 4-5, 5-6, *18,* 30, 31, 40, 50, 70, 71, 91, 97, 120, *128,* 174, 183, 271, 302, 324

    inspiration to play golf, 32

    Belle Meade golf shop regular, 28-29

    talent and potential, 27, 35

        natural swing and effortless power, 29

        "anchoring," 68

        risk of over-coaching, 65

        attending Masters, 80, 103, 167

    high school basketball, 33

    role model, 80

    Battle Ground Academy, 87-89

    record in junior tournaments

        Southern Junior Invitational (1974), 73-74

        U.S. Junior Boys Amateur (1975), Jerry Elam caddying, 86-87

        U.S. Junior Amateur (1976)

            qualifier, 92

            pre-tournament preparation, 95-96

            focused breathing, 97

King, Matt *(cont.)*
 record in junior tournaments *(cont.)*
  Quarter-final vs. Doug Clarke, 97-102
 Music City Classic, 103
 scholarship to Wake Forest University, 139
 mastering Claude Harmon's "Lily Pad" shot, 139-140
 namesake for Matthew Downing McIver, 144
King's Creek Golf Club, 296-300
Kite, Tom, 40, 43, 57, 157
Knox, Tillman, 20
Kuehne, Hank, 217

LaJolla Country Club, 96-98
Lakewood Golf Course at The Grand Hotel in Point Clear, Alabama, 25
Lanier, William, 220
Larkin, Bob, 146
Larkin, Jack, 6-8, *18*, 140, 152, 157, 219, 228
 last to join Belle Meade group, 70
 2 x 4 for short game practice, 76
 Battle Ground Academy team, 87, 88
 U.S. Junior (1979), 146-148
  Southern Junior, 147-148
  grip change 146-147
 playing for the University of Georgia, 147-148
 visiting Farmington Country Club, 214, 218
 practicing short game with metronome, 330
 PGA Tour, 330
 GSGA Public Links Amateur Championship, 331
Larkin, Lee Anne, 330
Leonard, Justin, 370
Lesher, Greg, 169, 214
Lewis, C.S., 279, 387
Lidell, Eric, 325
The Little Red Book, *see* Penick, Harvey
Littler, Gene, 96, 97, 101,
Lombardi, Vince, 134
Louisiana State University, 169, 170, 220, 231, 314, 362
Love III, Davis, 334, 370
Love Jr., Davis, 119, 334
Low, Peter, 187, 188-189

MacDonald, Charles Blair, 351
MacGregor Golf Company, 25

Index

Macomber, Megan, 314, 315, 351, 361

Magician (golf personality type), *see* McIver, Bobby, Self-Coaching

Margo, Marty, 105, 166

Margo, Robert, 105, 166

Marr, Dave, 137, 157

Martha White Foods, 102, 103, 131

Martin, Sandra, 28

Massey, Jack, 113

The Masters Golf Tournament, 27, 40, 51-52, 101, 103, 134, 167-168, 177, 180, 181-182, 206, 217-218, 372

Mathews, David, 145

Mathews, Pete, 200

Mayer, Dick, 137

McGraw, Mike, 47, 362-364

McIver, Bobby (Robert E. McIver), *17, 18, 58, 128, 129, 130, 131, 176, 243, 360, 380, 390*

> Coaching Experiences
> Belle Meade Country Club, Belle Meade, TN (1971-1977)
>> Belle Meade "crew," 29-30
>> young players as specialty, 43
>>> twelve-year-olds, 163, 225, 353, 373-373, 379
>>> withholding the ball, 32
>> spiritual focus, 72
>> short game 75-77
>> using data to lower scores, 79
>> rhythm and timing, 78-79, 81, 181
>> Seven Core Practices, 83-84
>> *see also* King, Matt; Keliher, Mike; Wolcott, Bob; Ward, Jimmy; Larkin, Jack
> River Oaks Country Club, Houston, TX (1977-1980), 133-148
>> *see also* Verplank, Scott; McMurrey, Mark; Harmon, Dick; Harmon, Claude
> Country Club of Jackson, Jackson, MS (1980-1988)
>> *see also* Crowder, Rett; Dearman, Buck; Travis, Bob; Sproul, R.C.; Grantham, Steve; Ware, Cobby
>> Intercollegiate Championship, 168-169
> Farmington Country Club, Charlottesville, VA (1988-1977)
>> Kenridge Cup, 212
>> Middle Atlantic Sectional Teacher of the Year, 219
>> Golf Magazine Top 100 Teacher, 219-220, 257
>> *see also* Rotella, Bob; McNamara, Rob; Youel, Robbye; Moraghan, Mike; Chitengwa, Lewis

McIver, Bobby *(cont.)*

Coaching Experiences *(cont.)*
Greenville Country Club, Greenville, SC (1997-2000), 76, 247-263
    servant leadership, 252-253
YMCA basketball
    twelve-year-olds, "best coaching story," 224-228
    fourteen-year-olds, 201-202
without a golf course, 289-290
long-distance golf coaching
    Harry McMurrey, 372-373
    George Creagh by phone and email, 374-377
see also High Road

Coaching Philosophy
Self-reliance as goal, 147, 165, 183, 228
"I do my best coaching when I'm not there," 228
"Know your players," 181
"I coach the player, not the swing," 311
"Less is more," 13, 32, 38, 308, 314
    "Paralysis by analysis," 42, 73, 118
    The Hippocratic Oath, 72, 165
    "Nothing left to take away," 45, 83
"encourager" coaching style, 136, 234
    "coaxing," 138, 345-346, 369, 379
    anchoring, 65, 68, 83
non-verbal communication, 28-29, 41

Self-Coaching
importance of belief in putting, 75-76
using sensory perceptions, 76, 82, 334
    preparing for extreme situations, 334-335
practicing at night, 77
    putting, 335-336
short game, 334-336
    practice with tournament balls, 75, 335
scoring vs. "pretty swing," 69, 173
practice inner and outer game simultaneously, 339
    pre-shot routine, 287
    making every shot a "tap-in," 334
    reprogramming, 320
"unlearning," 353
visualization, 83-84, 337-339

Index

McIver, Bobby *(cont.)*

Self-Coaching *(cont.)*
"Eagle" label, 338
    non-judgmental awareness, 353
    the Eagle vs. the Professor, 353
Magician (golf personality type), 11, 49
    "unconscious" play, 303-310
Interferences
    "Don't think about a pink elephant!" 55-56
    "Playing safe, not playing golf," 56
    "The Revolving Door" 36
taking breaks, 84
repetitions 50, 64, 328-329, 346
"showing up," 346
meditation
    breathing basis 352-353
see also golf, course management and tournament strategies

Larger Lessons
attitude
    act like a champion, 60-61, 168
    thinking well, 151
    having fun, 84
    "Can't quit," 298
    self-expectations, 60, 320
    "intention," 151
    gratitude journal, 347
    "Everything is a learning experience," 106, 347
goals
    setting goals, 61-62
    Nightingale exercise, 61
    coaching players to "Dream Bigger," 74-75, 369, 389
getting ready, 83
detaching Ego, 82
    "Professor" label, 82, 353
The Flow
    goal of coaching, 82
    spiritual aspects, 82
    "feeling of destiny," 317
    getting there vs. staying there, 347, 353-354
    the "zone," 347

McIver, Bobby *(cont.)*

    Larger Lessons *(cont.)*
    The Flow *(cont.)*
        overcoming "obstacles" and "interferences," 83, 151, 347, 373
        "the God within," 358

    Manuscripts, Unpublished
    Playing Great Golf: Less Is More, 13, 308, 314
    Swing More Efficiently and Play More Effectively, 187

McIver, Edwin Holt, 19-20, 26, 33, 46-47, 107, 112, 283-284
McIver, Elizabeth Gale (Armstrong), 20, 33-34, 50, 104, 118, 160, 221, 222-223, 260-261, 280
McIver, Elizabeth, *see* Cooper, Elizabeth McIver
McIver, Matthew Downing, *128*, 206, 210, 213, 223, 226, *243*, 252, 253, 259-260, *264*, 276, 293, 296, 307, 317, 365
McIver, Robert E., Jr., 148, 193, 200, 201-202, 205, 206, 235, *243*, 251
McIver, Ruth Johnson, 47, 51, *90*, 93-95, 103-104, 107-109, 112-115, 118-119, 121, 124, 127, *129*, 133, 139, 144-145, 147, 150, 152, 160-161, 174, 185, 195, 196-197, 204, 206, 208, 210-211, 221-223, 227, 232-233, 240-242, 248-254, 262-263, 267-268, 271, 274-277, *278*, 287-288, 290-294, 296-297, 299-300, 315, 323, 366, 377-379, 381, 384-385, 387
McKnight, Tom, 217-218
McLean, Jim, 317
McLean, Steve, 191, 199, 221
McLure, Libby, 200
McMurrey, Harry, 371-373
McMurrey, Mark, 5-6, *34*, 137-138, 139, 247, 305-306, 371-373
McNamara, Carrie, 220
McNamara, Rob, 169, 184, 215, 219, 220, 229-231, 252
McNeely, John, *128*, 133, 143, 151-152, 174, 186, 195-196, 247, 303
Meadowcreek Municipal Golf Course, 210
Melnyk, Steve, 32
Melville, Herman, 313, 388
Memphis Open, 200, 271-272
Mengert, Al, 170
Meredith, Gary 168
Metairie Country Club, 145-146, 189
Metropolitan Golf Association (MGA), 350, 362
Mickelson, Phil, 62
Middle Atlantic Amateur Championship 211-212

Index

Middle Atlantic Section Pro-Assistant Championship, 203-206, 229-230
Mize, Larry, 215
Montemayor, Felipe 308
Moore, Lewis, 23, 29
Moore, Miriam, 93, 121
Moore, Tommy, 154-155, 363
Moraghan, Mike, 201, 211, 234, 238, 286-287
Mosby, Bill, 300
Mosby, Karen, 300
Moser, Bob, 27, 122, 162
Mouton, Dr. Stephanie, 365-366
Murphy, Gunn, 248-250, 263
Myers-Briggs Personality Inventory, 56

Nashboro Golf Club, *see* Nashboro Village
Nashboro Village, 104-105, 108-109
Nashville Banner, 69
Nashville Tennessean, 69
Natural learning process (NLP), 103, 315, 340-341
    described in The Inner Game of Tennis, 63
    used in a lesson, 193, 372
    in YMCA basketball, 225
    as a training strategy, 346
        "NLP upside down" theory, 376
NCAA Rules governing athletes, 207, 210-211, 363
Neely, Jess, 125
Nelson, Byron, 39, 71
neurolinguistic programming, *see* Pearse, Wade
Neville, Sarah, 221
Newton's Laws, 202, 329
Nicklaus, Jack, 29, 71, 105, 120, 152, 162, 78, 181, 187, 228, 229, 327
Nicklaus, Jackie, 71
Nightingale, Earl, 59-60, 65, 374, 375, 383
Noble, Mark, 374
Norman, Greg, 134, 180

Oak Hill Country Club, 134, 180
O'Connor, Justice Sandra Day, 200
O'Grady, Mac, 181
Oklahoma State University, 47, 62, 140, 154-155, 156, 166, 168-169, 202, 347, 362-364
Ole Miss, *see* University of Mississippi
O'Meara, Mark, 155
The Open, *see* The British Open

The Orange Bowl World Junior Classic, *see* Junior Orange Bowl International Golf Championship

Paige, Satchel, 361
Palmer, Arnold, 183, 194, 296, 315, 371
Patterson, David, 114
Payne, Dr. Joel, 160
Peachtree Golf Club, 330
Pearl, Minnie, 120
Pearse, Wade, 340-342
 neuro-linguistic programming, 341-342
 "Circle of Excellence," 342
Pebble Beach, 190
Peege, Dave, 169
Penick, Harvey, 40-46, 50, 57, 72, 113, 133, 138, 146-147, 157, 220, 267, 383, 387
 TPGA seminar, 40
 on coaching Ben Crenshaw and Tom Kite, 43
 nonverbal "presence," 45-46
 skill at diagnosing swing problems, 41
  PGA National Club Pro Championship, 141-143, 341
 The Little Red Book, 42-43
 focus on scoring, not technique, 42
 simple words and small changes, 41
  "If I prescribe an aspirin . . . " 44, 213
 "Practicers hit the third shot," 43
 "Good players ask for putting lessons," 45, 75
  putter most important club, 77, 326
 teaching with stories, 46
Perry, Jack, 59-63, 74, 374, 382
PGA National Club Pro-Assistants Championship, 141
Pike, Steve, 228
Pinns, Gary, 86-87, 92, 99
Player, Gary, 153, 181-182
Playing Great Golf: Less Is More, *see* McIver, Bobby
Points, Josh, 213, 316-317
Police Athletic League (PAL), 272-273, 286
Pomeroy, Ewing, 24-25
Poppa, John, 119
Powers, Greg, 334-335
Price, Charles, 147
Price, Nick, 207, 209, 271-272
Princeton University, 241, 313

Index

The Pro, *see* Harmon, Butch
Professor label, *see* McIver, Bobby, Larger Lessons

Quaker Ridge Golf Club, 135

Randolph, Sam, 165-167
Ravielli, Anthony, 37
Record, Kevin, 306-307
Rein, Max, 213, 235-236
Rethinking the Future, 373
Reynolds, Erika, 224
Reynolds, Tim, 224, 227
Rice University, 125, 133
River Oaks Country Club, *see* McIver, Bobby, Coaching Experiences
The Riverview School, 240-241, 254, 258-259
Robinson, Jackie, 209
Rodgers, Phil, 98
Rodriguez, Chi Chi, 153
Ross, Donald, 28, 120, 122
Ross, Lock, 93-94
Rotella, Bob, 218-219, *243*
Runyan, Paul, 98
Russell, Fred, 69
Russell, Kelly, 378
Ryan, Skip, 239
Ryun, Jim, 62

Sales, Jeff, 26, 73
Saint-Exupery, Antoine de, 45
Scheller, Dr. Jim, 365
Scheller, Mary Dale, 365, *390*
Schroeder, John, 98
Scopes Trial, 46
Scott, Adam, 9
Seabiscuit: An American Legend, *see* Hillenbrand, Laura
Sea Island Golf Club, 114-115, 118-119
Seminole Golf Club, 134-135
Sigma Alpha Epsilon, 24, 259-260
Sinsel, Betsy, 221
Shaw, Tom, 103
Shinnecock Hills Golf Club, 177-178; *see also* Verplank, Scott, U.S. Open
Shorehaven Country Club, 348, 349, 361, 364
Sisson, Clark, 256
Smith, Stuart, 324

Snead, Sam, 43, 329, 330, 333
Souchak, Mike, 137
South African Amateur Championship, *198*, 207, 209, 317, *344*
Southern Junior Invitational, 71
The Sporting News, 49
Sports Illustrated, 27, 40
Sproul, R.C., 163-164, 206
    "like a 12-year-old," 163
    Private Board of Directors, 164
    advising Bobby McIver to write a book, 184-185, 202
    ethical advice 262, 266, 297
The Square to Square Golf Swing, 36, 41, 42
Staub, Rusty, 137
Stoneybrook Golf Course, 338
Stewart, Payne, 179
Strange, Allen, 195
Strange, Curtis, 195, 214, 371
Sullivan, Chip, 169
Swindoll, Chuck, 263
Swing More Efficiently and Play More Effectively, *see* McIver, Bobby

Tallent, Pat, 212
The Temptations, 313
The Ten Thousand Hours to Mastery Theory, 10, 67, 370
Tennessee Golf House, 267-268, 288-289
Tennessee State Junior Boys Championship, 87
Terrell, Tammi, 314
The Texas Open, 370-371
Texas State Amateur, 155-156
Thunderbird Country Club, 134
Tillinghast, A.W., 135
Titleist VI debut, 258
Toffler, Alvin, 373
Toms, David, 169-170, 370
Travis, Bob, 164, 188, 189, 190, 196
Turner, David, 239
Twain, Mark, 295
Tway, Scott, 183, 316, 343, 385

UCLA, 47-50, 362, 383
Unbroken, *see* Hillenbrand, Laura
University of Florida, 67, 362
University of Mississippi, 23, 24, 93, 94, 152, 160, 161, 169, 301, 401

Index

University of Texas, 137, 154

University of Virginia (UVA), 187, 201, 207, 210-211, 213, 235, *244*, 252, 253, 257, 268, 286-287, 288, 291, 292, 306

    see also Chitengwa, Lewis, UVA golf team and Dixon Brooke Award

Union Theological Seminary, 107, 313

U.S. Amateur, 37, 140, 141, 156, 165-167, 168, 170, 183, 217, 228, 309, 311, 316, 348, 382

U.S. Golf Association (USGA), 86, 96, 166, 179, 183, 196, 200, 348

U.S. Junior Amateur Championship, 85-87, 91-92, 95, 97-102, 120; *see also* King, Matt; Wolcott, Bob

U.S. Junior, *see* U.S. Junior Amateur Championship

U.S. Open, 8, 27, 53, 78, 135, 167, 168, 170-172, 177-181, 182-183, 184, 274-275, 334-335 ; *see also* Verplank, Scott

U.S. Senior Amateur, 374-377

U.S. Senior Open, 11, 82, 315-316, 317, 320, 341, 345

Vanderbilt Legends Club, 267-268, 288

Vanderbilt University, 33, *90*, 119, 213, 365

Van Gogh, Vincent, 257

Vaughan, Vicki, 377-278

Verplank, Robert, 138

Verplank, Scott, 6, 127, *131*, 138-139, *176*, 216-217, 218, 219, 231, 253, 305, 315, 318, 320, 324

    first lessons at twelve, 138-139

    Juvenile Diabetes, 138

    Waitley tapes, 151

    slow but steady progress, 155

    "Never let 'em see you sweat," 173

    self-reliance as goal of coaching, 165, 228

    "Recruited" by Tommy Moore for Oklahoma State University, 154

    Amateur career

        AJGA All American and Player of the Year (1982), 155-156

        Texas State Amateur, 173

        Winning Western Open (as an amateur), 62, 172-173

        NCAA All American (1984), 157

        U.S. Amateur (1984), 165-167

        Masters (1985), 167-168

        U.S. Open (1985), 170-173, 181-182

        CCJ Intercollegiate Championship, 168-169

    Professional career

        U.S. Open (1986), 177-180

        Florida visit from Bobby McIver 181

        U.S. Open (1987), 182-183

Verplank, Scott *(cont.)*
    Professional career *(cont.)*
        on the PGA Tour with Bob Wolcott 214-215
        Scott Tway, caddy, 183
        Arnold Palmer Bay Hill Classic (2007), 316-317
        Texas Open (2011), 370-373
    Work ethic, 209
    Winner's mindset, 173, 183
visualization, *see* McIver, Bobby, Self-Coaching

Wade, Bill, 22-23, 29, 63-65, 72, 150, 226, 401
Wadkins, Lanny, 32, 181, 195, 214-215, 371
Waitley, Dennis, 151
Wake Forest University, 5-6, 138, 139, 140, 200, 274, 306, 371
The Walker Cup, 101, 200
Walton, Bill, 48-49
Ward, Jimmy, *18*, 29, 31, 33, 40, 56, 70, 71, 87, 268, 321, 324
Ware, Cobby, 162-163, 164, 206
Ware, Mark, 162
Watkins, Randy, 152, 169
Watson, Bubba, 228
Watson, Tom, 38, 39, 57, 102, 332
Watts, Brian, 155
Webster, Leland, 223
Webster, Willie Earl, 279
Weeks, Willie, 336-337, 340
West, Cornel, 313-315
West, Mike, 200, 203-206, 220, 229, 231, 387
Western Open, 62, 172, 177, 181
"What's Going On," 314, 329-330, 340, 349
Whiteside, Mike, 8, 25, 33, *58*, 387, 402
    Columbia, TN, "local phenom," 8
    at Belle Meade with Bobby McIver, 26
    offered PGA Tour sponsorship, 28
    playing Augusta National with Bobby McIver, 51-55
    benefit to young players, 73
    humor under the gun, 73-74
Williams, Cohen, 103
Wingate Park Golf Club, 291
Winged Foot Golf Club, 27, 133-135, 136, 137, 139, 158, 177, 350, 351
Wiren, Gary, 153
The Wisdom of the Ages, 316
Wolcott, Benjamin, 375-376

Index

Wolcott, Bob, *110*, 138, 210, 218, 333, 375
    High school basketball, 33
    arrival at Belle Meade, 70, 324
    practicing short game with tournament balls, 75
        Titleist VI balls, 336, 340
    Tennessee State Junior and Southern Junior (1976-77), 87
    U.S. Junior Amateur (1976), 91-92, 120, 147
    widely recruited, 120
    U.S. Junior (1977), 120
    visiting River Oaks, 140
    AJGA All American (1978), 154
    U.S. Amateur (1982), 156
    University of Georgia, 140, 157
    NCAA All American (1984), 157
    PGA Tour, 214-217; "Iron Man," 217
    tendency to narrow stance, 342
    fundraiser for hometown of Dickson, TN, 336-337
Woodberry Forest School, 206, 208, 213, 217, 241, 252, 253, 317
Wooden, John, 47-50
    Coach's Wooden's Pyramid of Success, 47-48
    NCAA Championship record at UCLA, 47-48
    full-court press adapted by Bobby McIver for YMCA kids, 201
    coaching philosophy, 48
    correction vs. criticism, 48
    definition of success, 50
    wife Nellie, 112
    They Call Me Coach, 47
    love as a coach's primary motivator, 64
Woodholme Country Club, 205-206
Woods, Tiger, 134, 182, 207, 209, 233
Wootten, Morgan, 49
Worsham, Grant, 290

Yale University, 11, 161, 241, 313, 351
Yank, Glenn Dr., 312
YMCA Basketball, *see* McIver, Bobby, Coaching Experiences
Youel, Ellen, 14, 192-194
Youel, Robbye, 191, 193, 195, 249, 250-251

Zaruba, Harry, 86
Zen, 92, 353
Zimbabwe Amateur Championship, 209
Zoeller, Fuzzy, 135, 170

CPSIA information can be obtained at www.ICGtesting.com
Printed in the USA
BVOW08s0216220216

437582BV00001B/63/P